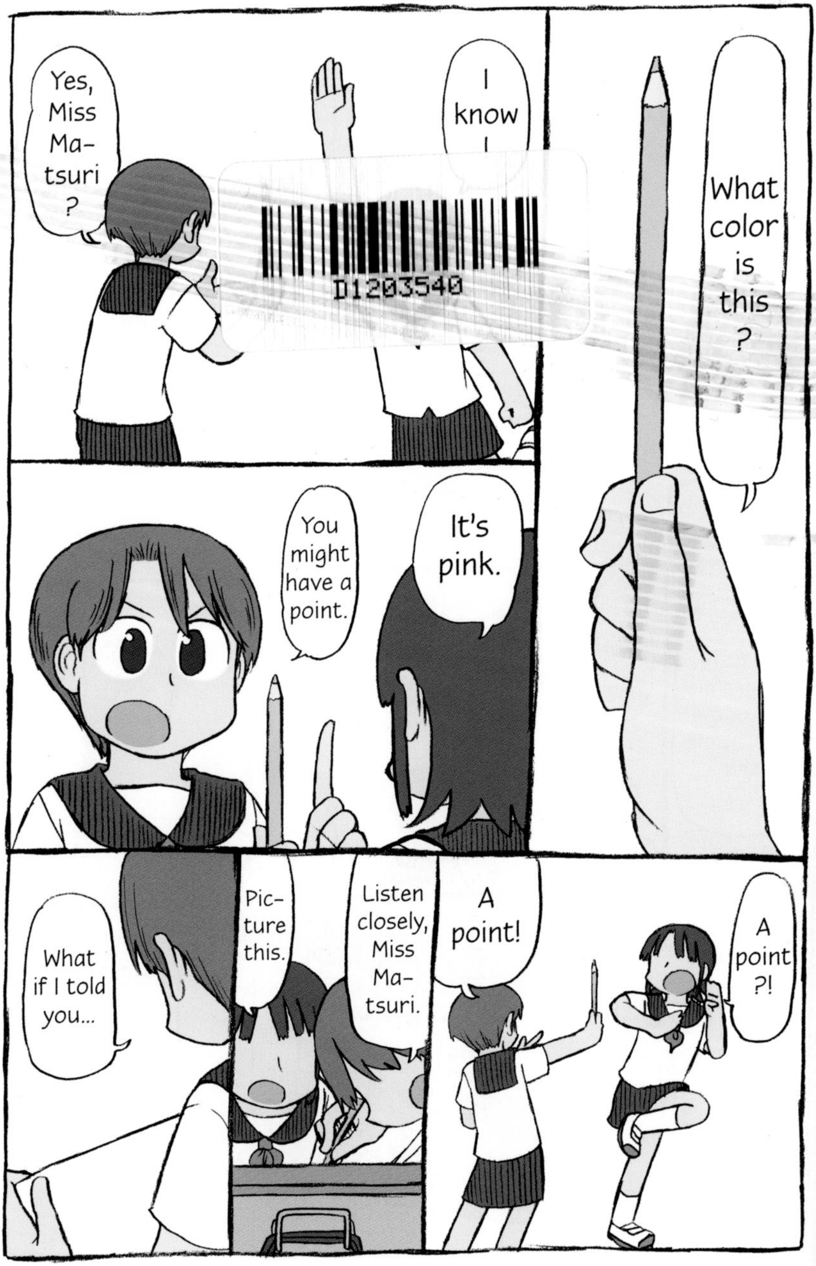
What color is this?
I know
Yes, Miss Ma-tsuri?
It's pink.
You might have a point.
A point?!
A point!
Listen closely, Miss Ma-tsuri.
Pic-ture this.
What if I told you...

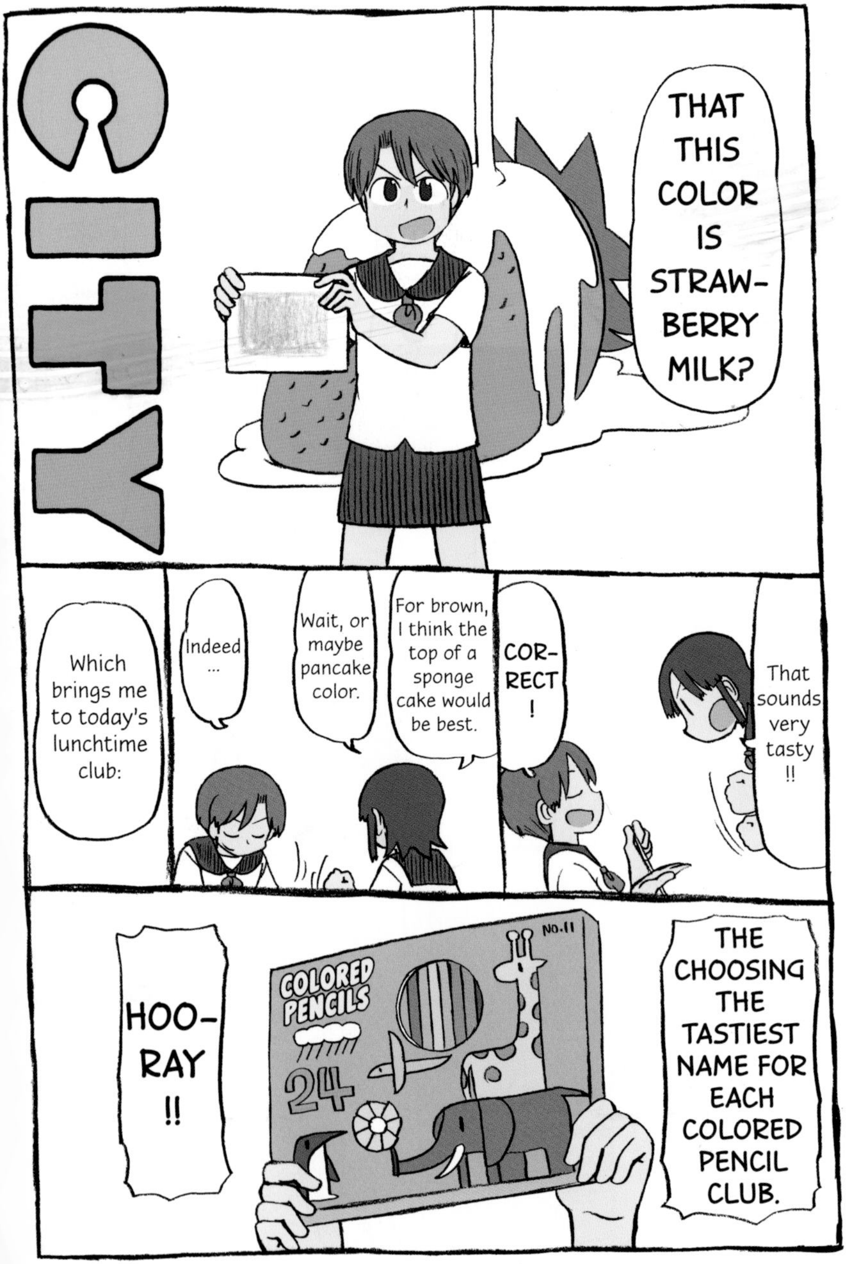
CITY
THAT THIS COLOR IS STRAW-BERRY MILK?
That sounds very tasty !!
COR-RECT !
For brown, I think the top of a sponge cake would be best.
Wait, or maybe pancake color.
Indeed ...
Which brings me to today's lunchtime club:
THE CHOOSING THE TASTIEST NAME FOR EACH COLORED PENCIL CLUB.
NO.11
COLORED PENCILS
24
HOO-RAY !!

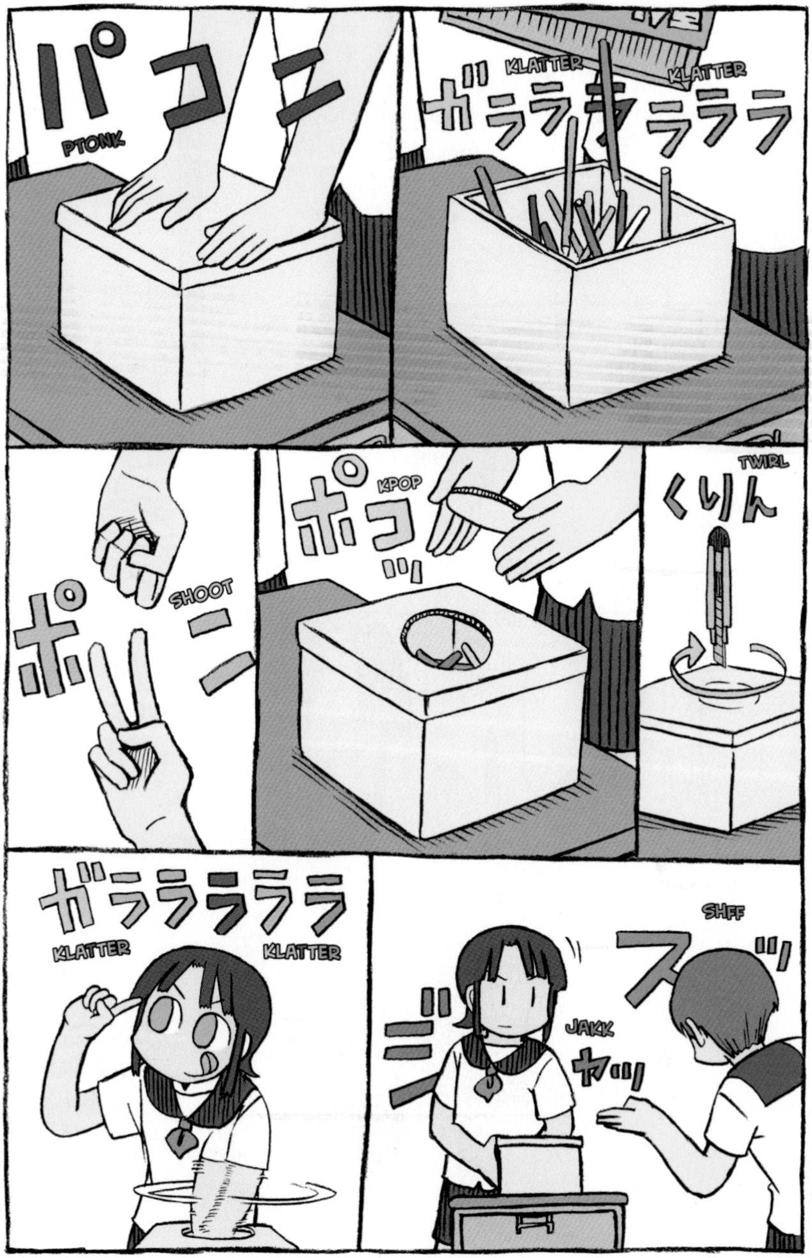
ガラララララララ
KLATTER
KLATTER
パコ
PTONK
くりん
TWIRL
ポコッ
KPOP
ポン
SHOOT
ズッ
SHFF
ジャッ
JAKK
ガラララララ
KLATTER
KLATTER

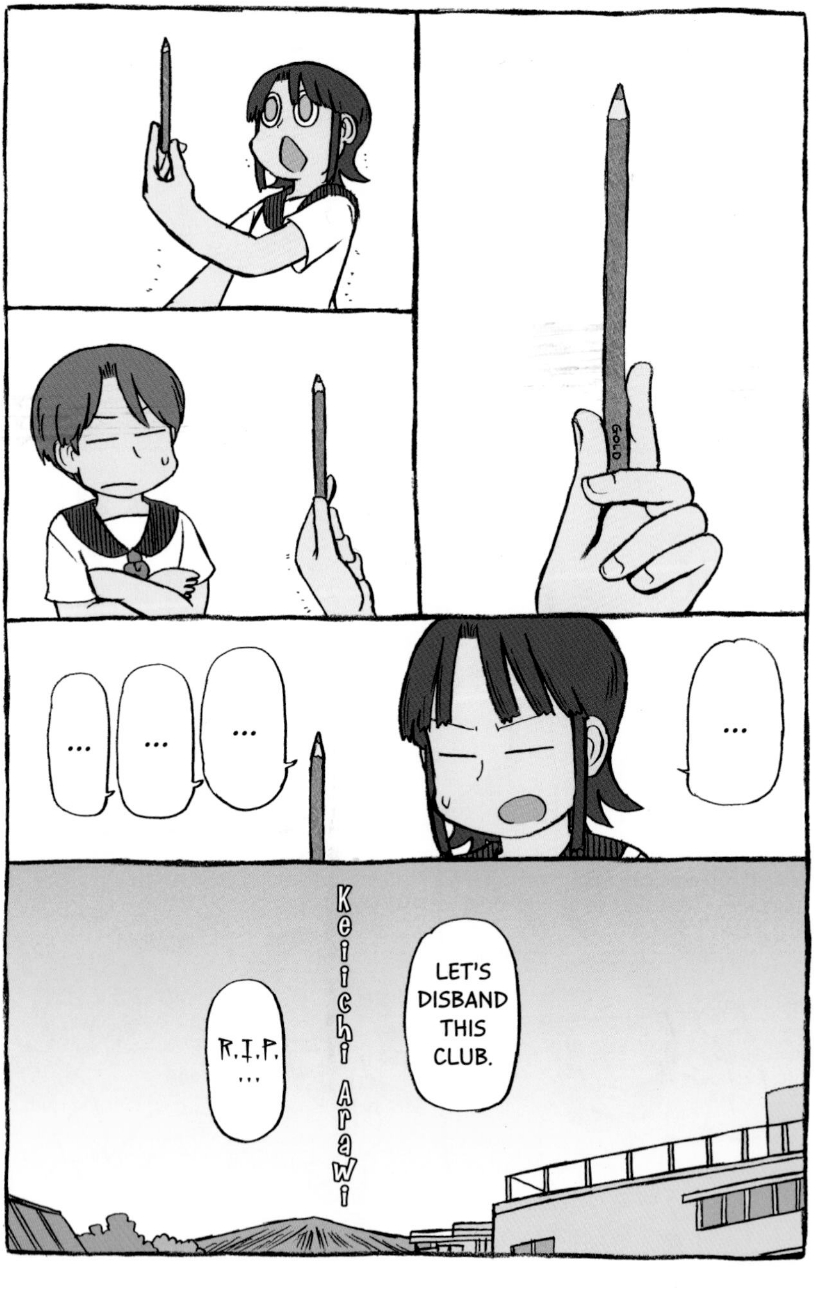
GOLD
...
...
...
...
LET'S DISBAND THIS CLUB.
Keiichi Arawi
R.I.P. ...

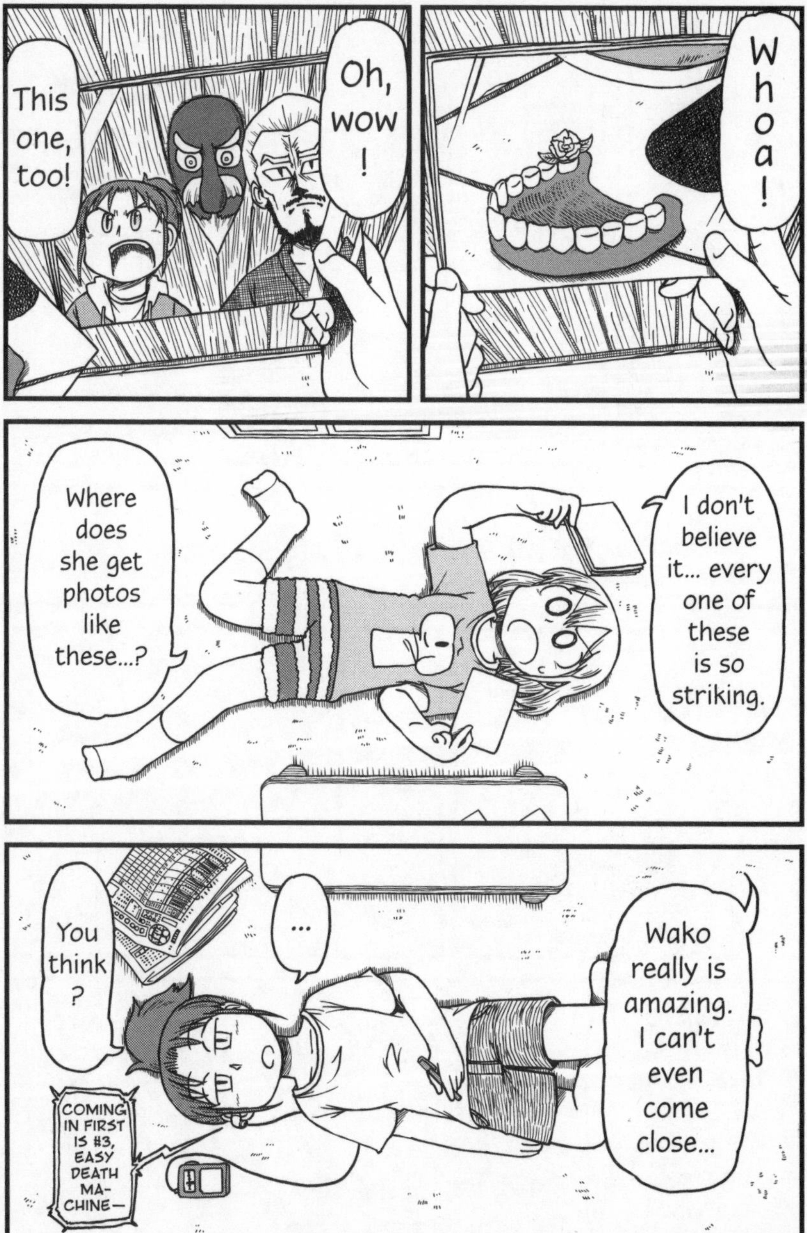
Whoa!
Oh, wow!
This one, too!
I don't believe it... every one of these is so striking.
Where does she get photos like these...?
Wako really is amazing. I can't even come close...
...
You think?
COMING IN FIRST IS #3, EASY DEATH MA-CHINE—

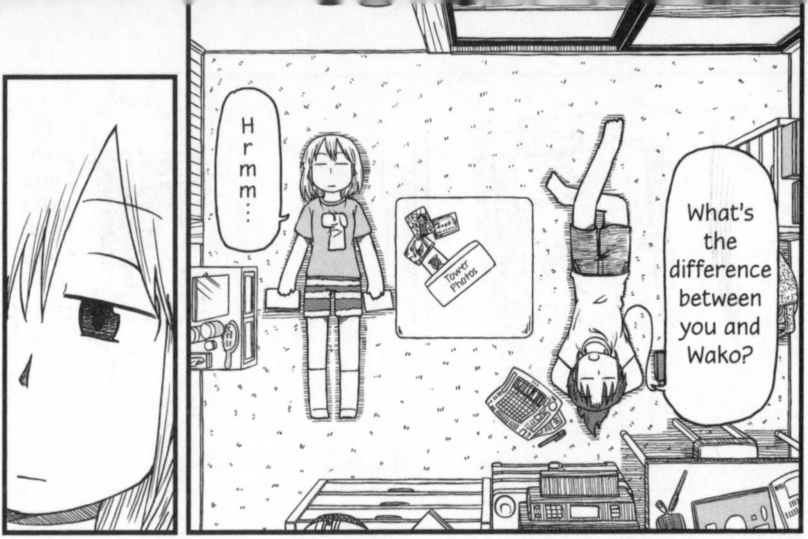
What's the difference between you and Wako?
Tower Photos
Hrmm…

Chapter 54 On a Lazy Afternoon

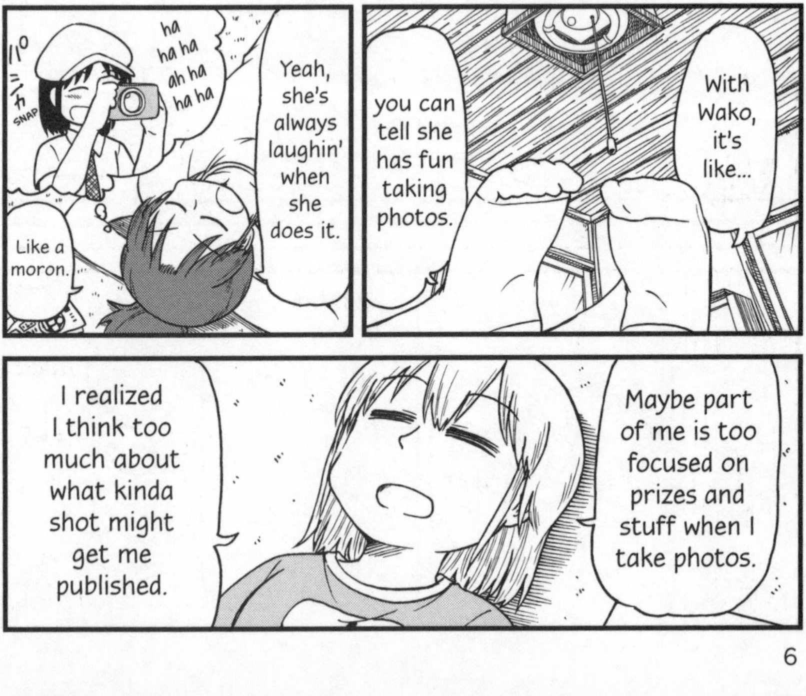
With Wako, it's like...
you can tell she has fun taking photos.
Yeah, she's always laughin' when she does it.
ha ha ha ah ha ha ha
SNAP
Like a moron.
Maybe part of me is too focused on prizes and stuff when I take photos.
I realized I think too much about what kinda shot might get me published.

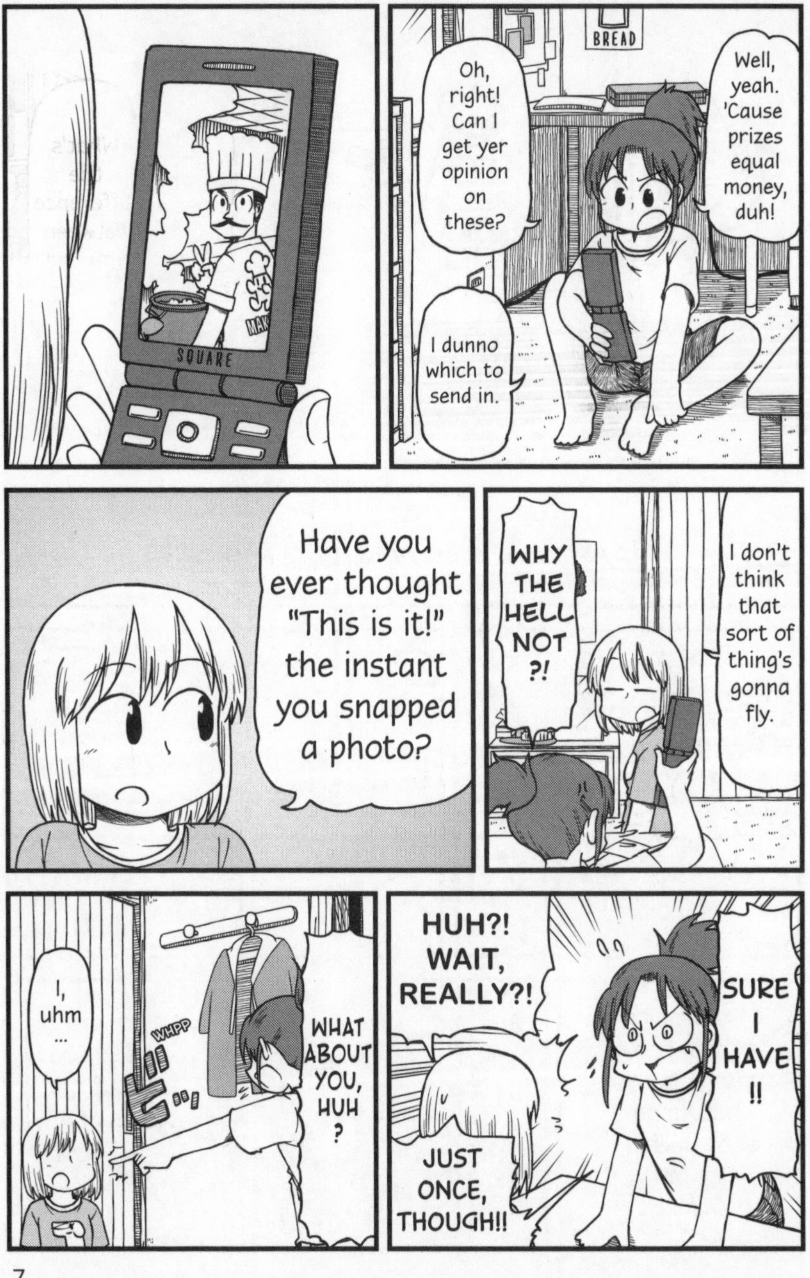
BREAD
Well, yeah. 'Cause prizes equal money, duh!
Oh, right! Can I get yer opinion on these?
I dunno which to send in.
SQUARE
I don't think that sort of thing's gonna fly.
WHY THE HELL NOT?!
Have you ever thought "This is it!" the instant you snapped a photo?
SURE I HAVE!!
HUH?! WAIT, REALLY?!
JUST ONCE, THOUGH!!
WHAT ABOUT YOU, HUH?
WHPP
I, uhm ...

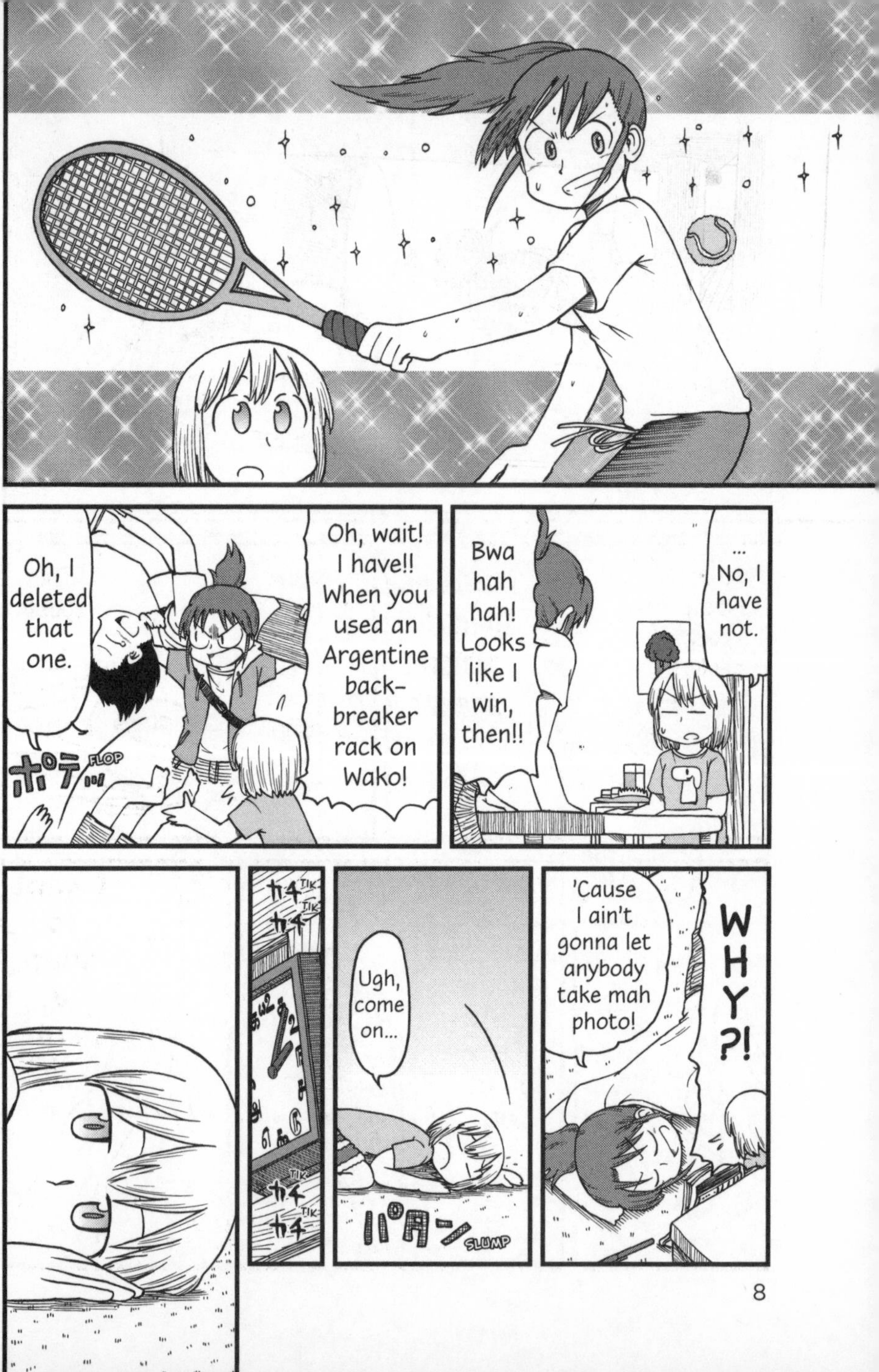

... No, I have not.
Bwa hah hah! Looks like I win, then!!
Oh, wait! I have!! When you used an Argentine back-breaker rack on Wako!
Oh, I deleted that one.
ポテッ FLOP
WHY?!
'Cause I ain't gonna let anybody take mah photo!
Ugh, come on...
パタン SLUMP
カチ TIK
カチ TIK
カチ TIK
カチ TIK

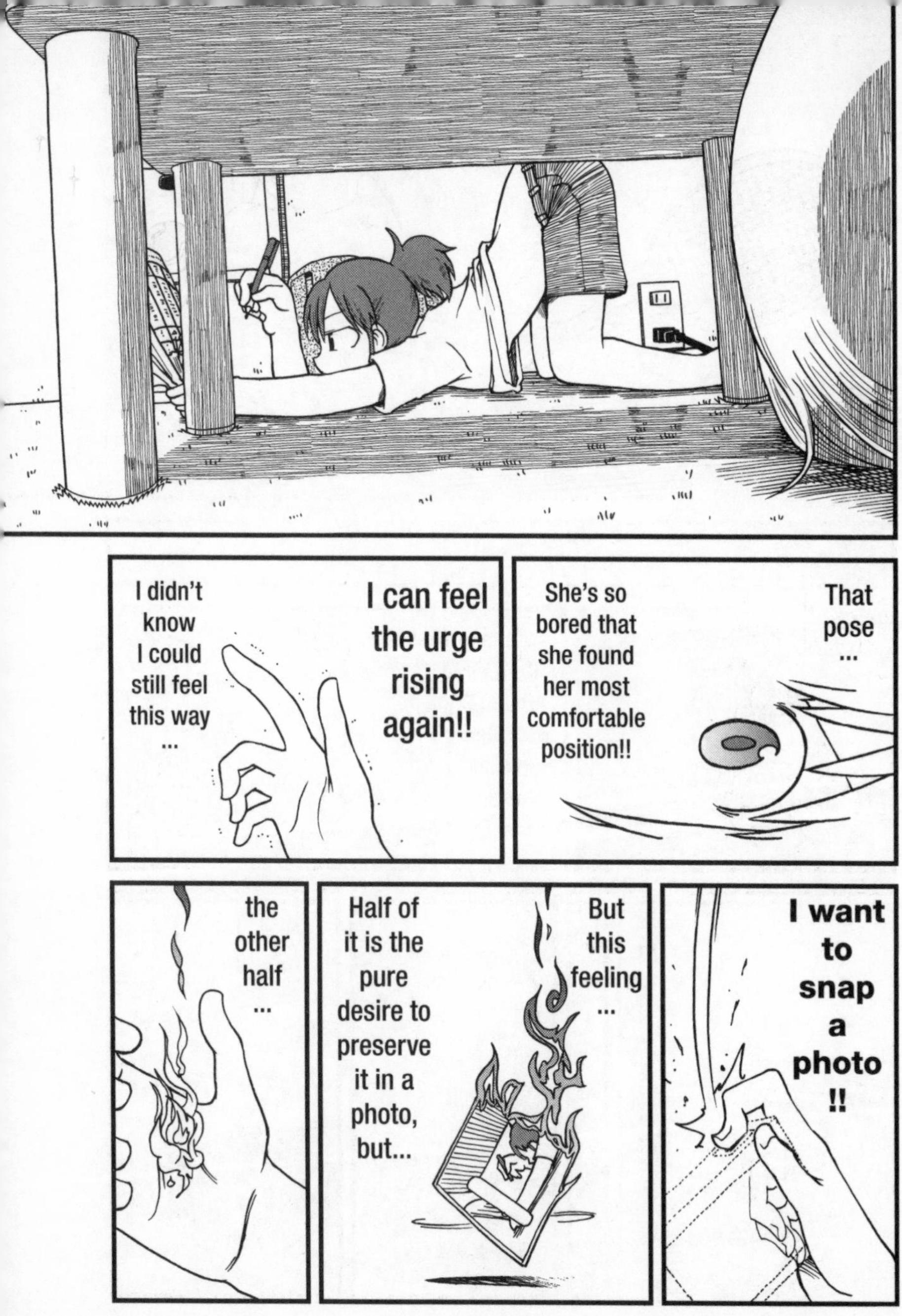
That pose ...
She's so bored that she found her most comfortable position!!
I can feel the urge rising again!!
I didn't know I could still feel this way ...
I want to snap a photo !!
But this feeling ...
Half of it is the pure desire to preserve it in a photo, but...
the other half ...

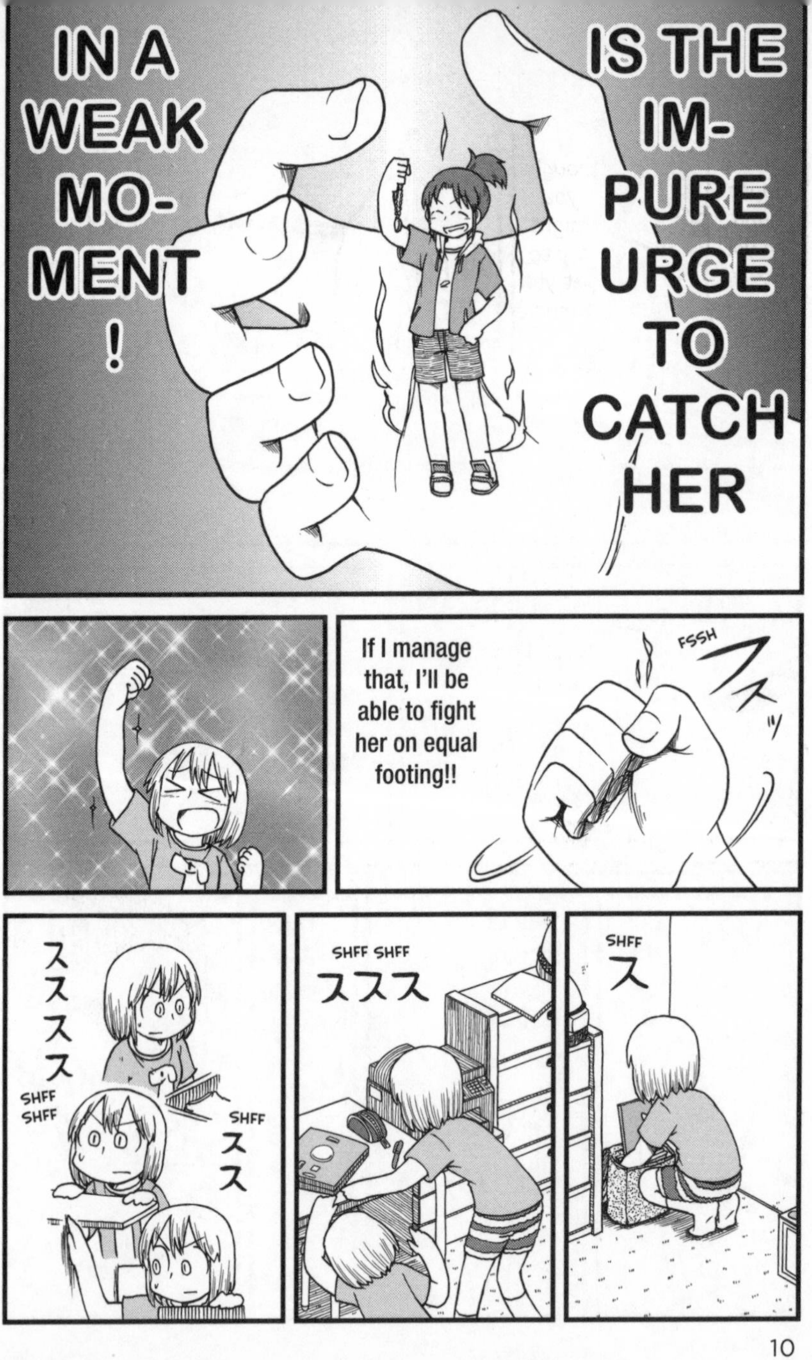
IS THE IM-PURE URGE TO CATCH HER
IN A WEAK MO-MENT!
FSSH
フスッ
If I manage that, I'll be able to fight her on equal footing!!
SHFF
ス
SHFF SHFF
ススス
スススス
SHFF SHFF
SHFF
スス

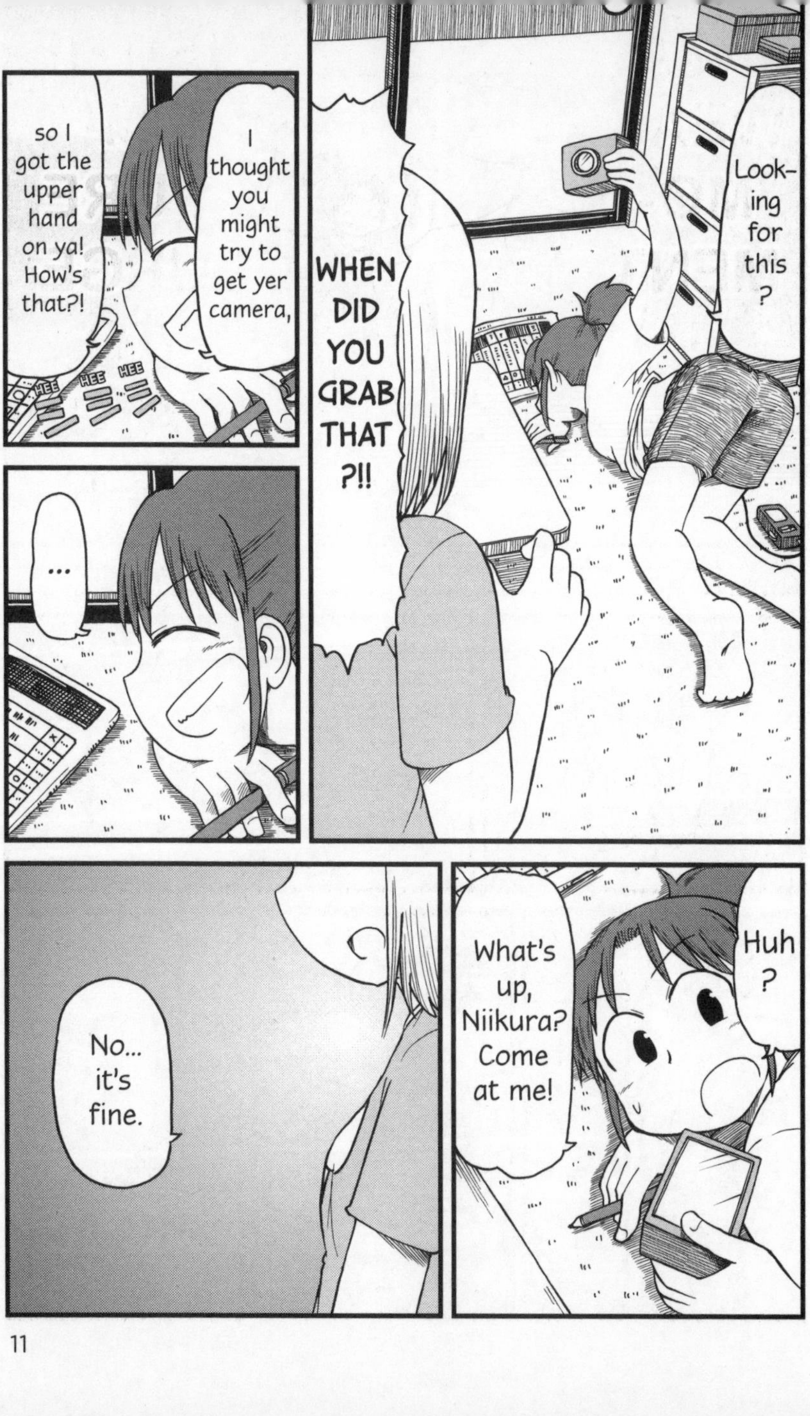

Looking for this?
WHEN DID YOU GRAB THAT?!!
I thought you might try to get yer camera,
so I got the upper hand on ya! How's that?!
HEE HEE HEE
...
Huh?
What's up, Niikura? Come at me!
No... it's fine.

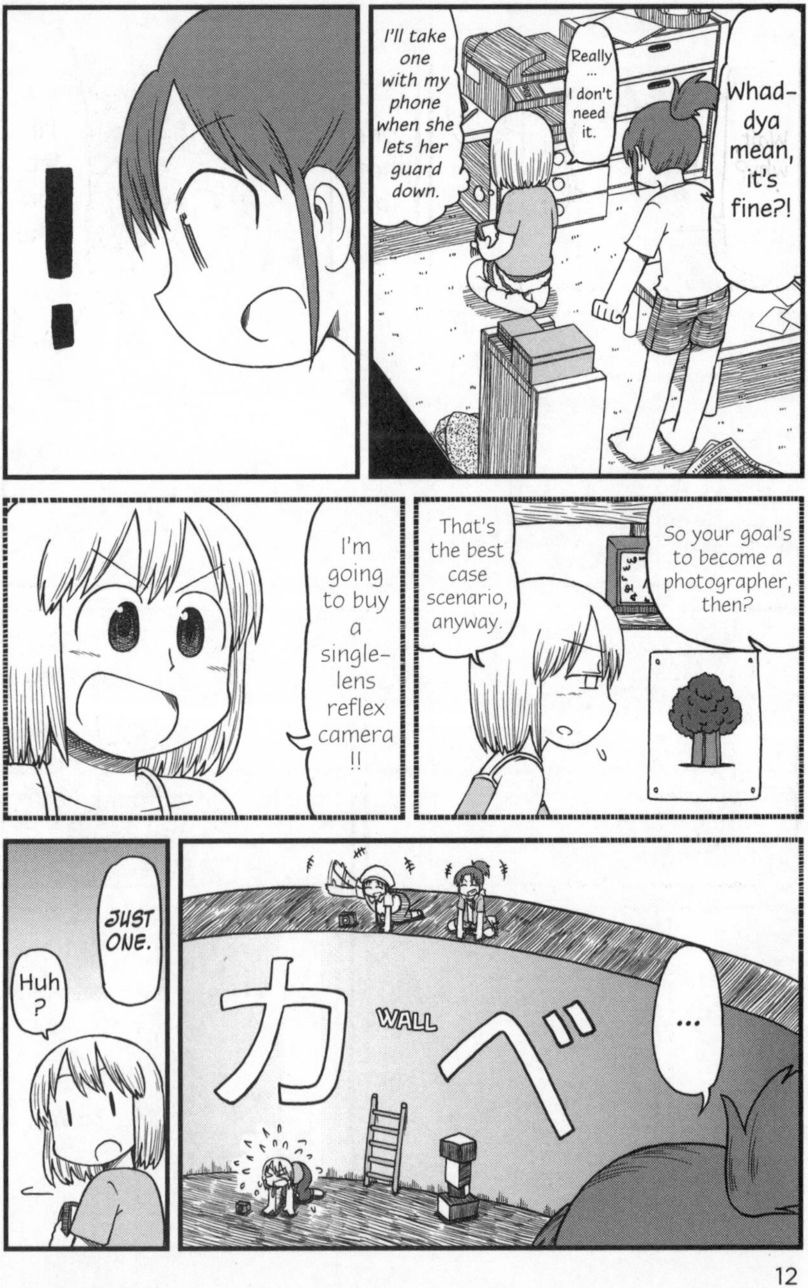
Whaddya mean, it's fine?!
Really... I don't need it.
I'll take one with my phone when she lets her guard down.
!
So your goal's to become a photographer, then?
That's the best case scenario, anyway.
I'm going to buy a single-lens reflex camera!!
...
カベ
WALL
JUST ONE.
Huh?

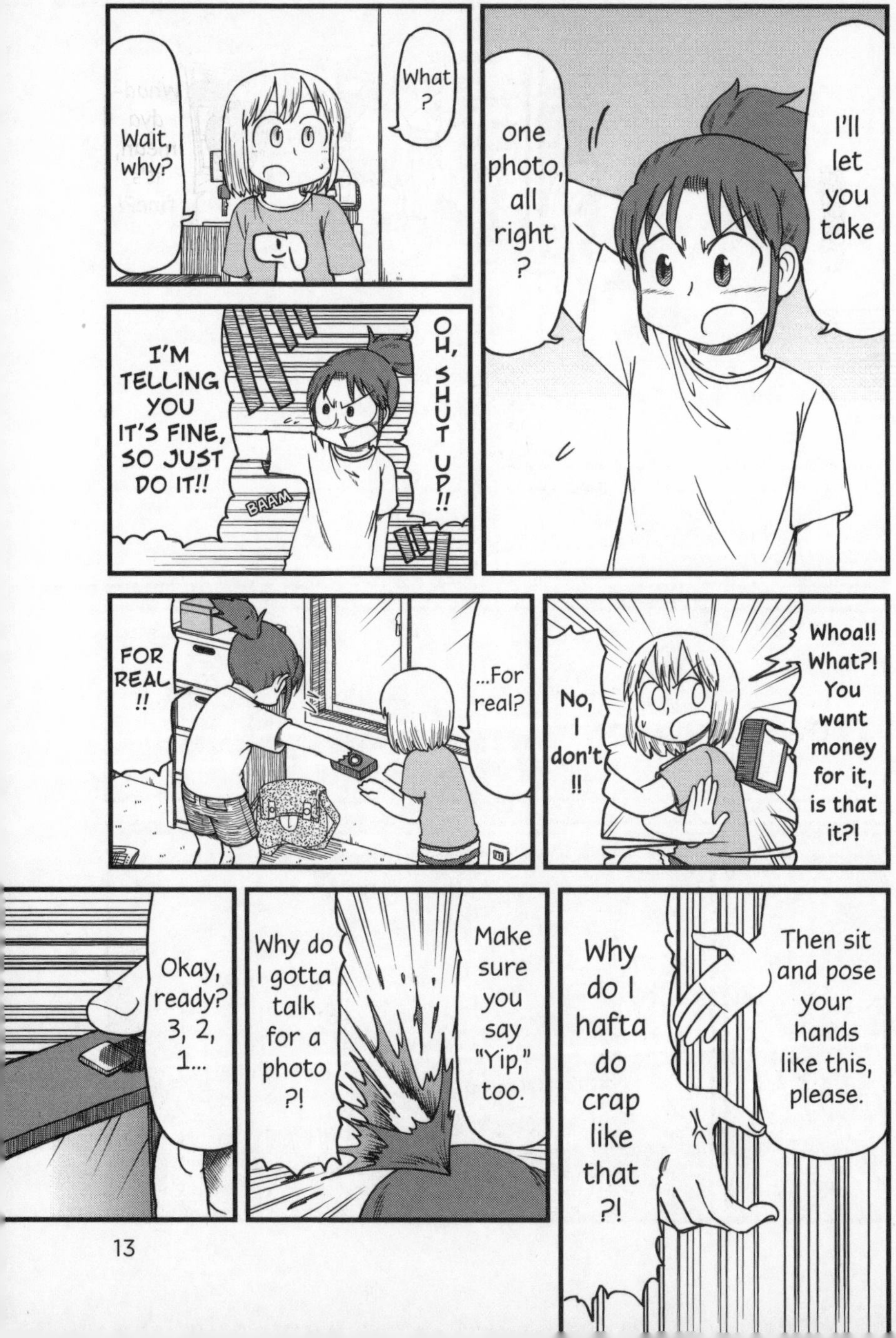
I'll let you take
one photo, all right?
What?
Wait, why?
OH, SHUT UP!!
I'M TELLING YOU IT'S FINE, SO JUST DO IT!!
BAAM
Whoa!! What?! You want money for it, is that it?!
No, I don't!!
...For real?
FOR REAL!!
Then sit and pose your hands like this, please.
Why do I hafta do crap like that?!
Make sure you say "Yip," too.
Why do I gotta talk for a photo?!
Okay, ready? 3, 2, 1...

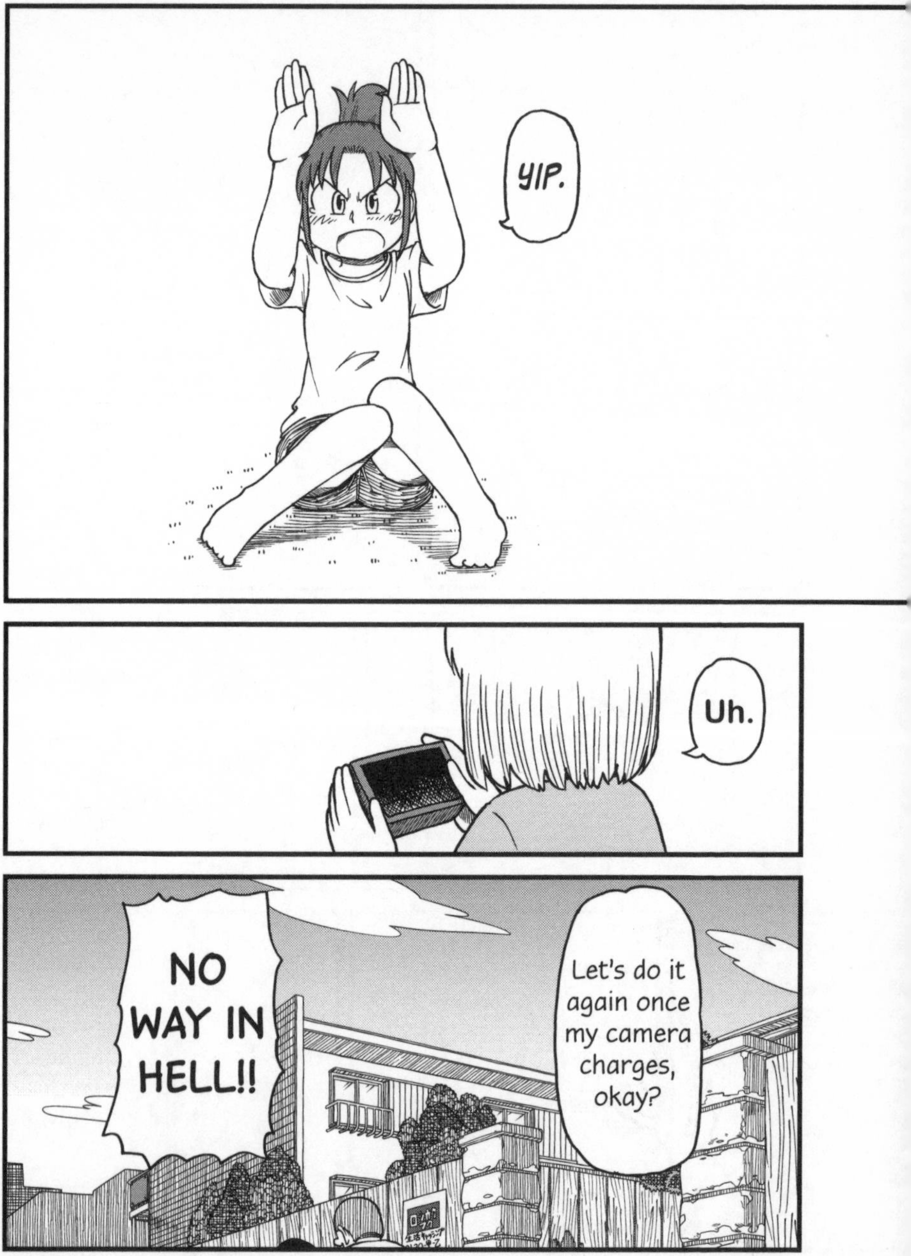
YIP.
Uh.
Let's do it again once my camera charges, okay?
NO WAY IN HELL!!

CITY

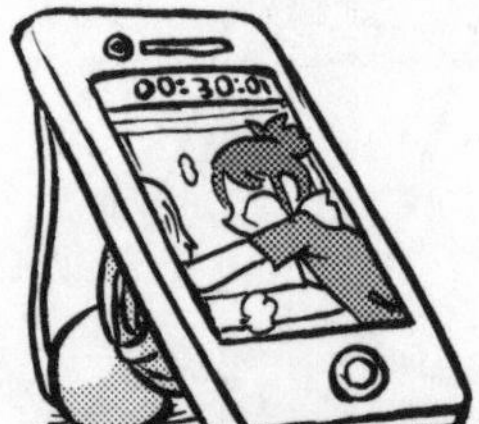

CITY

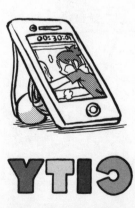

Mr. Delight ~On Par with Mr. Dylan~ Wako Izumi

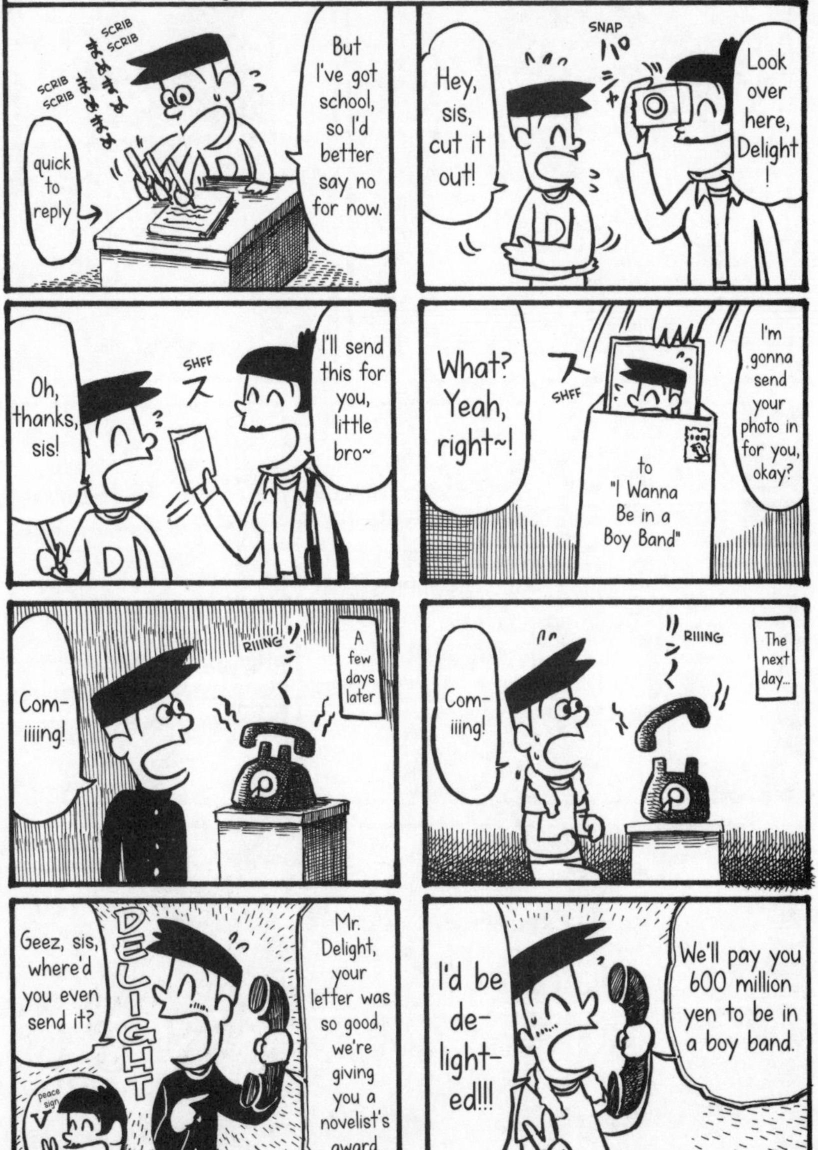
Look over here, Delight!
SNAP
パシャ
Hey, sis, cut it out!
I'm gonna send your photo in for you, okay?
SHFF
ス
to "I Wanna Be in a Boy Band"
What? Yeah, right~!
The next day...
RIIING
Com-iiing!
We'll pay you 600 million yen to be in a boy band.
I'd be de-light-ed!!!
But I've got school, so I'd better say no for now.
SCRIB SCRIB
まめまめ
SCRIB SCRIB
まめまめ
quick to reply
I'll send this for you, little bro~
SHFF
ス
Oh, thanks, sis!
A few days later
RIIING
Com-iiing!
Mr. Delight, your letter was so good, we're giving you a novelist's award.
DELIGHT
Geez, sis, where'd you even send it?
peace sign
V

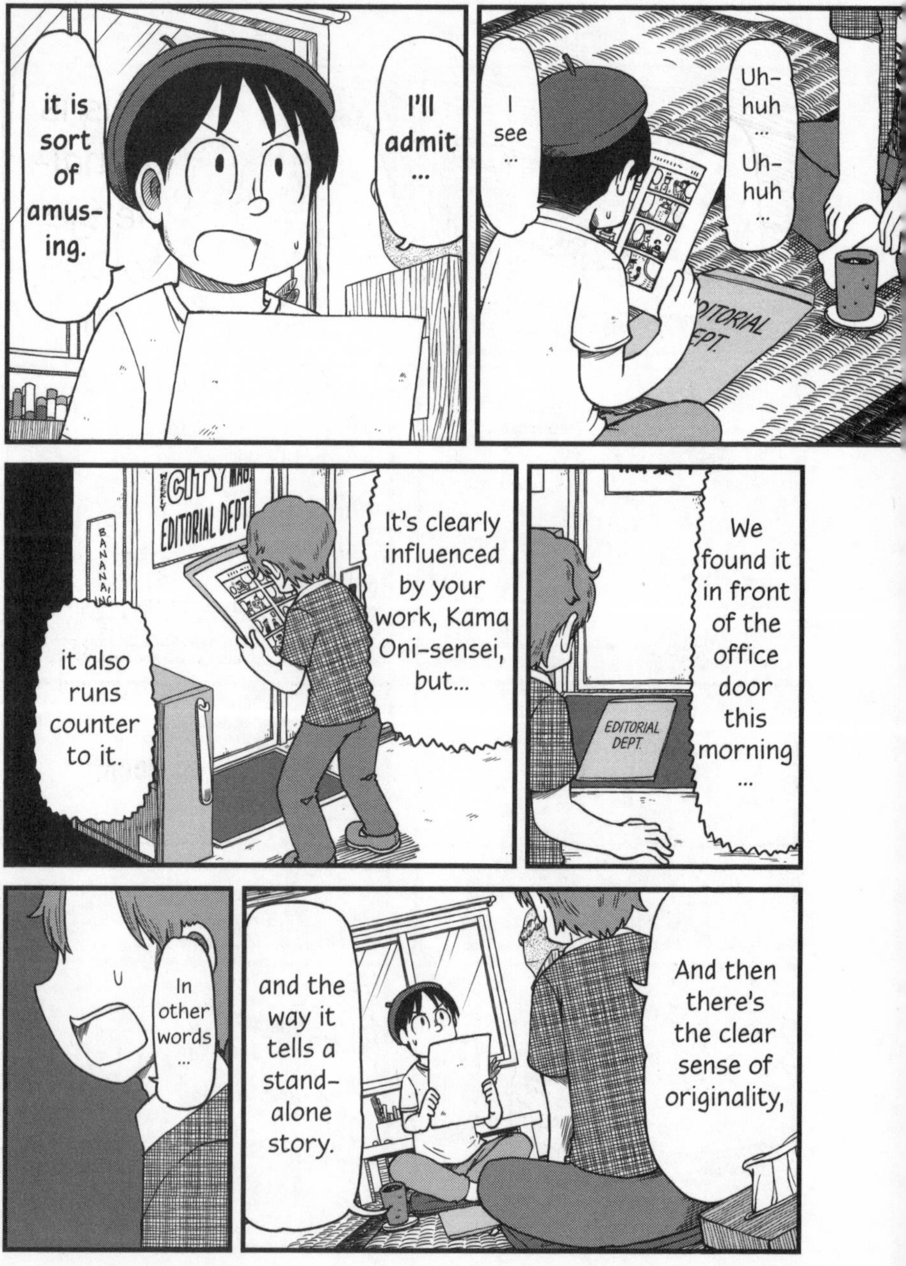
Uh-huh ... Uh-huh ...
I see ...
EDITORIAL DEPT.
I'll admit ...
it is sort of amusing.
We found it in front of the office door this morning ...
EDITORIAL DEPT.
It's clearly influenced by your work, Kama Oni-sensei, but...
WEEKLY CITY MAG.
EDITORIAL DEPT
it also runs counter to it.
And then there's the clear sense of originality,
and the way it tells a stand-alone story.
In other words ...

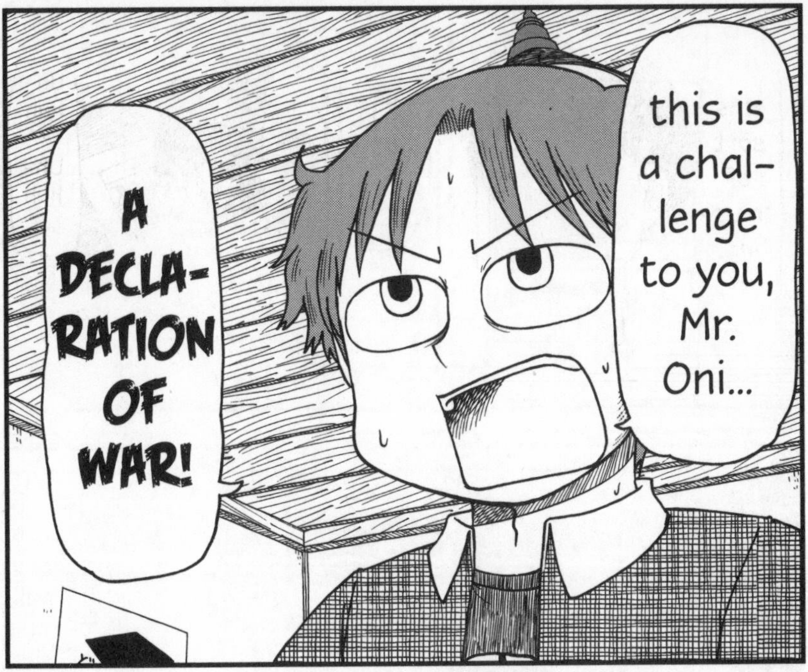
this is a chal-lenge to you, Mr. Oni...
A DECLA-RATION OF WAR!

Chapter 55 ◇ Freesia in the Tatami Room

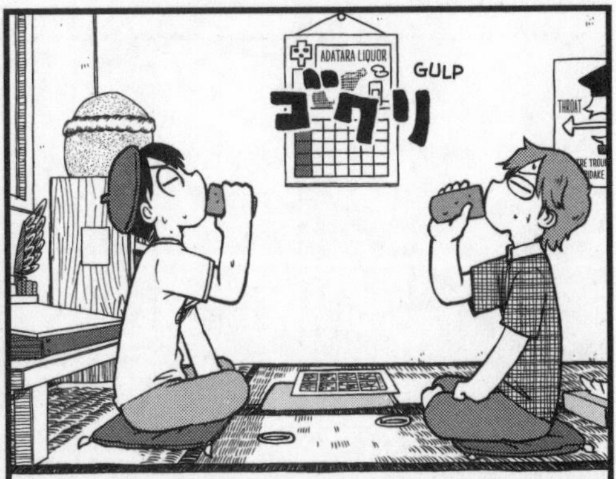
ADATARA LIQUOR
GULP
ゴクリ
THROAT

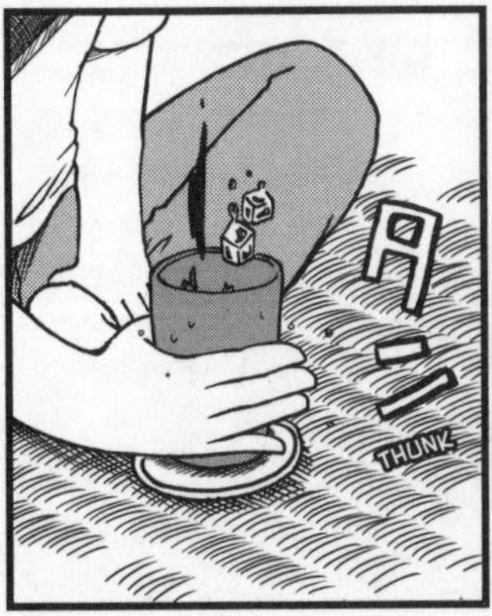
THUNK

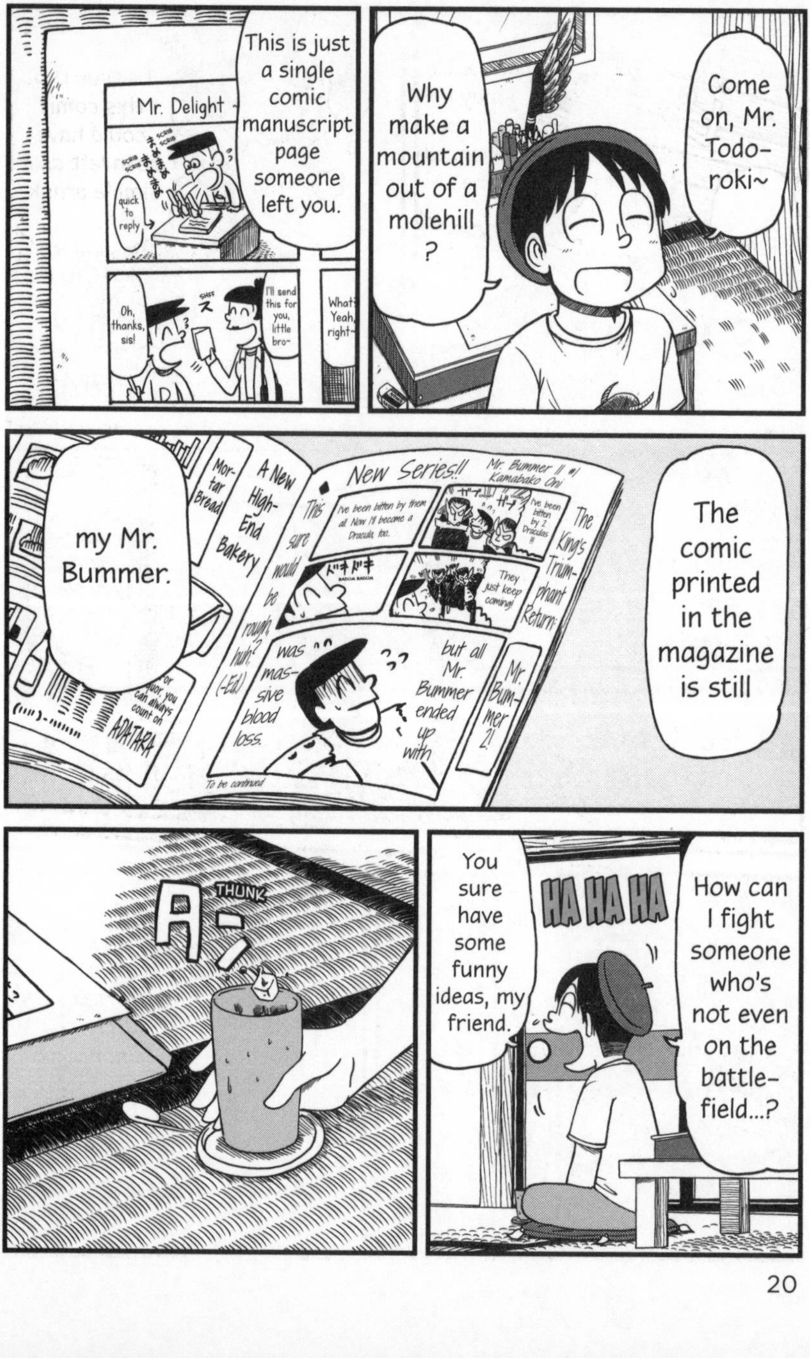
Come on, Mr. Todoroki~
Why make a mountain out of a molehill?
This is just a single comic manuscript page someone left you.
Mr. Delight~
SCRIB SCRIB
quick to reply
I'll send this for you, little bro~
What? Yeah, right~
SHFF
Oh, thanks, sis!
The comic printed in the magazine is still
New Series!!
Mr. Bummer II #1
Kamabako Oni
The King's Triumphant Return: Mr. Bummer 2!
I've been bitten by 2 Draculas!!!
I've been bitten by them all. Now I'll become a Dracula, too.
They just keep coming!
BADUM BADUM
but all Mr. Bummer ended up with
was massive blood loss.
This sure would be rough, huh? (-Ed.)
To be continued
A New High-End Bakery
Mortar Bread
can always count on
ADATARA
my Mr. Bummer.
How can I fight someone who's not even on the battlefield...?
HA HA HA
You sure have some funny ideas, my friend.
THUNK

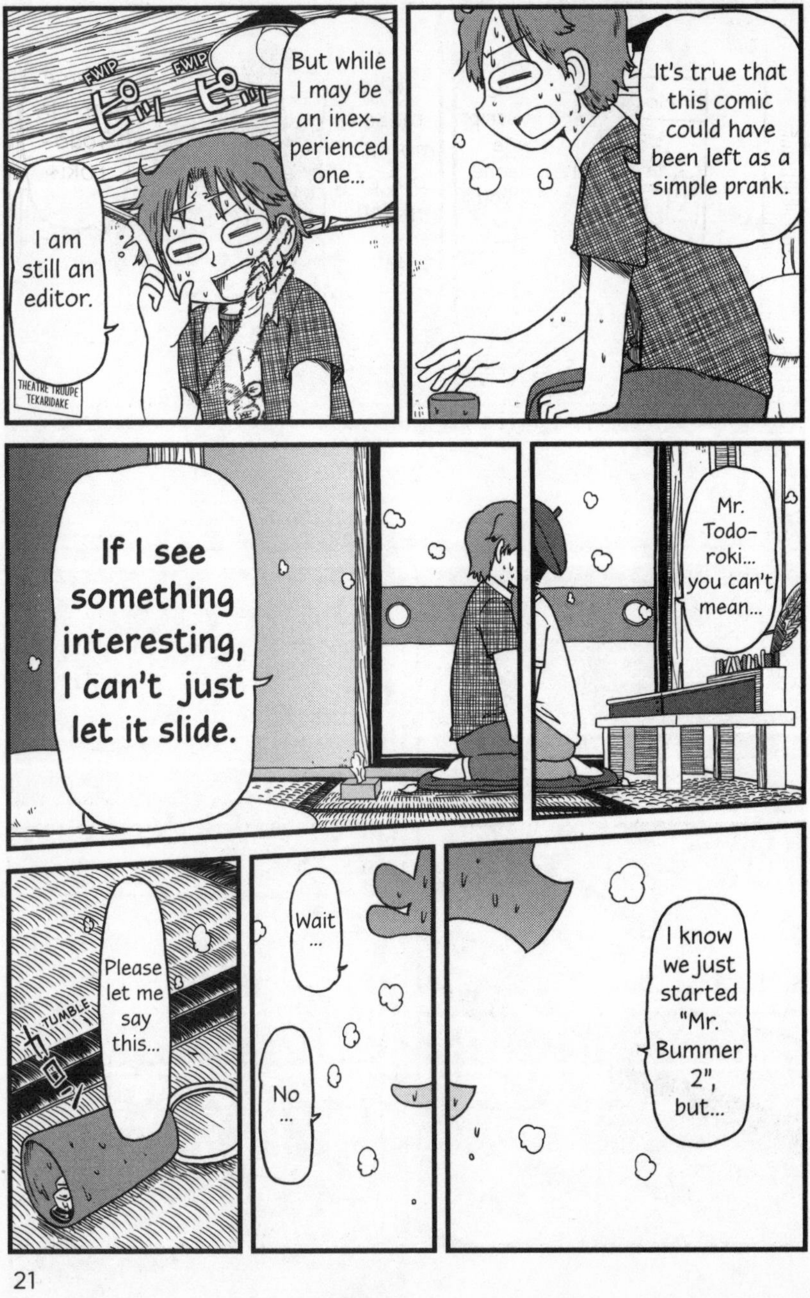
It's true that this comic could have been left as a simple prank.
But while I may be an inex-perienced one...
FWIP FWIP
ピッ ピッ
I am still an editor.
THEATRE TROUPE TEKARIDAKE
Mr. Todo-roki... you can't mean...
If I see something interesting, I can't just let it slide.
I know we just started "Mr. Bummer 2", but...
Wait...
No...
Please let me say this...
TUMBLE

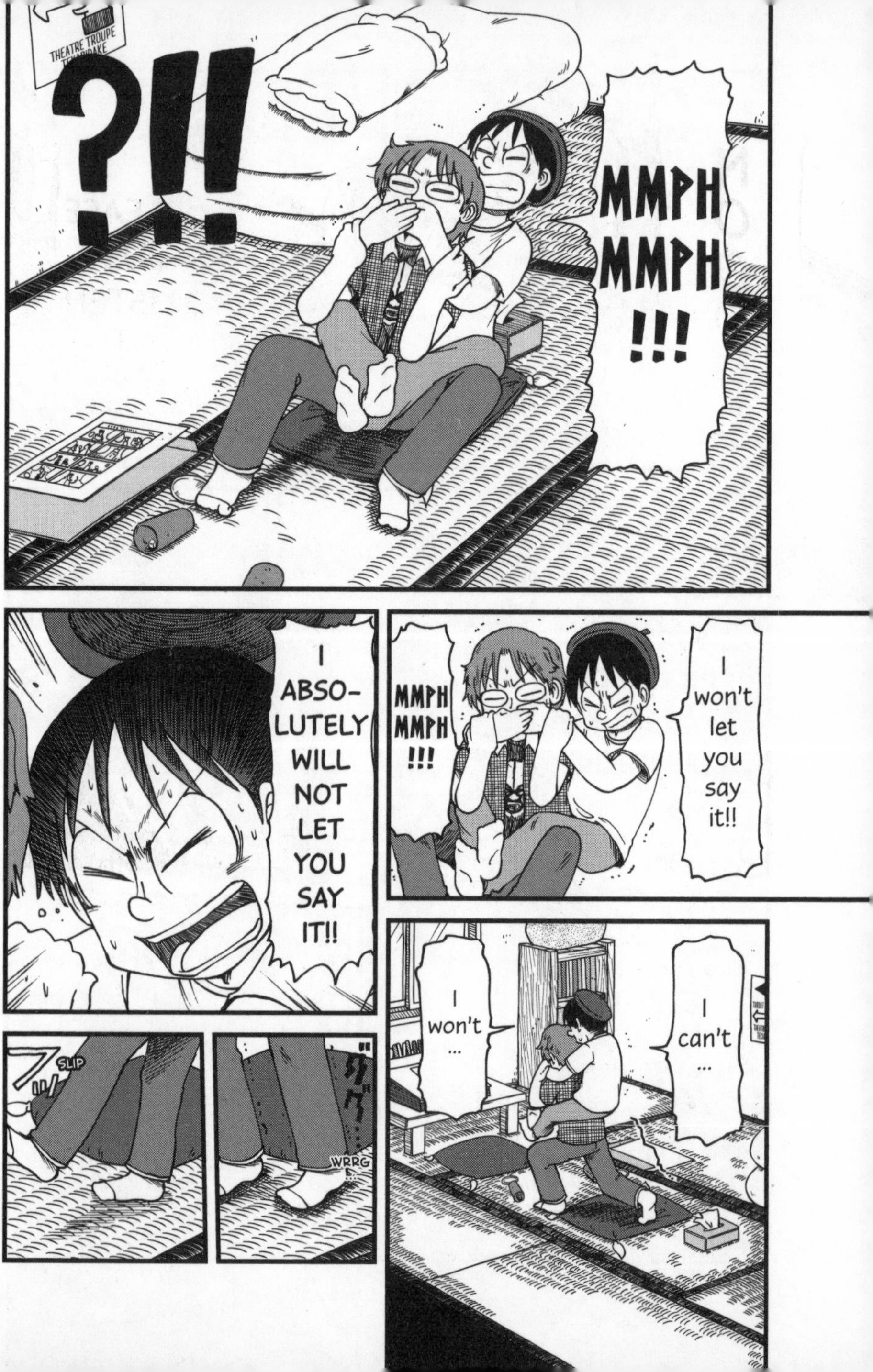
MMPH
MMPH
!!!
?!!
THEATRE TROUPE
I won't let you say it!!
MMPH
MMPH
!!!
I ABSOLUTELY WILL NOT LET YOU SAY IT!!
WRRG
SLIP
I can't ...
I won't ...

NOOOOO!!

PLEASE JUST LISTEN!

KRAASH

Why?!

I can't hear you!!

GRA GRA GRA GRA WRRG

No, no, no!

Why...

Why...

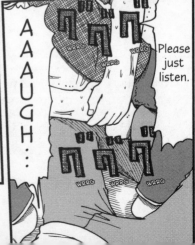

AAAUGH...

WRRG WRRG WRRG WRRG WRRG WRRG

Please just listen.

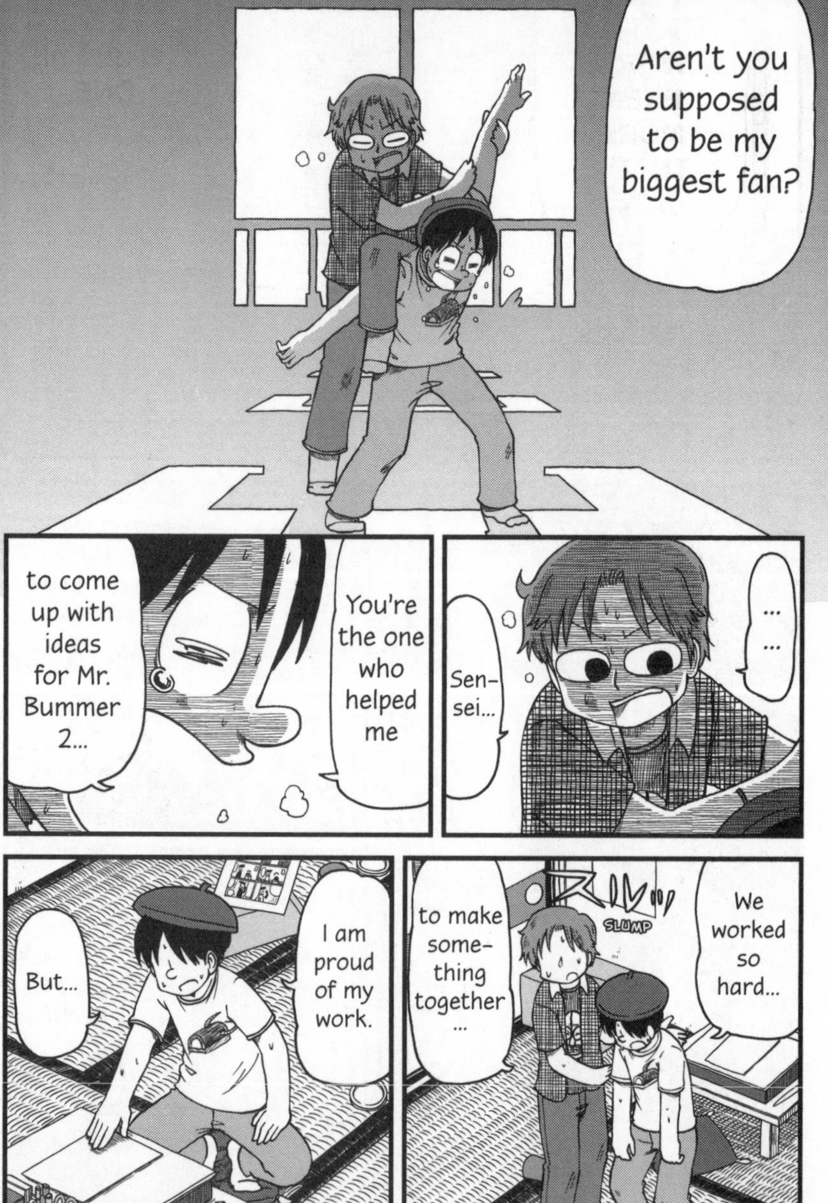
Aren't you supposed to be my biggest fan?
......
Sen-sei...
You're the one who helped me
to come up with ideas for Mr. Bummer 2...
We worked so hard...
SLUMP
to make some-thing together...
I am proud of my work.
But...

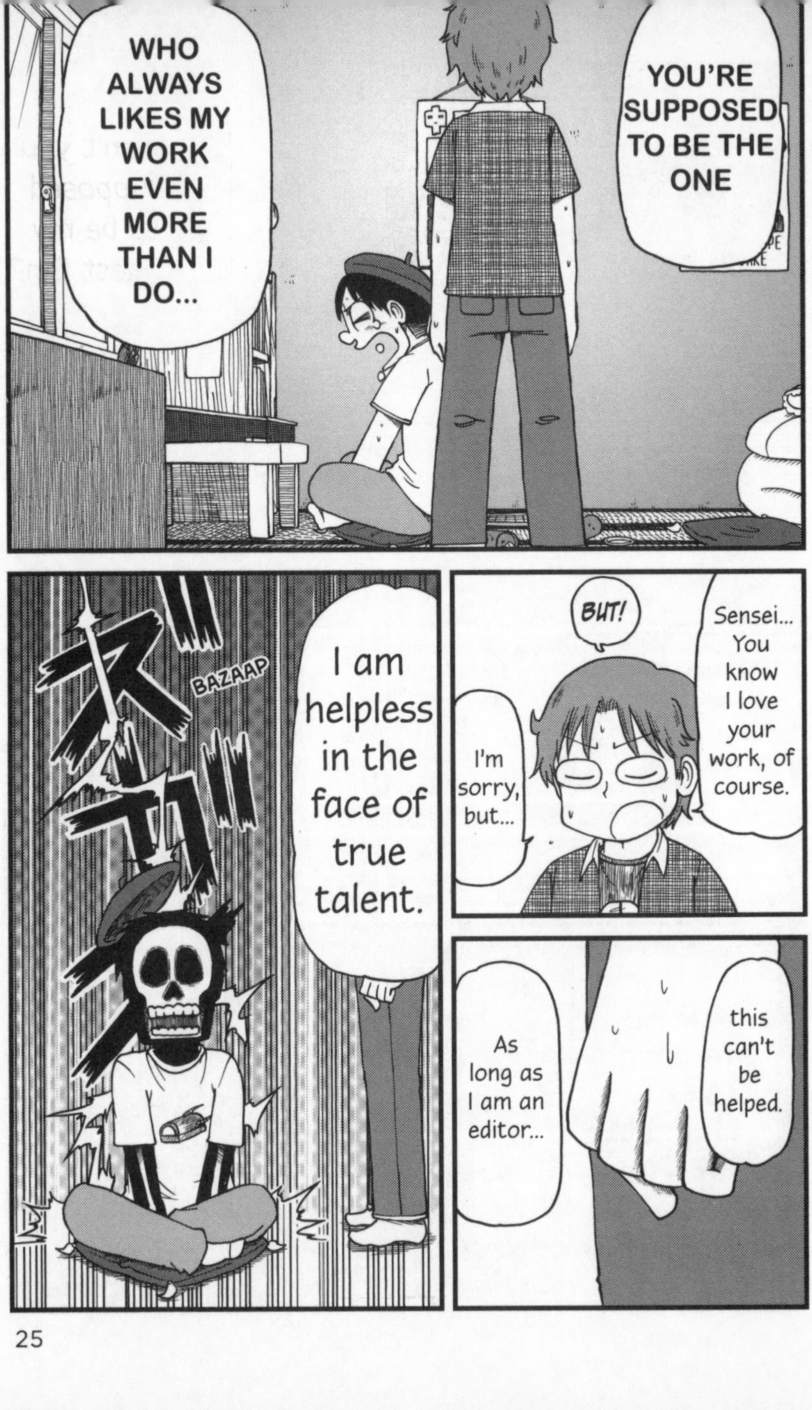
YOU'RE SUPPOSED TO BE THE ONE
WHO ALWAYS LIKES MY WORK EVEN MORE THAN I DO...
Sensei... You know I love your work, of course.
BUT!
I'm sorry, but...
this can't be helped.
As long as I am an editor...
I am helpless in the face of true talent.
BAZAAP

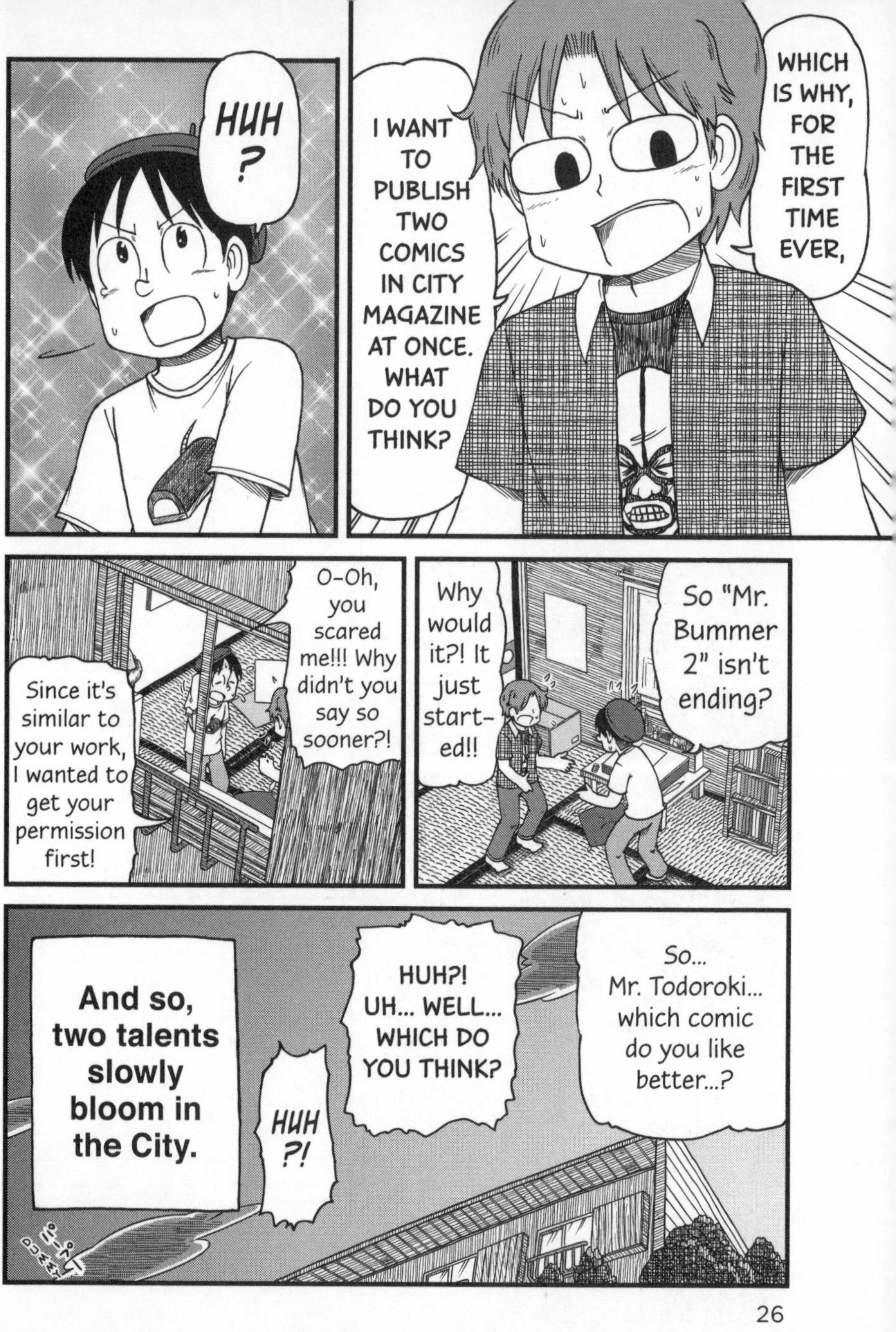
WHICH IS WHY, FOR THE FIRST TIME EVER,
I WANT TO PUBLISH TWO COMICS IN CITY MAGAZINE AT ONCE. WHAT DO YOU THINK?
HUH?
So "Mr. Bummer 2" isn't ending?
Why would it?! It just start-ed!!
O-Oh, you scared me!!! Why didn't you say so sooner?!
Since it's similar to your work, I wanted to get your permission first!
So... Mr. Todoroki... which comic do you like better...?
HUH?! UH... WELL... WHICH DO YOU THINK?
HUH?!
And so, two talents slowly bloom in the City.

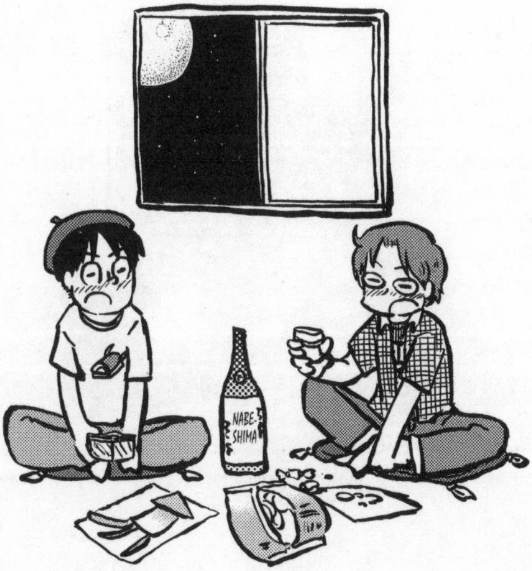
NABE-
SHIMA

CITY

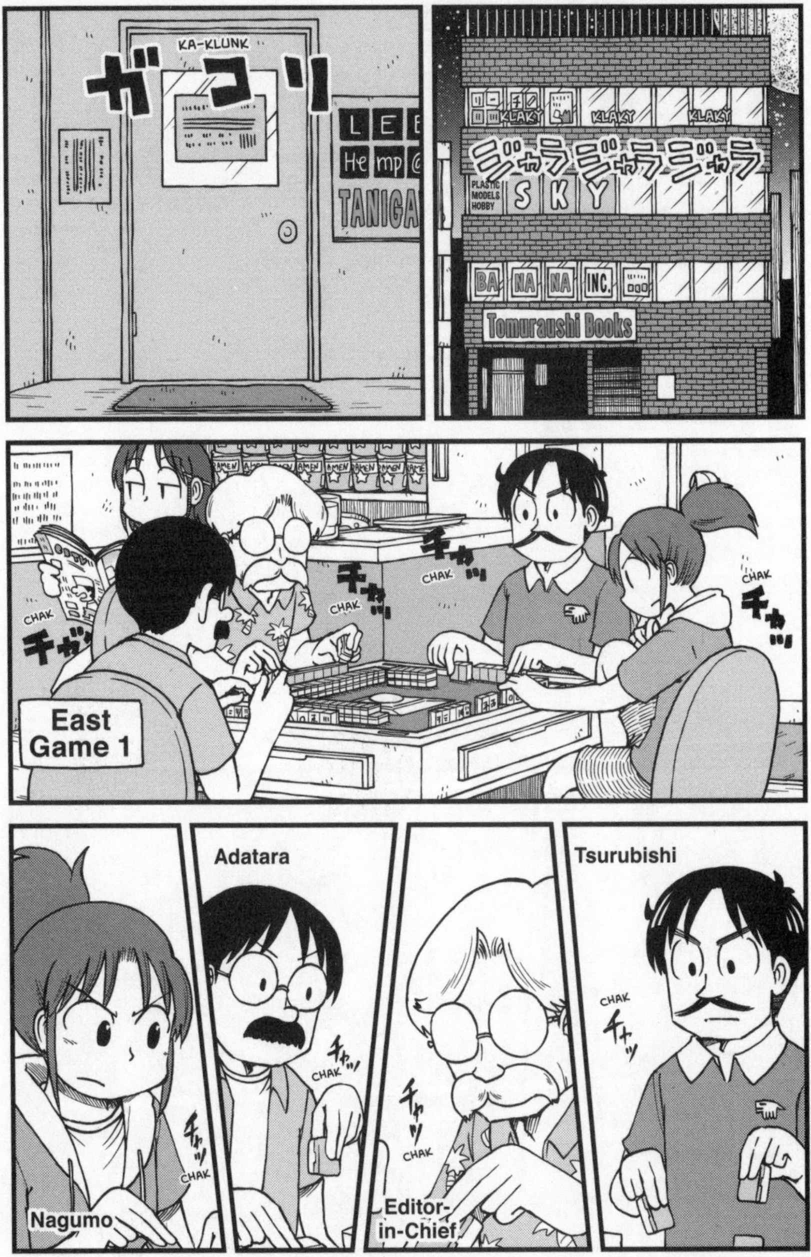
KLAKY
KLAKY
KLAKY
ジャラジャラジャラ
PLASTIC MODELS HOBBY
S K Y
BA NA NA INC.
Tomuraushi Books
ガコッ
KA-KLUNK
CHAK
チャッ
CHAK
チャッ
CHAK
チャッ
CHAK
チャッ
East Game 1
Tsurubishi
チャッ
CHAK
チャッ
CHAK
Editor-in-Chief
Adatara
チャッ
CHAK
チャッ
CHAK
Nagumo

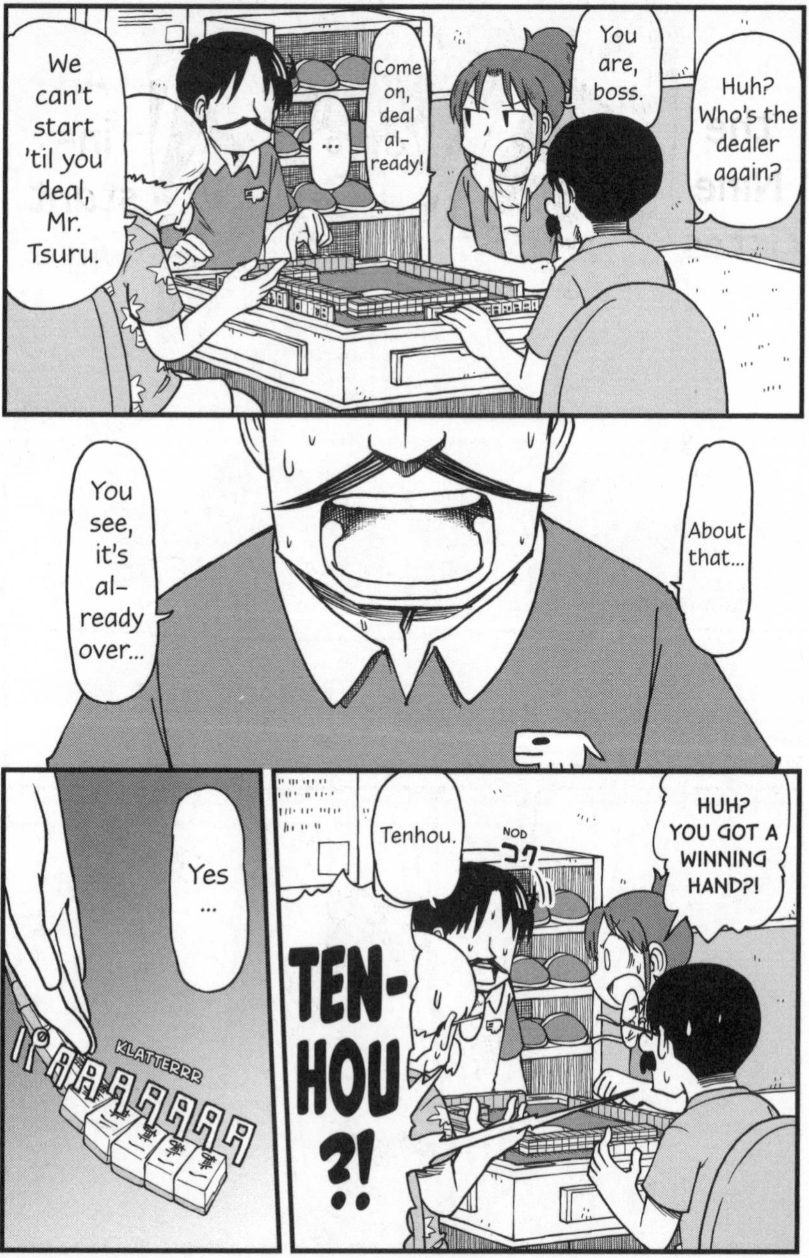
Huh? Who's the dealer again?
You are, boss.
Come on, deal al-ready!
...
We can't start 'til you deal, Mr. Tsuru.
About that...
You see, it's al-ready over...
HUH? YOU GOT A WINNING HAND?!
NOD
Tenhou.
TEN-HOU ?!
Yes ...
KLATTERRR

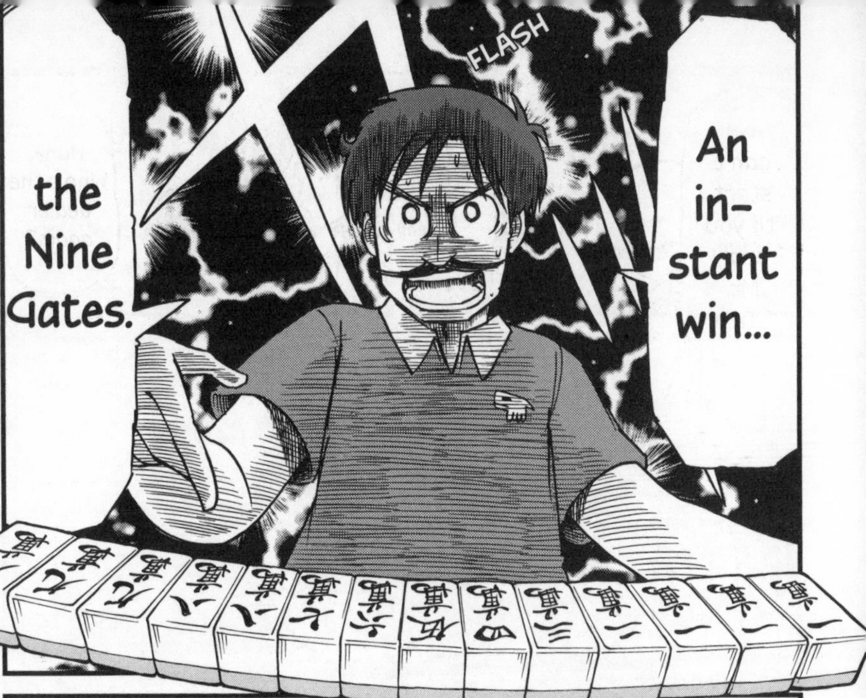
FLASH
An in-stant win...
the Nine Gates.

Chapter 56 Death of Tsurubishi?!

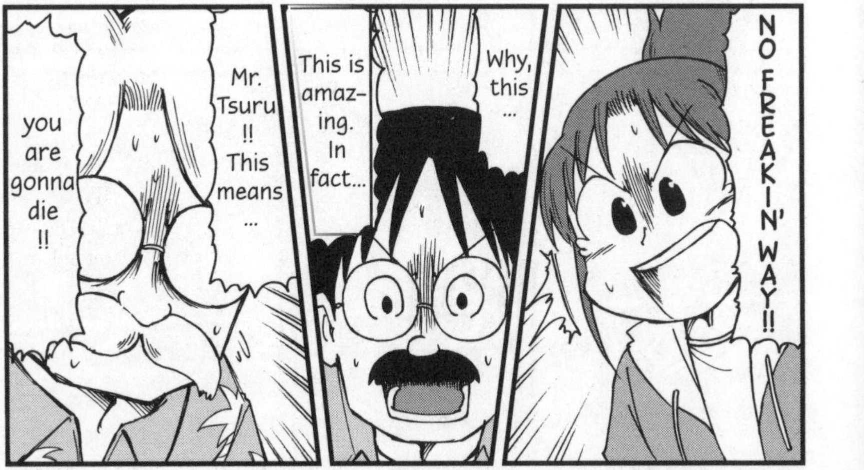
NO FREAKIN' WAY!!
Why, this ...
This is amaz-ing. In fact...
Mr. Tsuru!! This means ...
you are gonna die!!

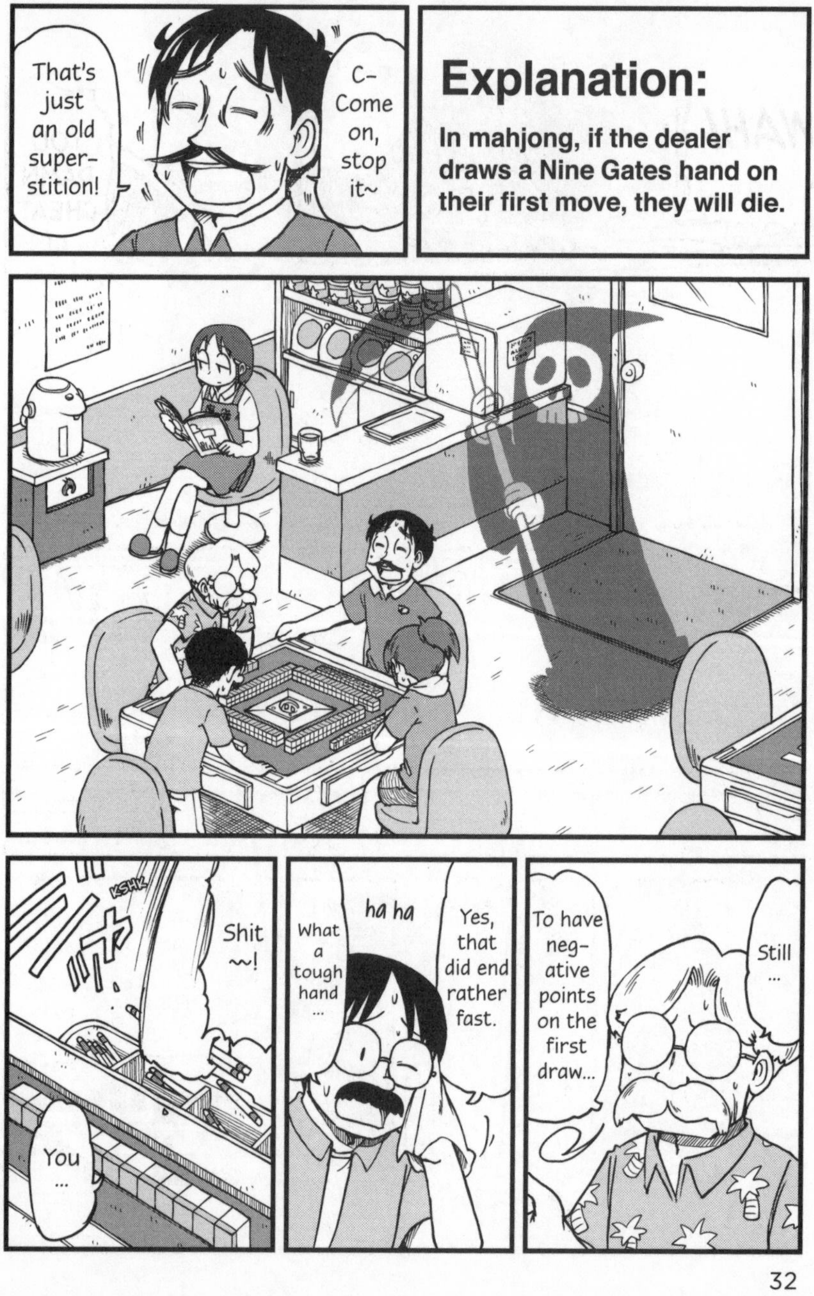
Explanation:
In mahjong, if the dealer draws a Nine Gates hand on their first move, they will die.
C- Come on, stop it~
That's just an old super-stition!
Still ...
To have neg-ative points on the first draw...
Yes, that did end rather fast.
ha ha
What a tough hand ...
Shit ~!
KSHK
You ...

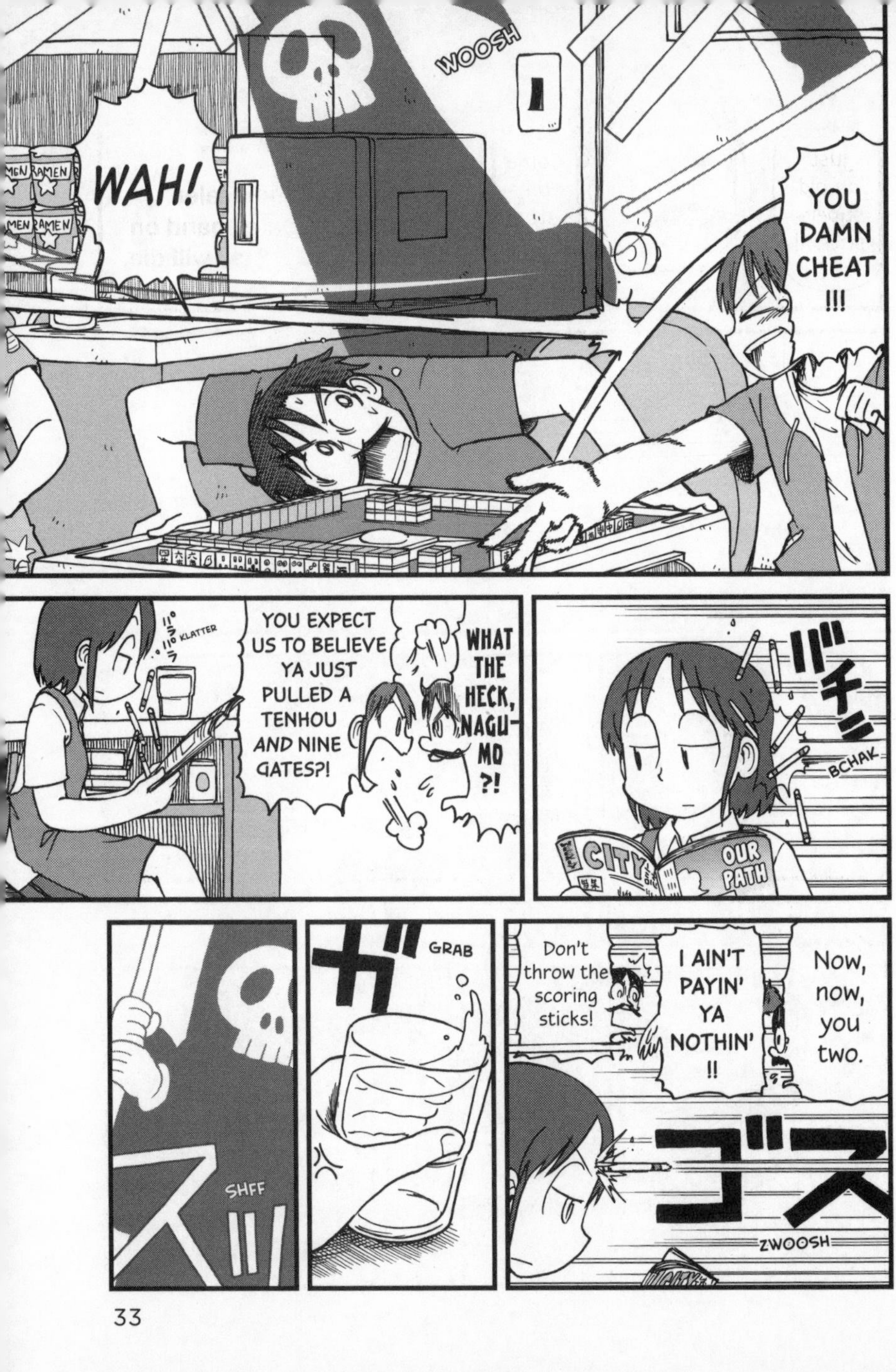
YOU DAMN CHEAT !!!
WOOSH
WAH!
BCHAK
CITY
OUR PATH
WHAT THE HECK, NAGUMO ?!
YOU EXPECT US TO BELIEVE YA JUST PULLED A TENHOU AND NINE GATES?!
KLATTER
Now, now, you two.
I AIN'T PAYIN' YA NOTHIN' !!
Don't throw the scoring sticks!
ゴス
ZWOOSH
GRAB
SHFF

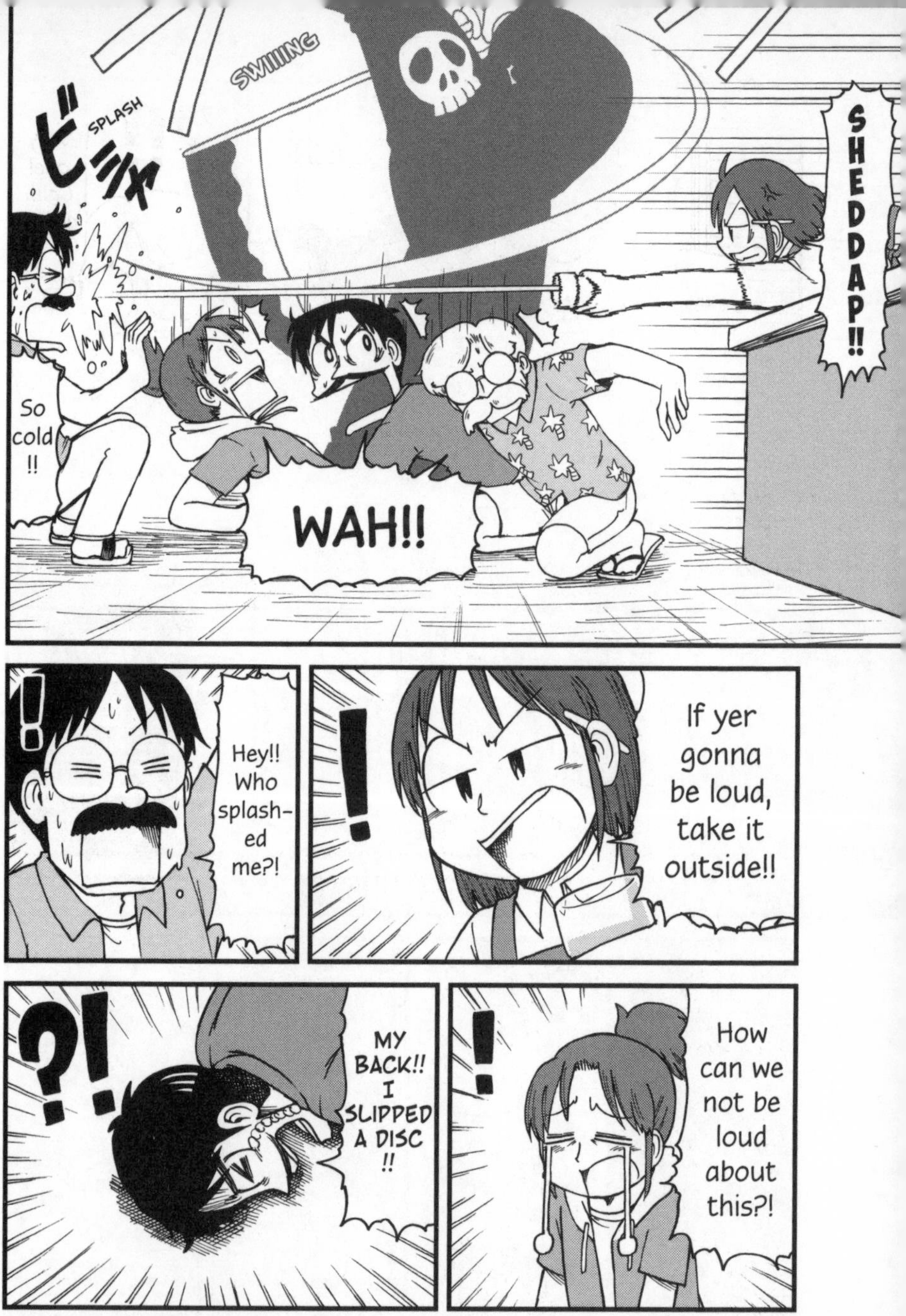
SHEDDAP!!
SWIIIING
ビシャ
SPLASH
WAH!!
So cold!!
If yer gonna be loud, take it outside!!
Hey!! Who splash-ed me?!
How can we not be loud about this?!
MY BACK!! I SLIPPED A DISC!!

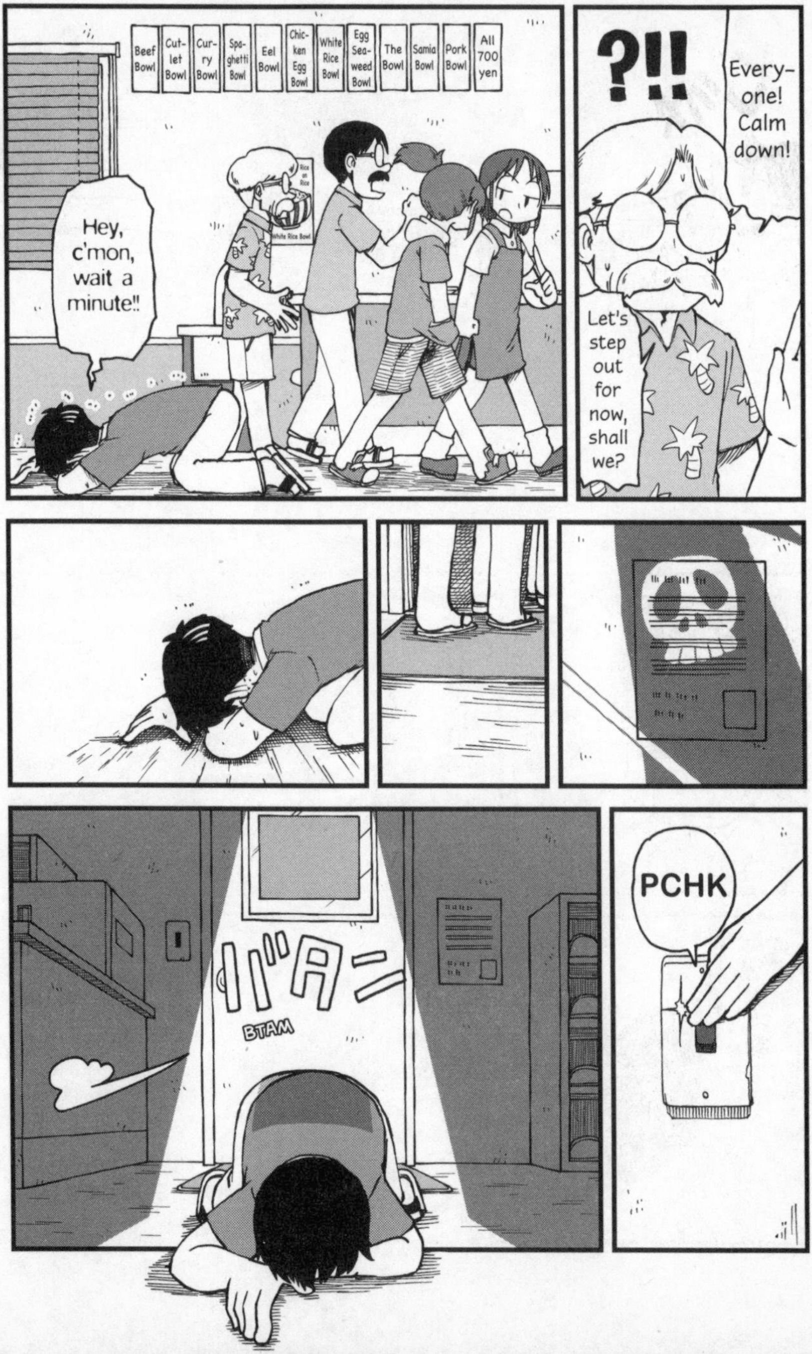
?!!
Everyone! Calm down!
Let's step out for now, shall we?
Beef Bowl
Cutlet Bowl
Curry Bowl
Spaghetti Bowl
Eel Bowl
Chicken Egg Bowl
White Rice Bowl
Egg Seaweed Bowl
The Bowl
Samia Bowl
Pork Bowl
All 700 yen
Rice on Rice
White Rice Bowl
Hey, c'mon, wait a minute!!
PCHK
バタン
BTAM

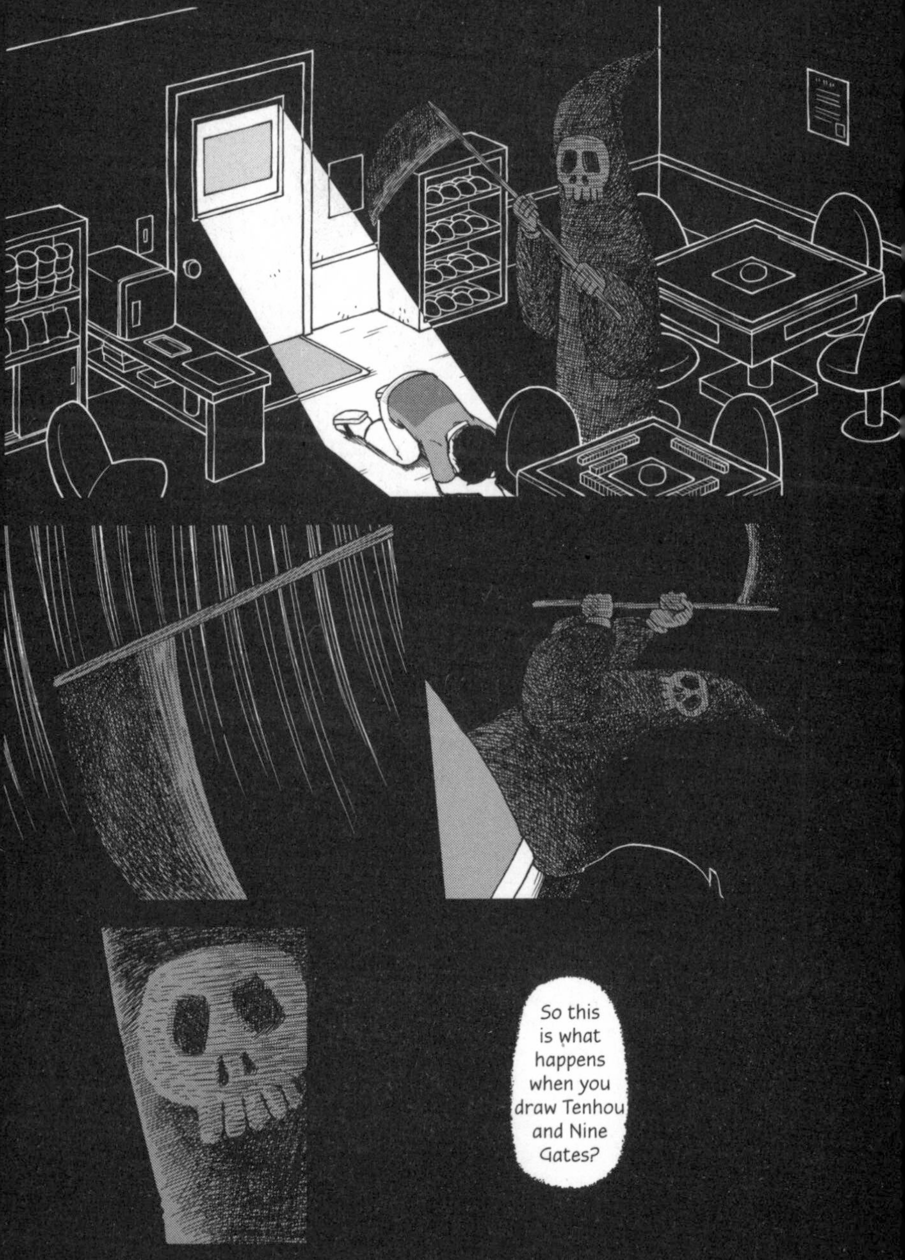
So this is what happens when you draw Tenhou and Nine Gates?

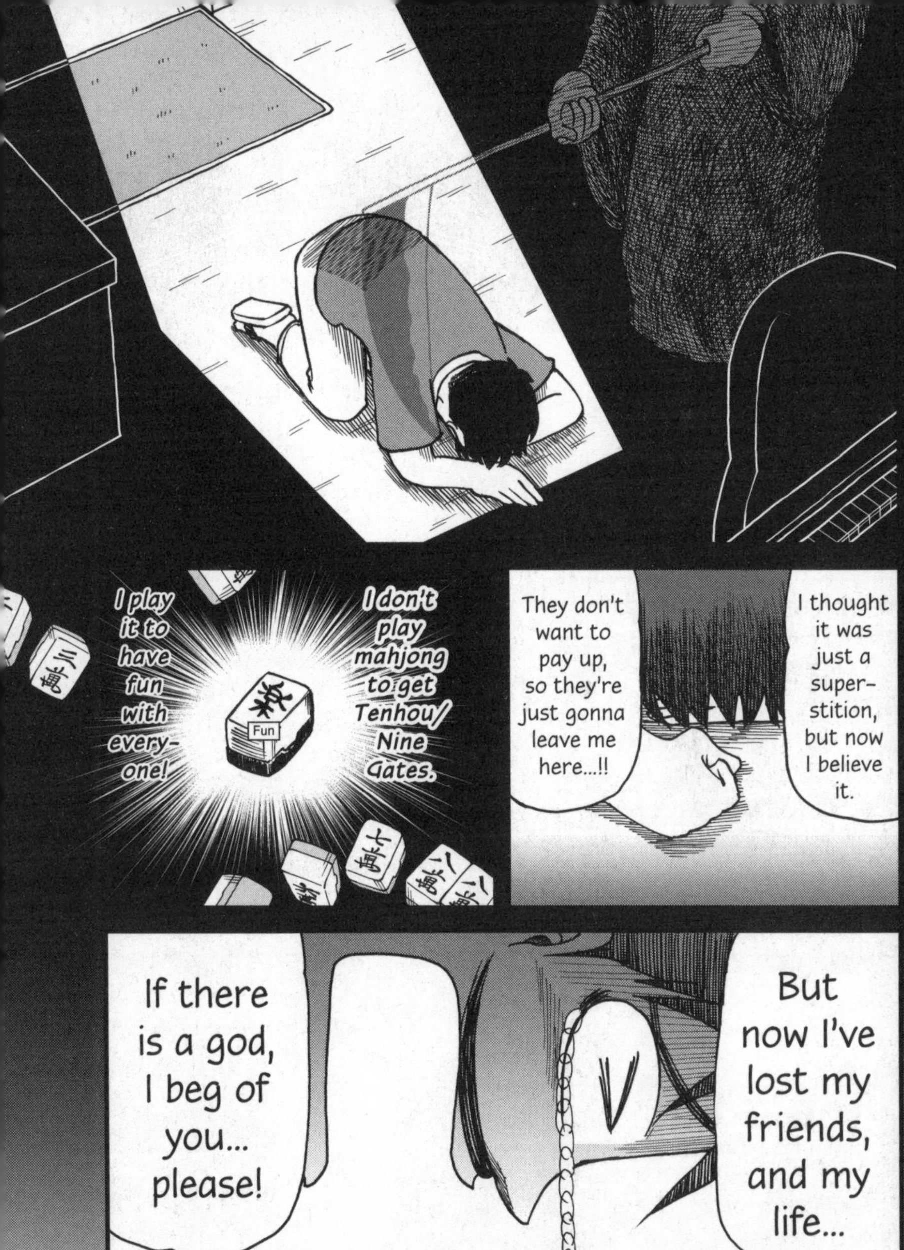
I thought it was just a super-stition, but now I believe it.
They don't want to pay up, so they're just gonna leave me here...!!
I don't play mahjong to get Tenhou/ Nine Gates.
Fun
I play it to have fun with every-one!
But now I've lost my friends, and my life...
If there is a god, I beg of you... please!

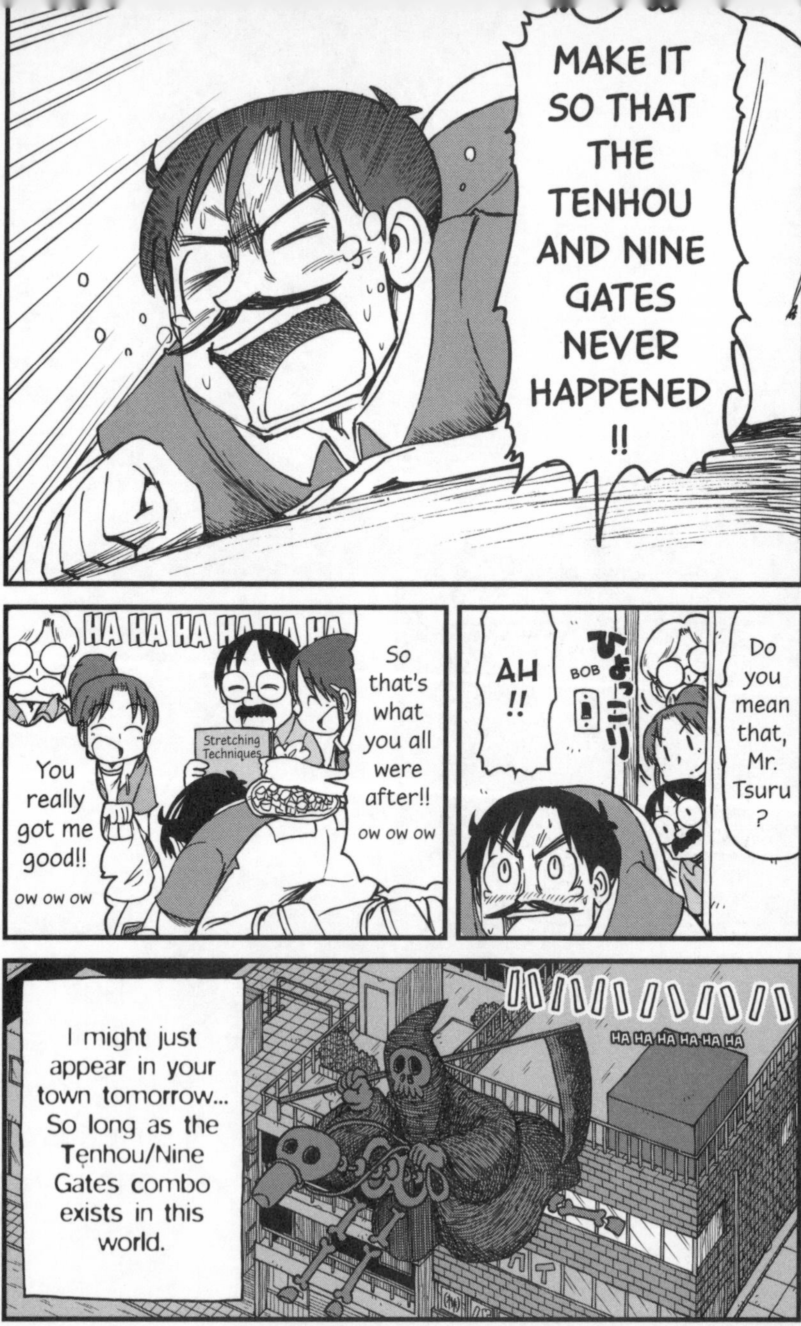

MAKE IT SO THAT THE TENHOU AND NINE GATES NEVER HAPPENED !!
Do you mean that, Mr. Tsuru ?
ひょっこり
BOB
AH !!
HA HA HA HA HA HA
So that's what you all were after!!
OW OW OW
Stretching Techniques
You really got me good!!
OW OW OW
I might just appear in your town tomorrow... So long as the Tenhou/Nine Gates combo exists in this world.
HA HA HA HA HA HA

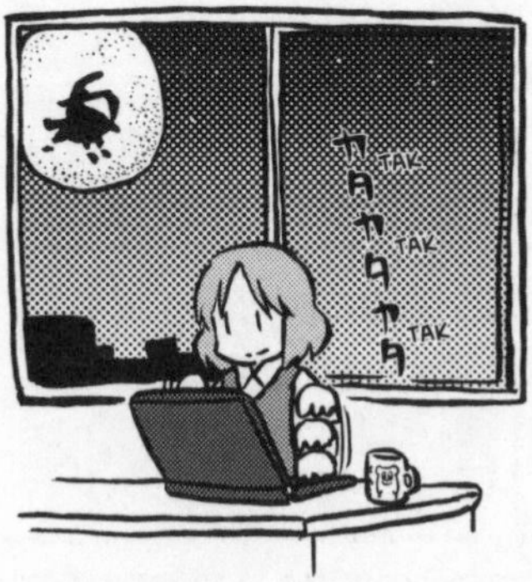
カタカタカタ
TAK
TAK
TAK

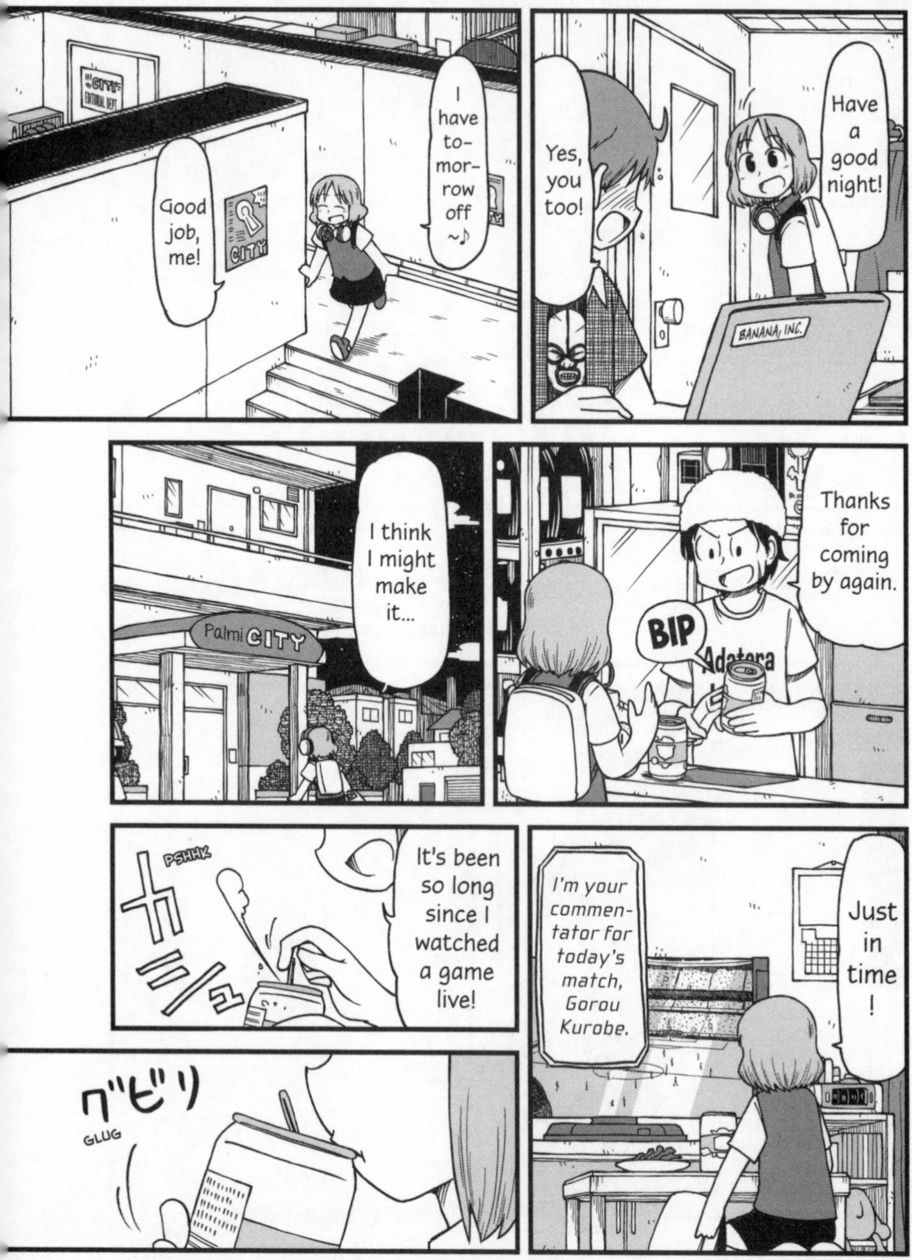
Have a good night!
Yes, you too!
BANANA, INC.
I have to-mor-row off ~♪
Good job, me!
CITY
EDITORIAL DEPT
Thanks for coming by again.
BIP
Adatora
I think I might make it...
Palmi CITY
Just in time!
I'm your commen-tator for today's match, Gorou Kurobe.
It's been so long since I watched a game live!
PSHHK
カシュ
グビリ
GLUG

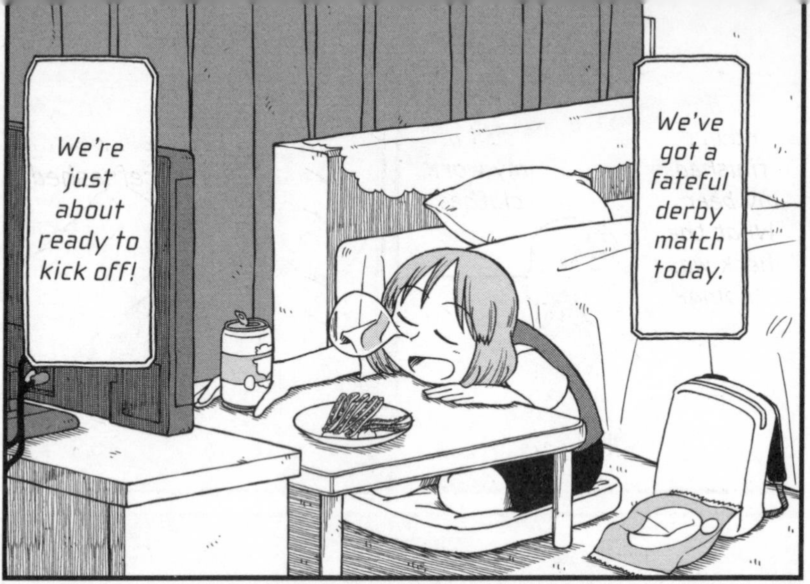
We've got a fateful derby match today.
We're just about ready to kick off!

Chapter 57 Single 28-year-old Office Lady: Ms. Arama's Path to the Perfect Day Off

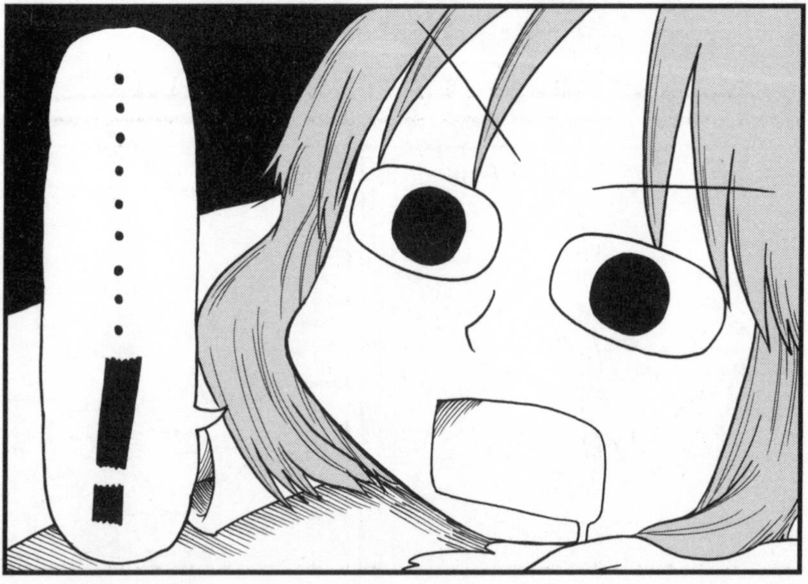
.........!

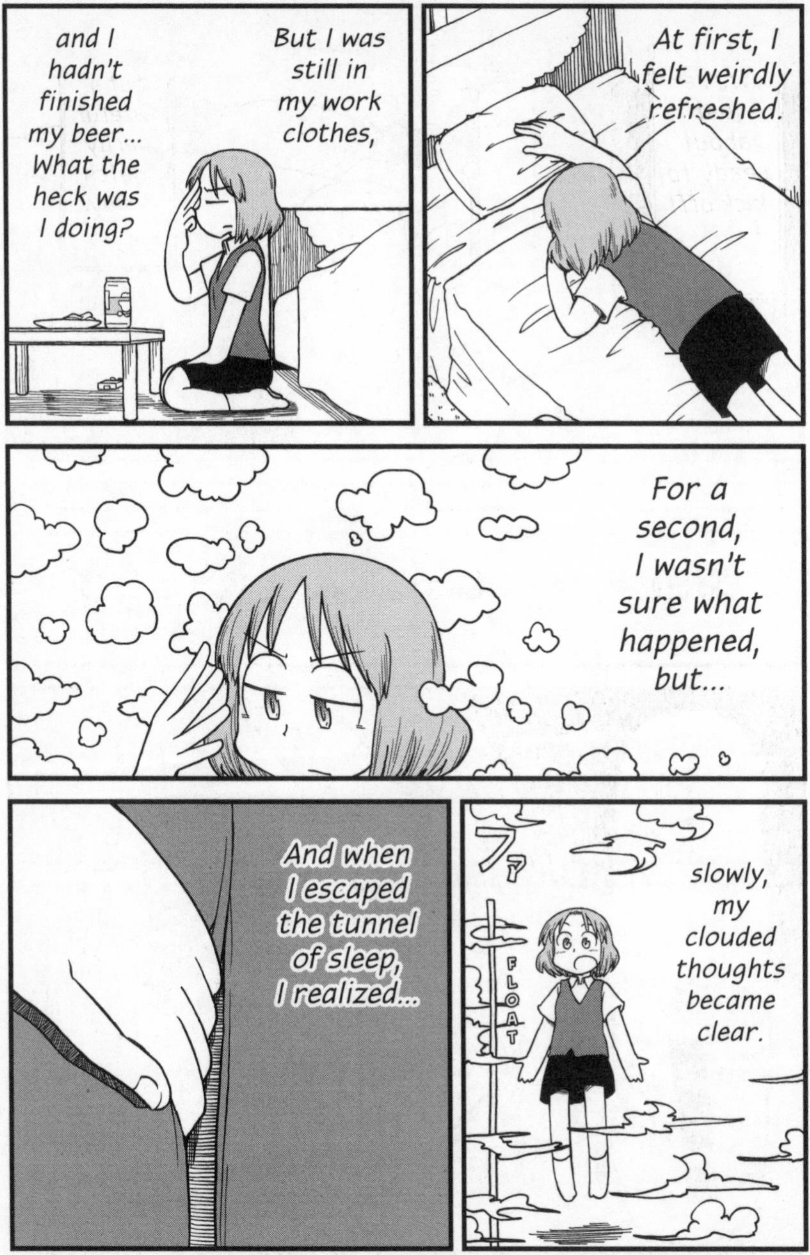
At first, I felt weirdly refreshed.
But I was still in my work clothes,
and I hadn't finished my beer... What the heck was I doing?
For a second, I wasn't sure what happened, but...
ファ
slowly, my clouded thoughts became clear.
FLOAT
And when I escaped the tunnel of sleep, I realized...

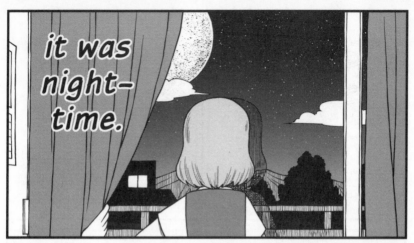

it was night-time.
19:16
I had slept the day away.
I was supposed to clean in the morning,
POOF
ポン
SPARKLE
シャラン
SHINE
ピカー
スイー
SWEEEEEEE
then have brunch at a river-side café,
and then I'd get a slice of their famous light and airy chocolat cake to go.

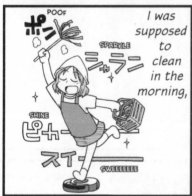

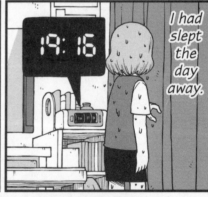

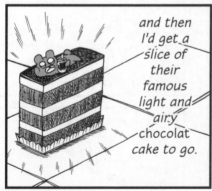

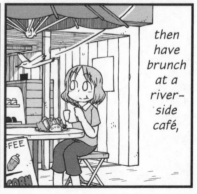

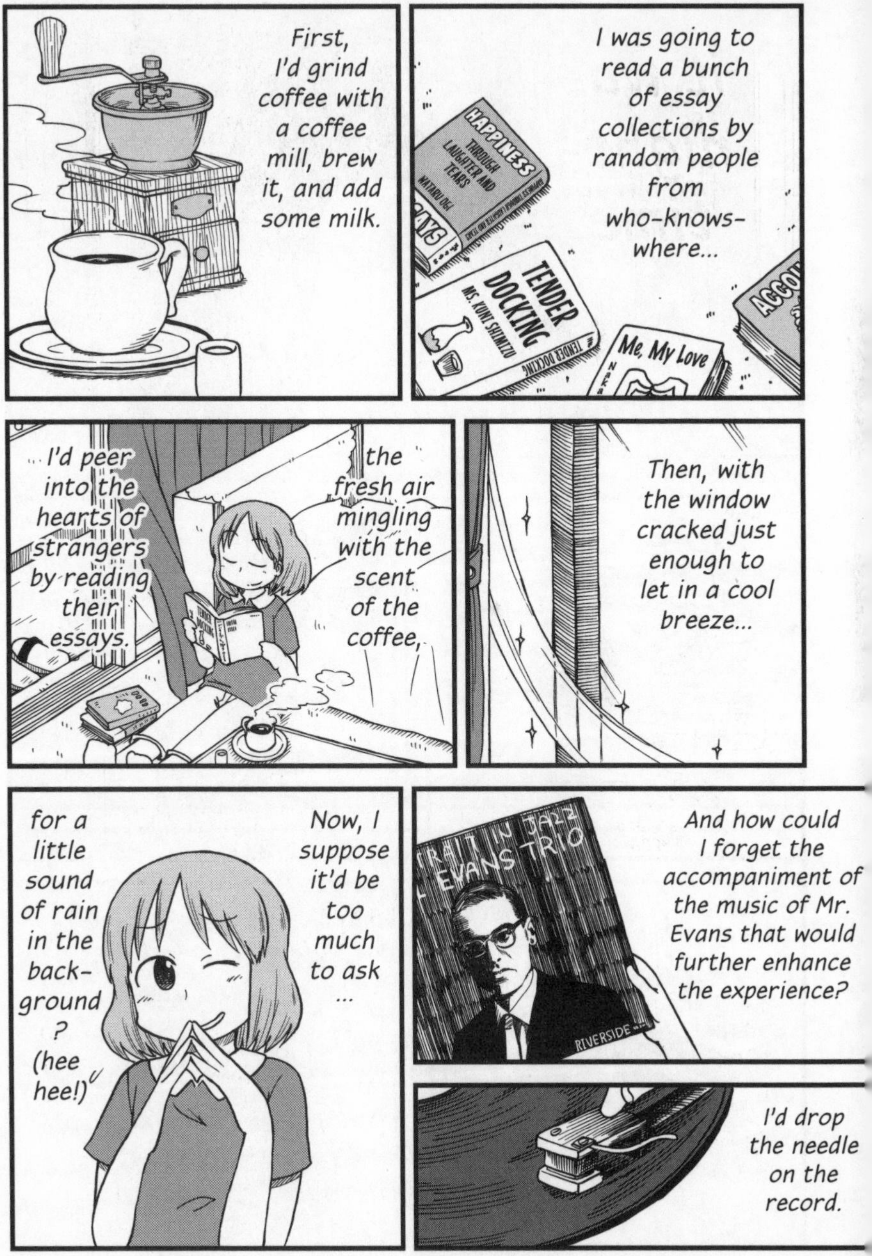
I was going to read a bunch of essay collections by random people from who-knows-where...
HAPPINESS THROUGH LAUGHTER AND TEARS
TENDER DOCKING
MS. KUNI SHIMIZU
Me, My Love
First, I'd grind coffee with a coffee mill, brew it, and add some milk.
Then, with the window cracked just enough to let in a cool breeze...
the fresh air mingling with the scent of the coffee,
...I'd peer into the hearts of strangers by reading their essays.
And how could I forget the accompaniment of the music of Mr. Evans that would further enhance the experience?
EVANS TRIO
RIVERSIDE
I'd drop the needle on the record.
Now, I suppose it'd be too much to ask ...
for a little sound of rain in the background?
(hee hee!)

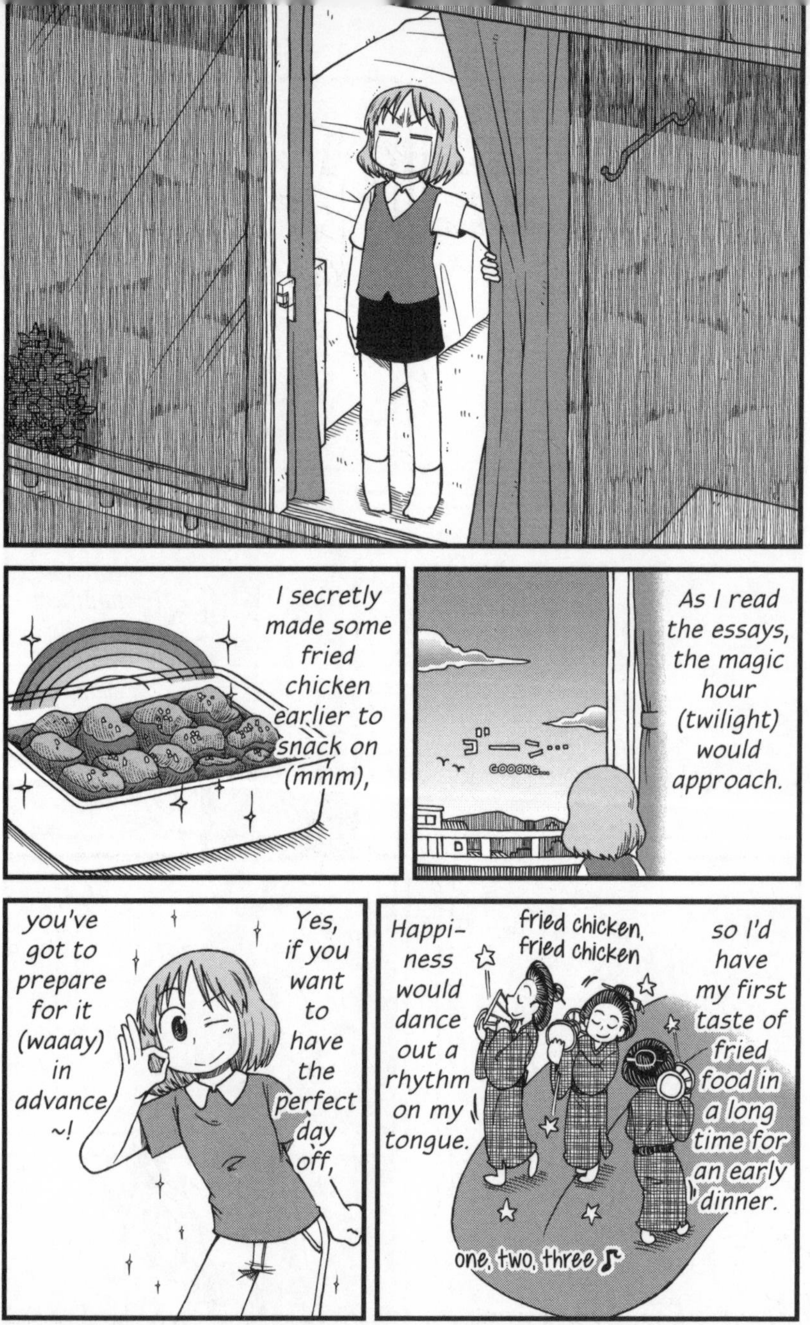
As I read the essays, the magic hour (twilight) would approach.
ゴーン…
GOOONG...
I secretly made some fried chicken earlier to snack on (mmm),
so I'd have my first taste of fried food in a long time for an early dinner.
fried chicken, fried chicken
Happiness would dance out a rhythm on my tongue.
one, two, three ♪
Yes, if you want to have the perfect day off,
you've got to prepare for it (waaay) in advance~!

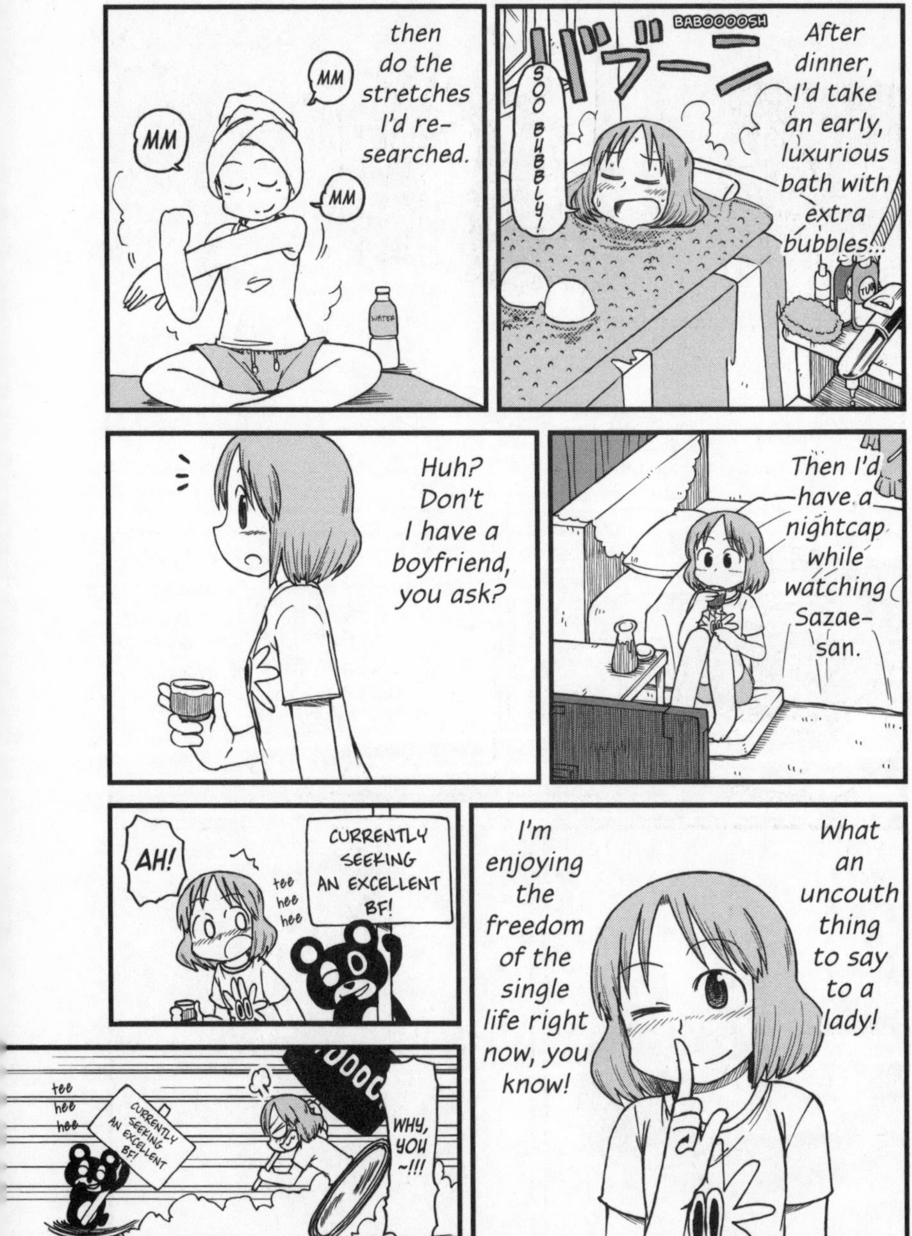
BABOOOOSH
After dinner, I'd take an early, luxurious bath with extra bubbles...
SOO BUBBLY!
then do the stretches I'd re-searched.
MM
MM
MM
WATER
Then I'd have a nightcap while watching Sazae-san.
Huh? Don't I have a boyfriend, you ask?
What an uncouth thing to say to a lady!
I'm enjoying the freedom of the single life right now, you know!
CURRENTLY SEEKING AN EXCELLENT BF!
tee hee hee
AH!
WHY, YOU ~!!!
CURRENTLY SEEKING AN EXCELLENT BF!
tee hee hee

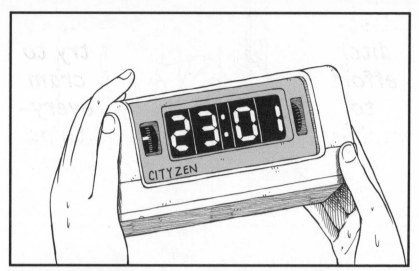

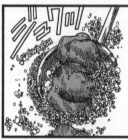

CITYZEN
23:01
I only get one shot at this.
ガリガリ
GRIND GRIND
ガリガリ
GRIND GRIND
ガリガリ
GRIND GRIND
If I don't act fast, my perfect day off will be ruined...!
ジュワッ
ZWASH
The despair of sleeping through my day off
テ
TROT
テテテ
TROT TROT
and the desperation of not being able to carry out my perfect plan...
スー
SHOOOOMF

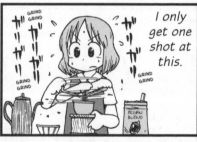

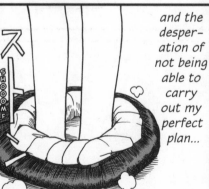

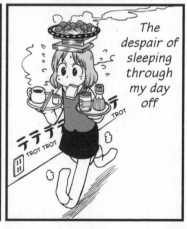

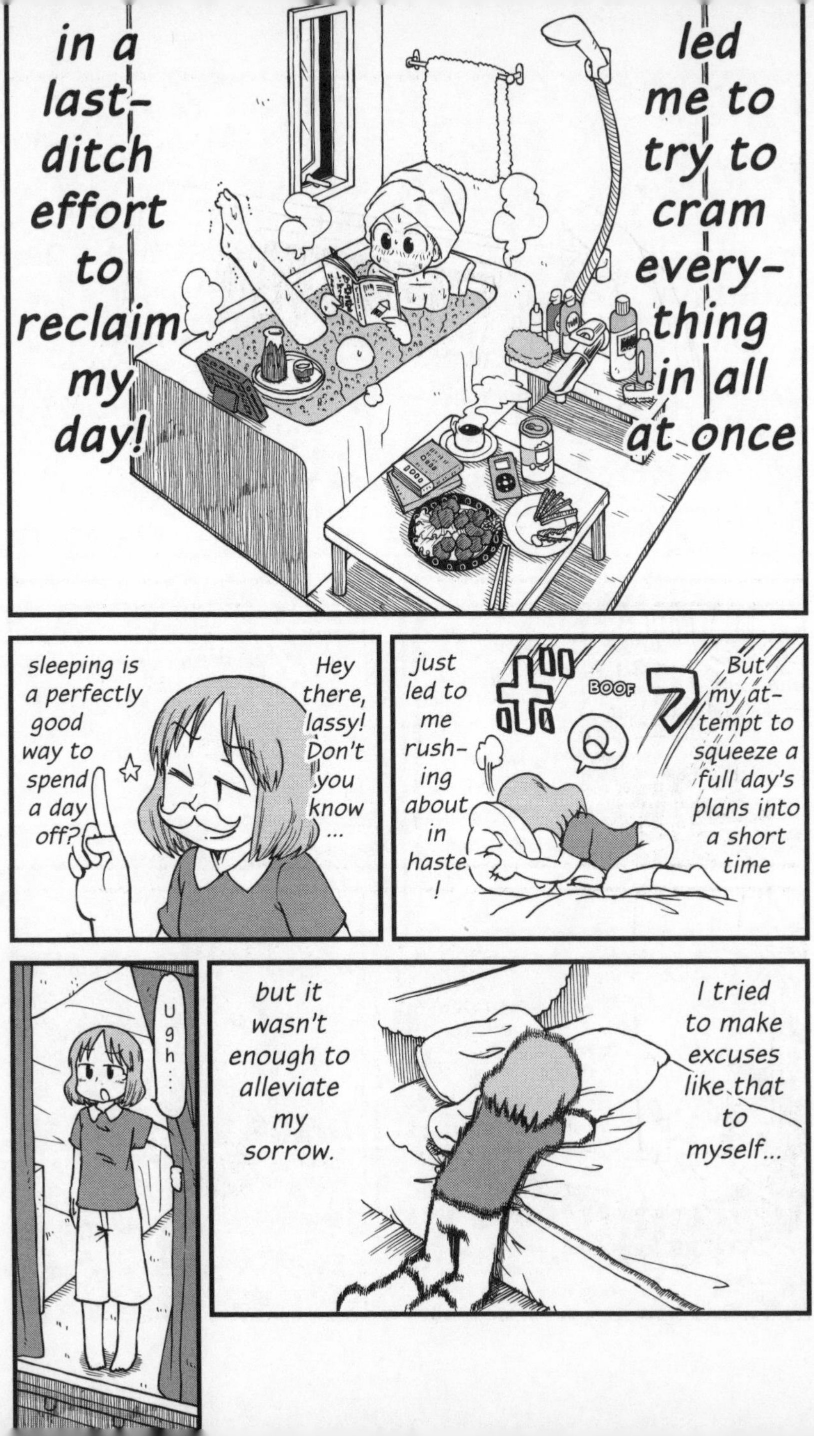
led me to try to cram everything in all at once
in a last-ditch effort to reclaim my day!
But my attempt to squeeze a full day's plans into a short time
BOOF
just led to me rushing about in haste!
Hey there, lassy! Don't you know ...
sleeping is a perfectly good way to spend a day off?
I tried to make excuses like that to myself...
but it wasn't enough to alleviate my sorrow.
Ugh...

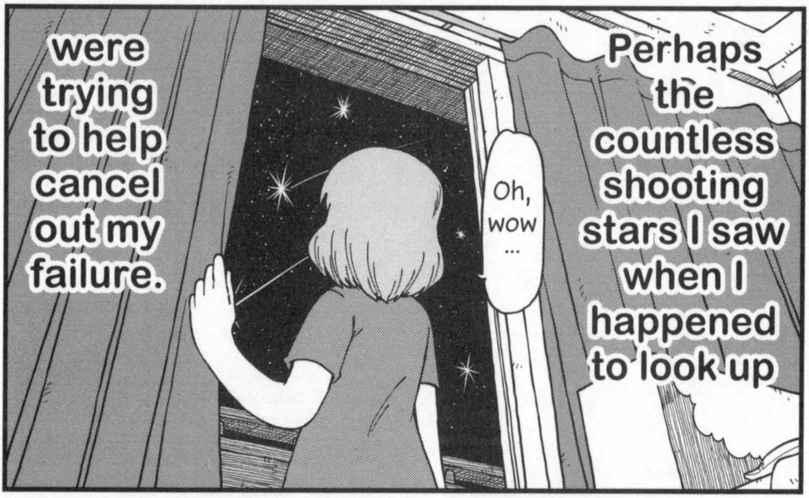
Perhaps the countless shooting stars I saw when I happened to look up
Oh, wow ...
were trying to help cancel out my failure.

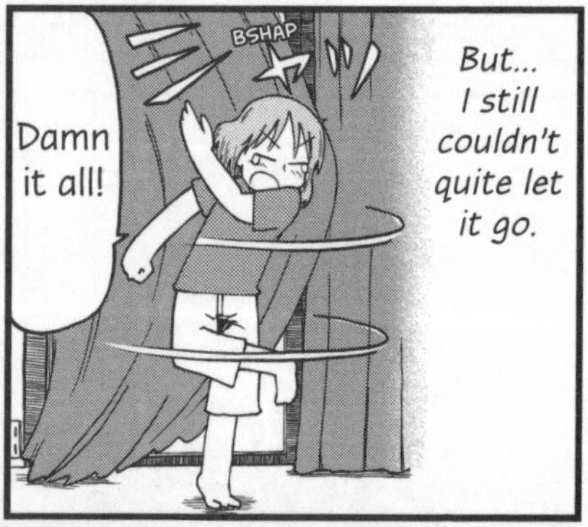
But... I still couldn't quite let it go.
BSHAP
Damn it all!

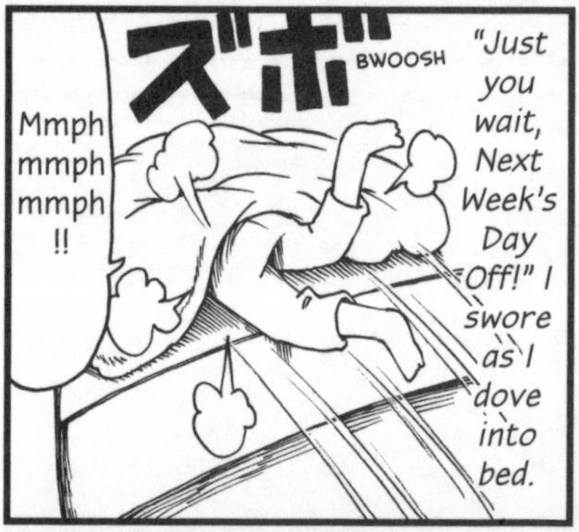
"Just you wait, Next Week's Day Off!" I swore as I dove into bed.
ズボ
BWOOSH
Mmph mmph mmph !!

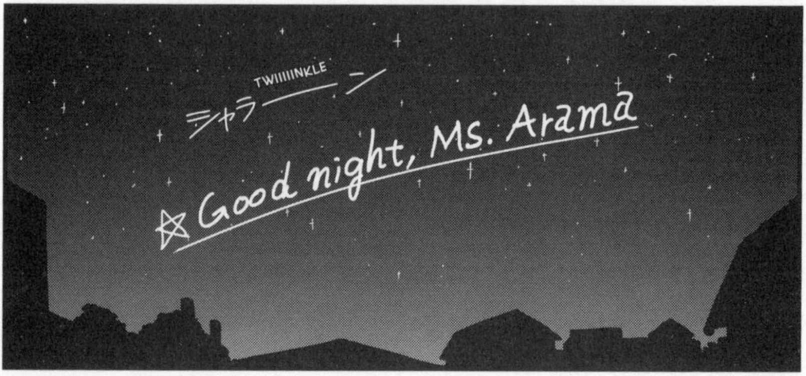
シャラ
TWIIIIINKLE
Good night, Ms. Arama

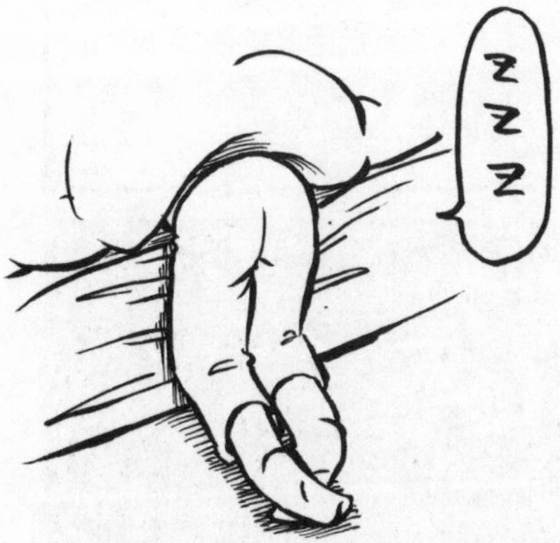
Z Z Z

CITY

BZZT
ジビー
BZZT
ジビー
BZZT
ジビー
BZZT
ジビー
BZZT
ジビー

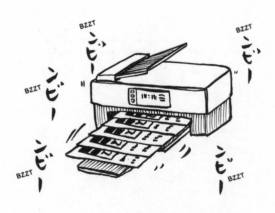

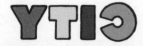

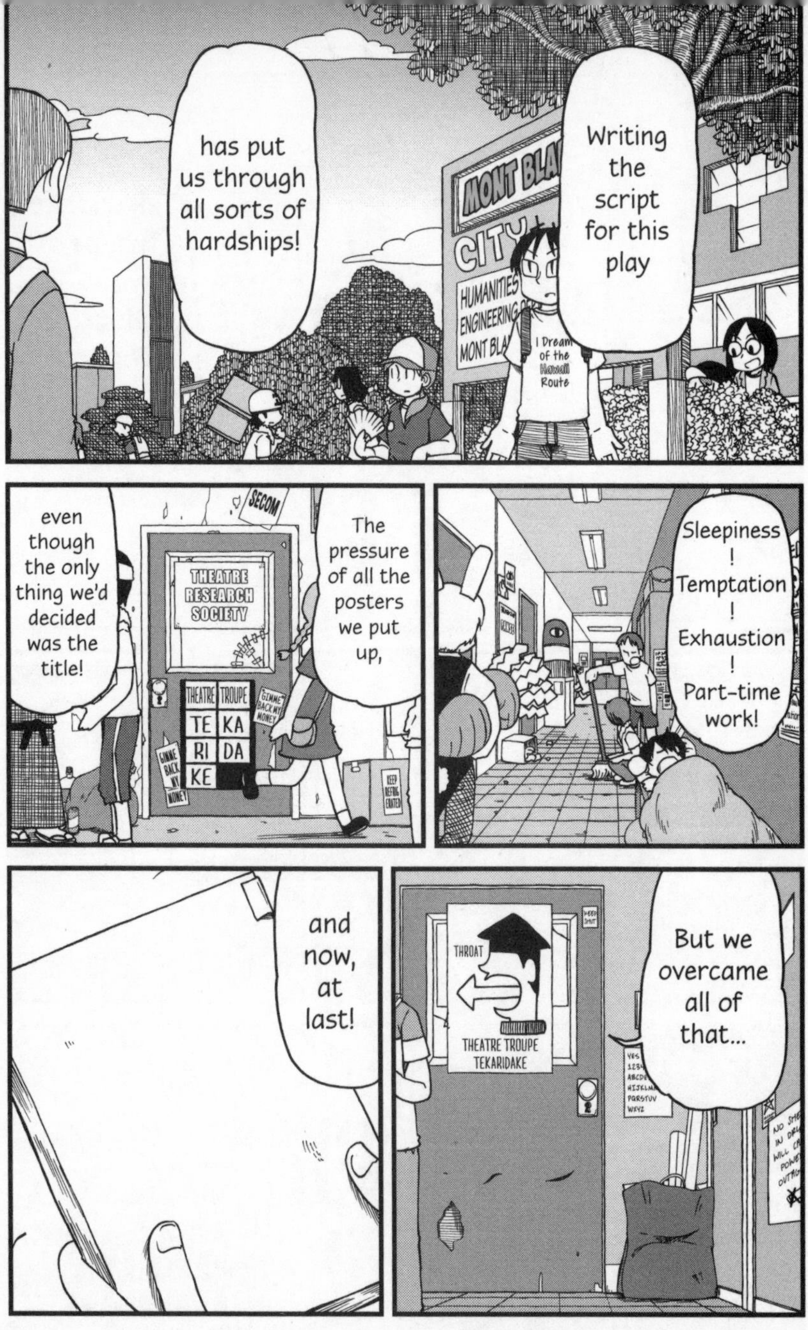
MONT BLA
CITY
HUMANITIES
ENGINEERING
MONT BLA
I Dream of the Hawaii Route
Writing the script for this play
has put us through all sorts of hardships!
Sleepiness! Temptation! Exhaustion! Part-time work!
SECOM
THEATRE RESEARCH SOCIETY
THEATRE TROUPE
TE KA RI DA KE
GIMME BACK MY MONEY
GIMME BACK MY MONEY
KEEP REFRIG ERATED
The pressure of all the posters we put up,
even though the only thing we'd decided was the title!
THROAT
THEATRE TROUPE TEKARIDAKE
But we overcame all of that...
and now, at last!

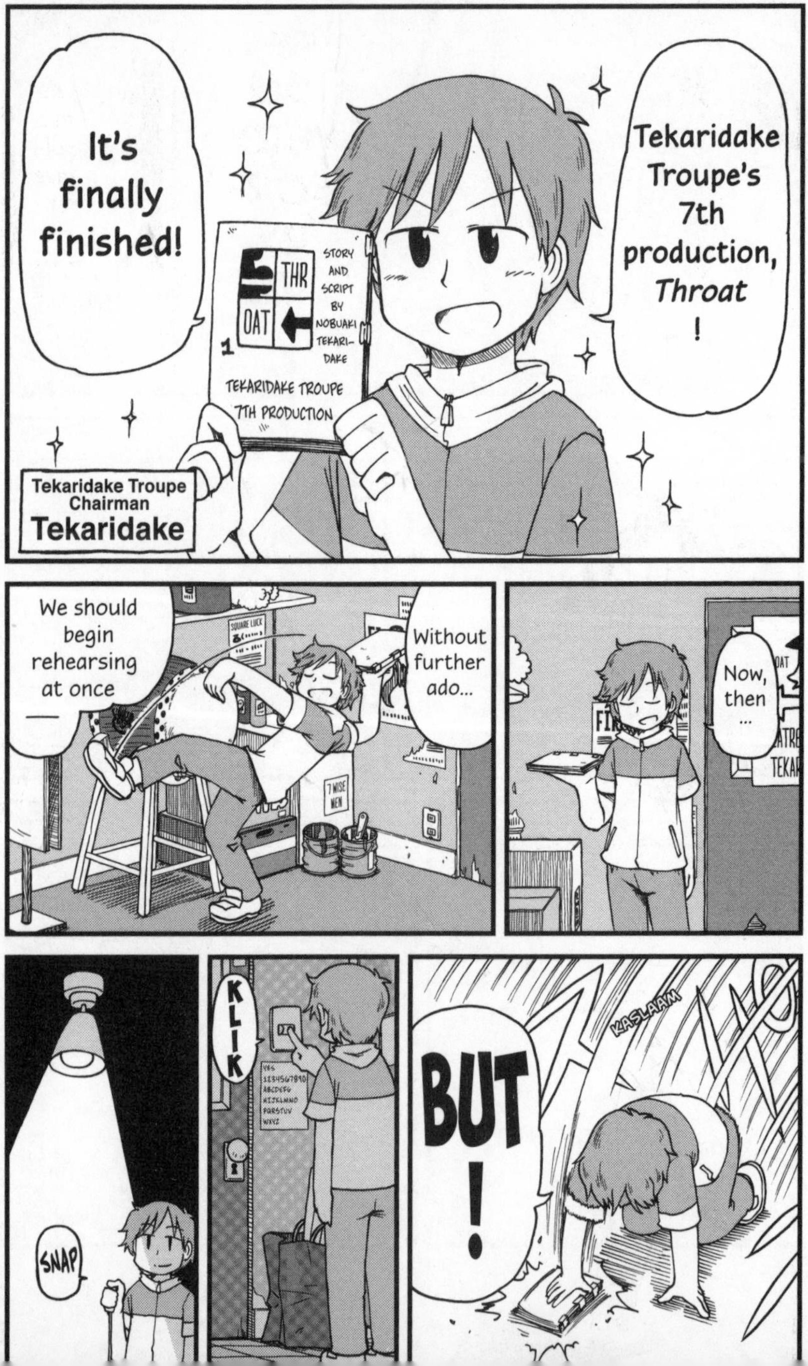
Tekaridake Troupe's 7th production, *Throat* !
THR OAT
1
STORY AND SCRIPT BY NOBUAKI TEKARIDAKE
TEKARIDAKE TROUPE 7TH PRODUCTION
It's finally finished!
Tekaridake Troupe Chairman
Tekaridake
Now, then ...
Without further ado...
We should begin rehearsing at once —
SQUARE LUCK
7 WISE MEN
KASLAAM
BUT !
KLIK
SNAP

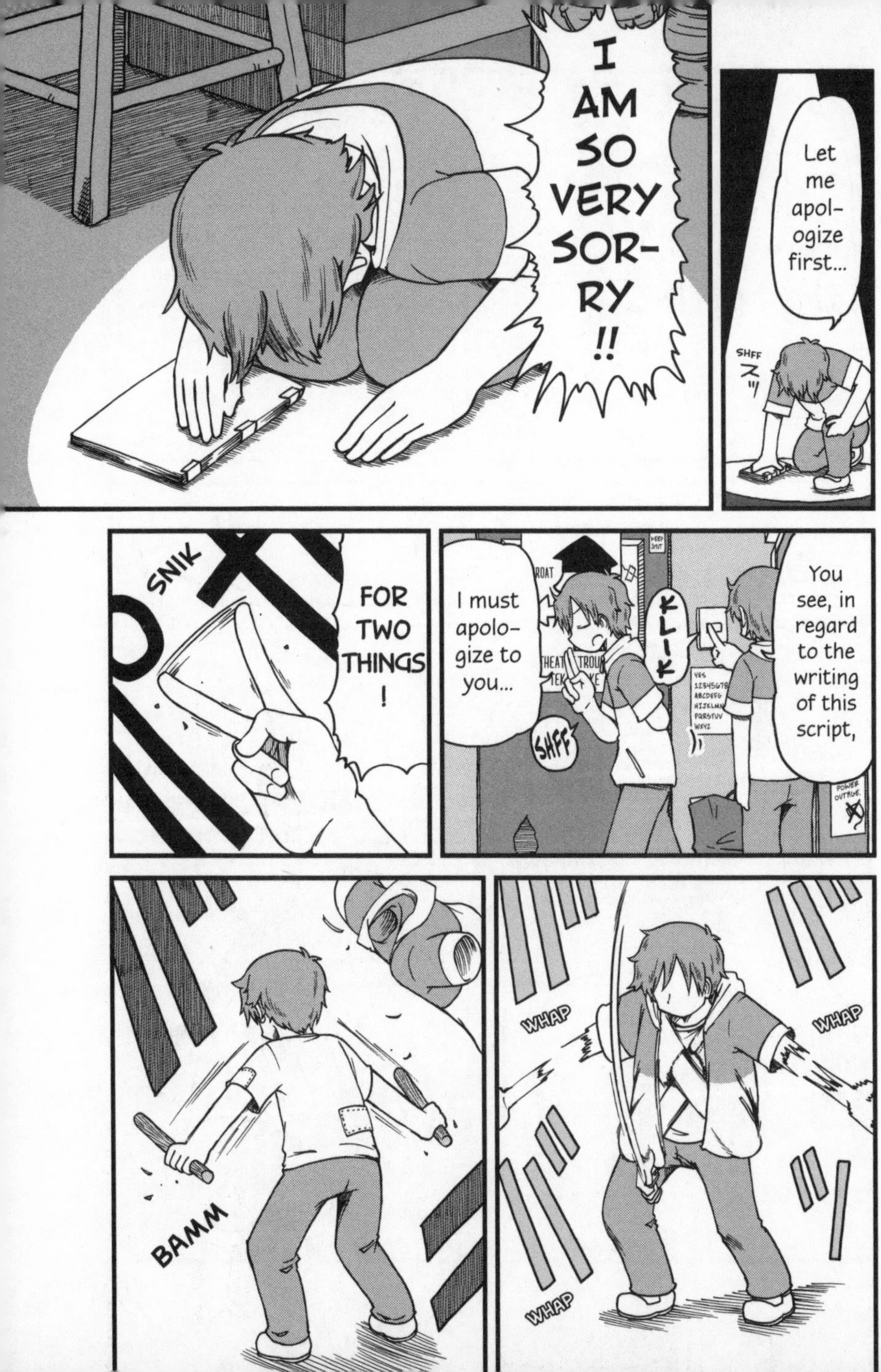
Let me apolo-gize first...
SHFF
ズッ
I AM SO VERY SOR-RY !!
You see, in regard to the writing of this script,
KLIK
I must apolo-gize to you...
SHFF
FOR TWO THINGS !
SNIK
WHAP
WHAP
WHAP
BAMM

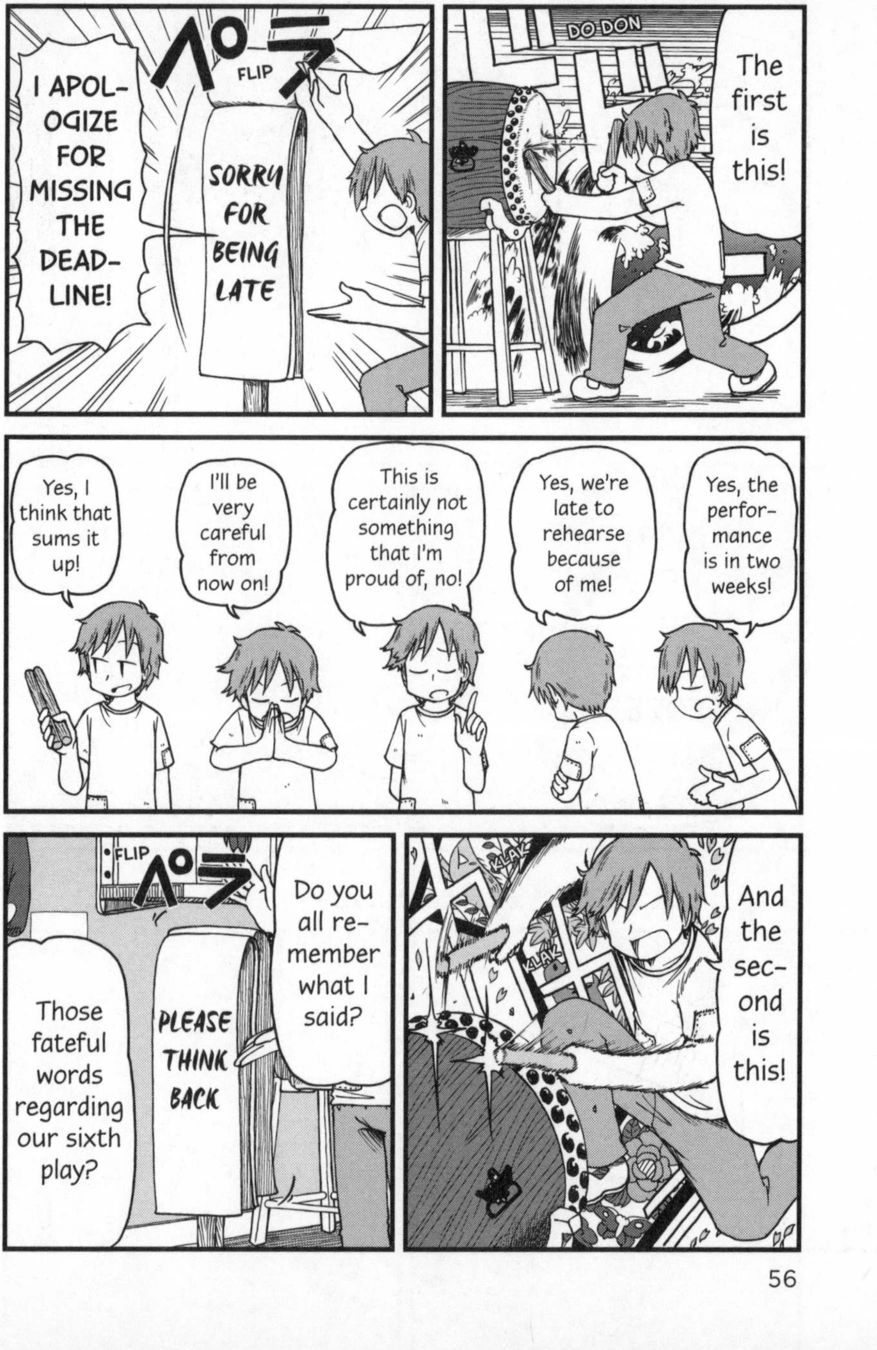
DO DON
The first is this!
ペラ
FLIP
SORRY FOR BEING LATE
I APOLOGIZE FOR MISSING THE DEADLINE!
Yes, the performance is in two weeks!
Yes, we're late to rehearse because of me!
This is certainly not something that I'm proud of, no!
I'll be very careful from now on!
Yes, I think that sums it up!
KLAK
KLAK
And the second is this!
ペラ
FLIP
Do you all remember what I said?
PLEASE THINK BACK
Those fateful words regarding our sixth play?

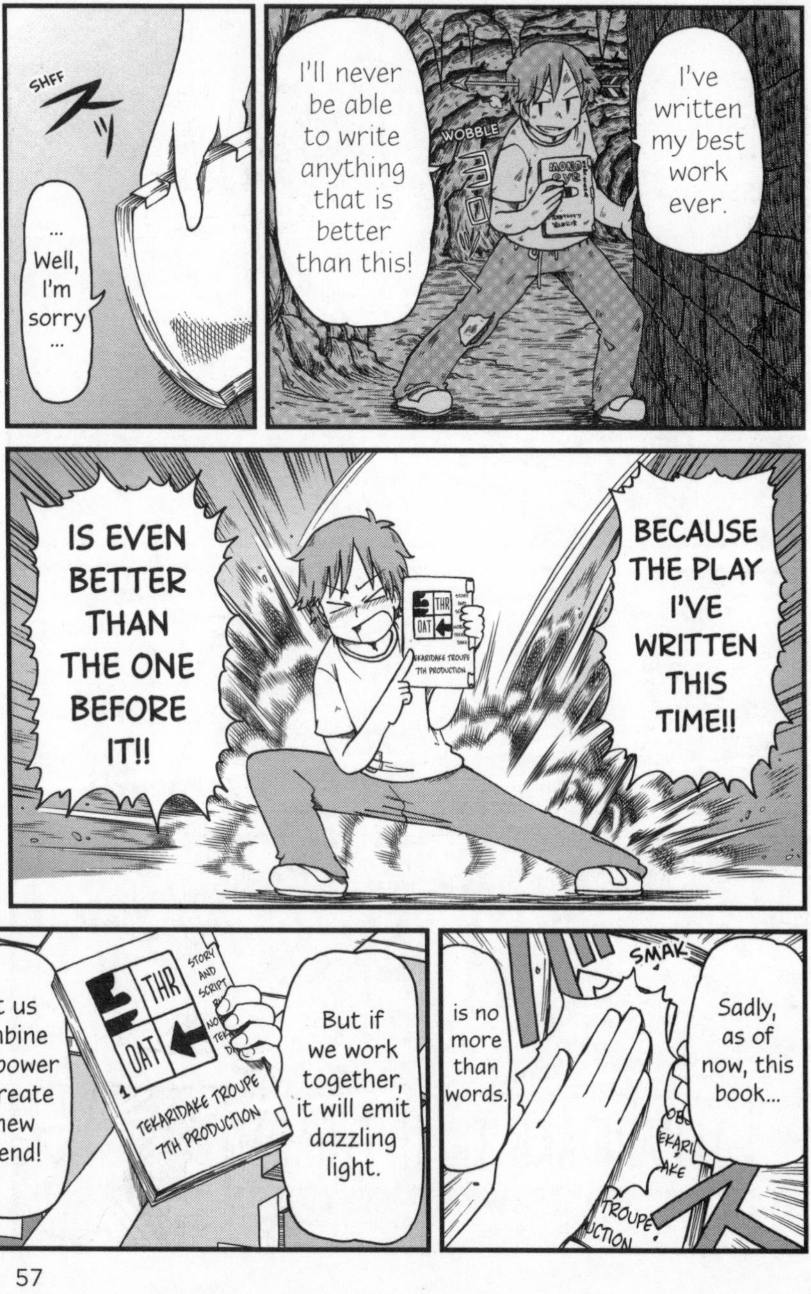
I've written my best work ever.
I'll never be able to write anything that is better than this!
WOBBLE
SHFF
... Well, I'm sorry ...
BECAUSE THE PLAY I'VE WRITTEN THIS TIME!!
IS EVEN BETTER THAN THE ONE BEFORE IT!!
TEKARIDAKE TROUPE 7TH PRODUCTION
SMAK
Sadly, as of now, this book...
is no more than words.
But if we work together, it will emit dazzling light.
Let us combine our power to create a new legend!
THR OAT
STORY AND SCRIPT
TEKARIDAKE TROUPE 7TH PRODUCTION

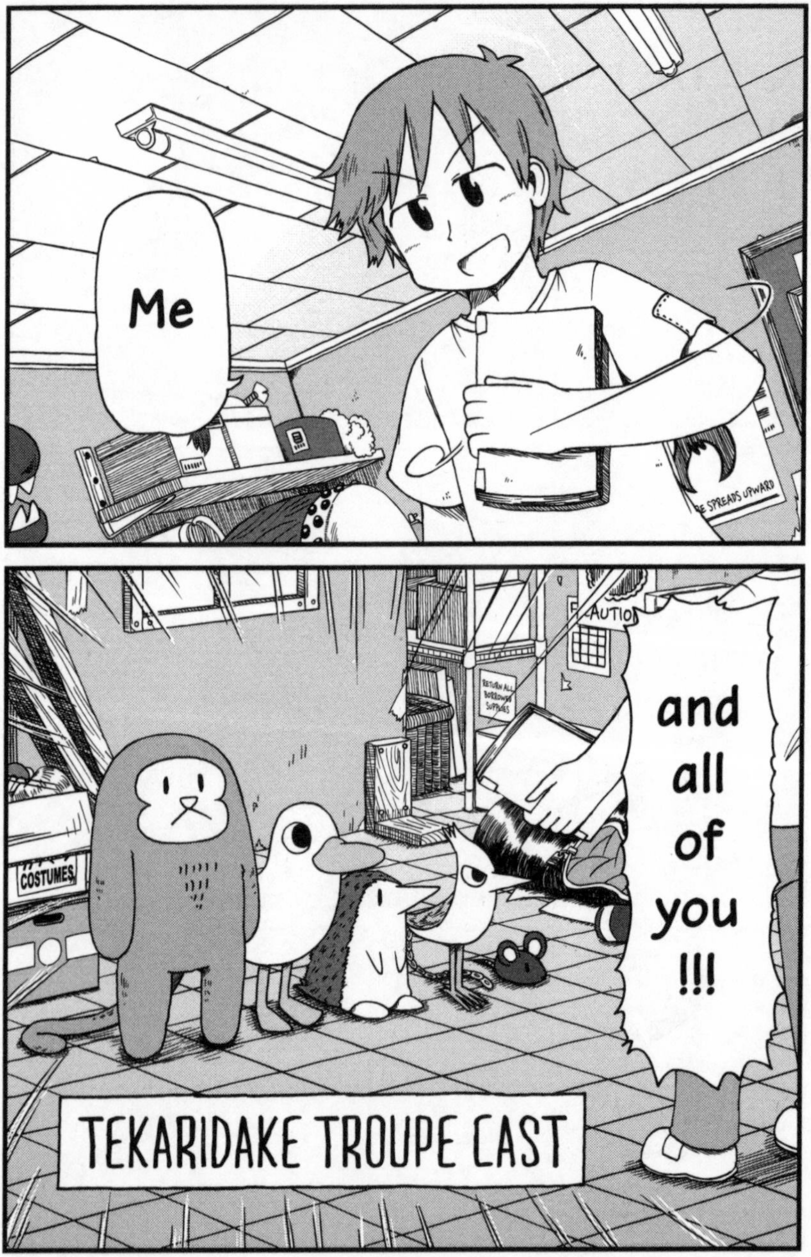
Me
and all of you !!!
COSTUMES
TEKARIDAKE TROUPE CAST

CHAPTER 58

THE LEGEND OF TEKARIDAKE TROUPE!

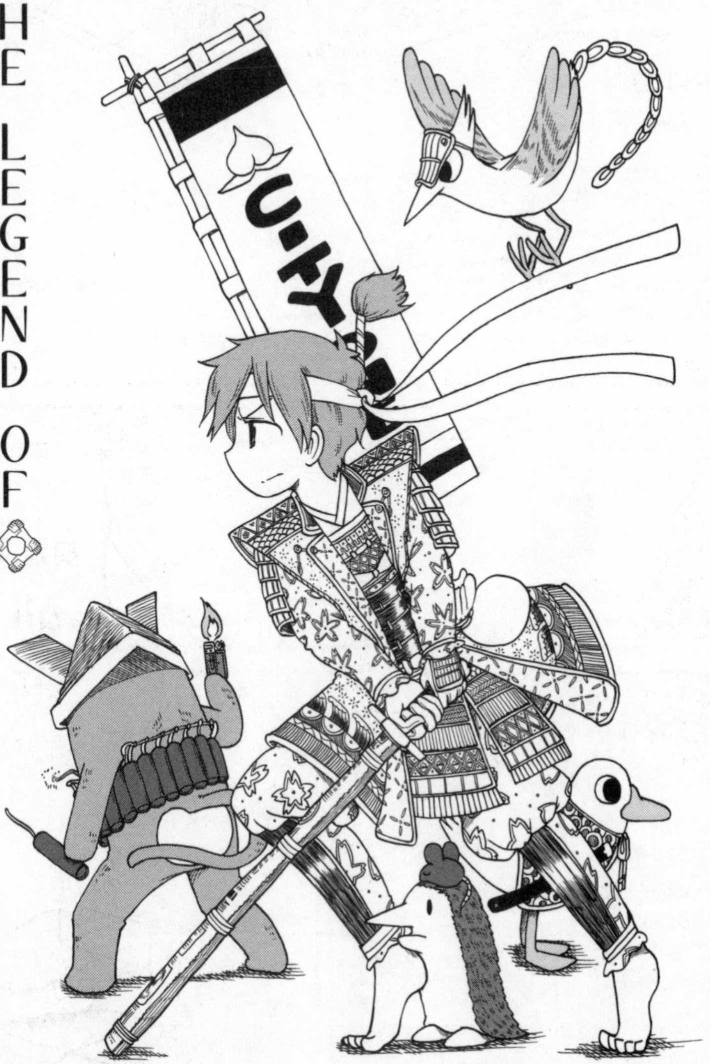

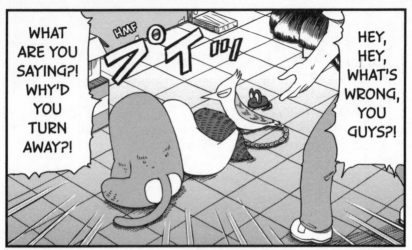

HEY, HEY, WHAT'S WRONG, YOU GUYS?!
HMF
WHAT ARE YOU SAYING?! WHY'D YOU TURN AWAY?!
Come on! I'm really sorry it was late!!
See? I mean it!!
I'll get all of you some bread crusts from my job!!
ALL RIGHT! I'LL TOTALLY SPLURGE!!
INSTANT NOO-DLES ALL 'ROUND! HOW ABOUT THAT?!

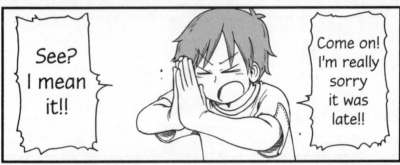

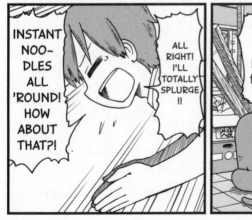

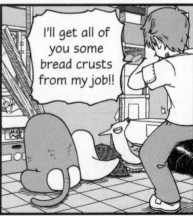

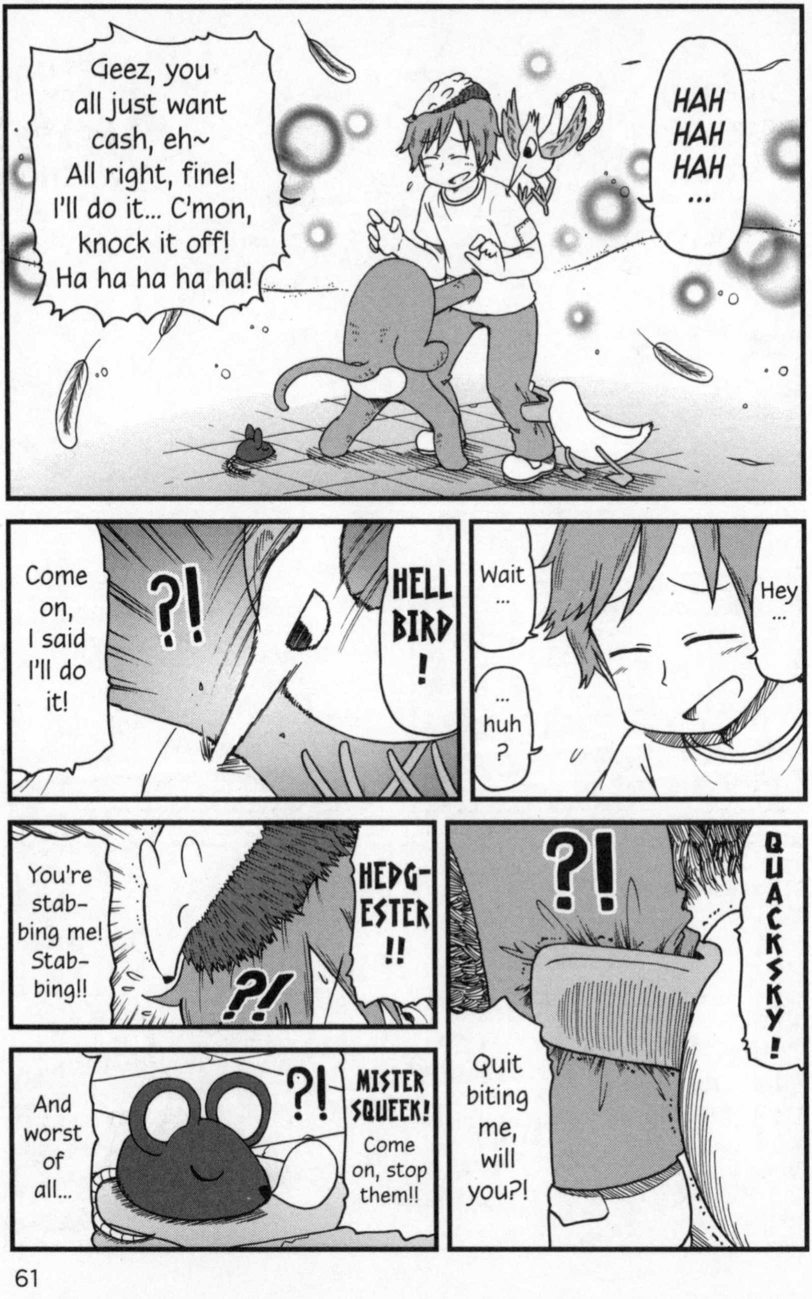
HAH HAH HAH ...
Geez, you all just want cash, eh~ All right, fine! I'll do it... C'mon, knock it off! Ha ha ha ha ha!
Hey ...
Wait ...
... huh ?
HELL BIRD !
?!
Come on, I said I'll do it!
QUACKSKY!
?!
Quit biting me, will you?!
HEDG-ESTER !!
?!
You're stab-bing me! Stab-bing!!
?!
MISTER SQUEEK!
Come on, stop them!!
?!
And worst of all...

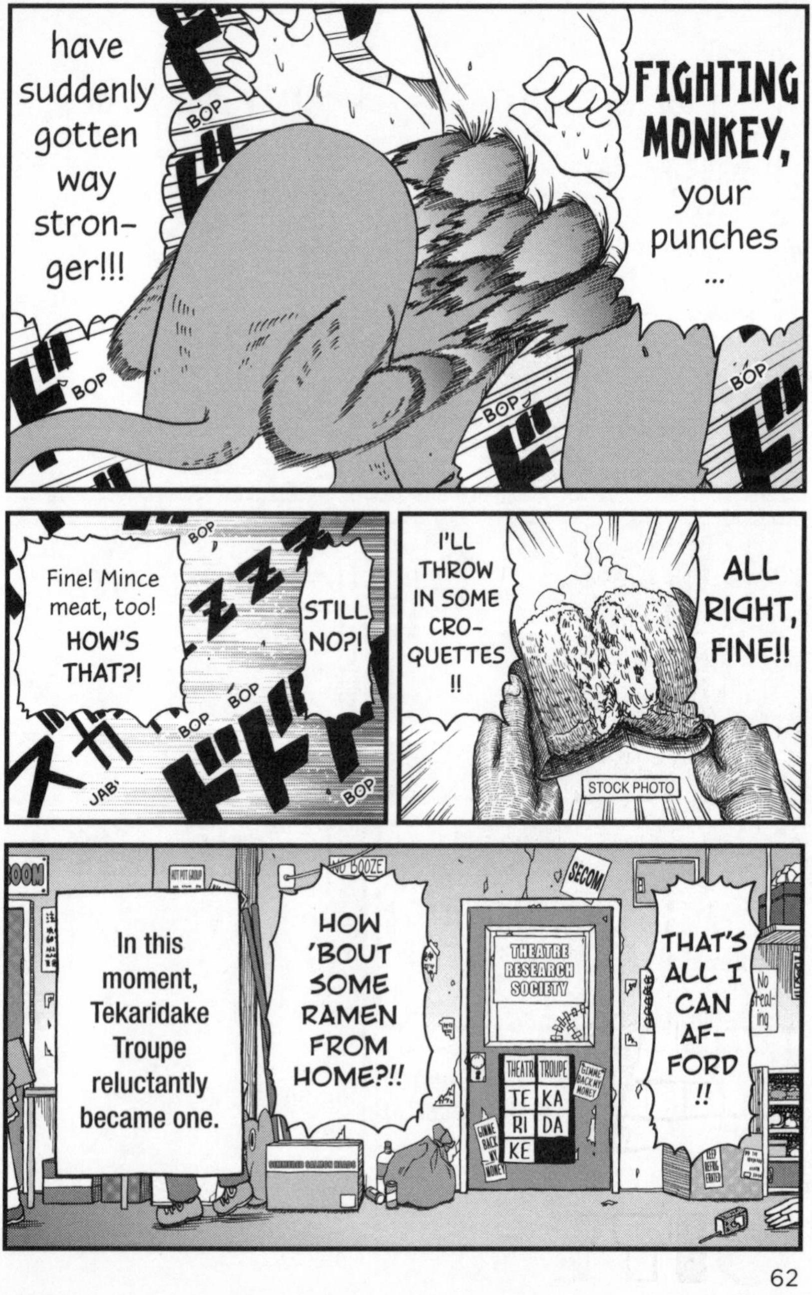
FIGHTING MONKEY, your punches ...
have suddenly gotten way stron-ger!!!
BOP
BOP
BOP
BOP
ALL RIGHT, FINE!!
I'LL THROW IN SOME CRO-QUETTES !!
STOCK PHOTO
STILL NO?!
Fine! Mince meat, too! HOW'S THAT?!
BOP
BOP
BOP
BOP
JAB
THAT'S ALL I CAN AF-FORD !!
No stealing
SECOM
THEATRE RESEARCH SOCIETY
THEATR TROUPE
TE KA RI DA KE
GIMME BACK MY MONEY
GIMME BACK MY MONEY
NO BOOZE
HOW 'BOUT SOME RAMEN FROM HOME?!!
In this moment, Tekaridake Troupe reluctantly became one.

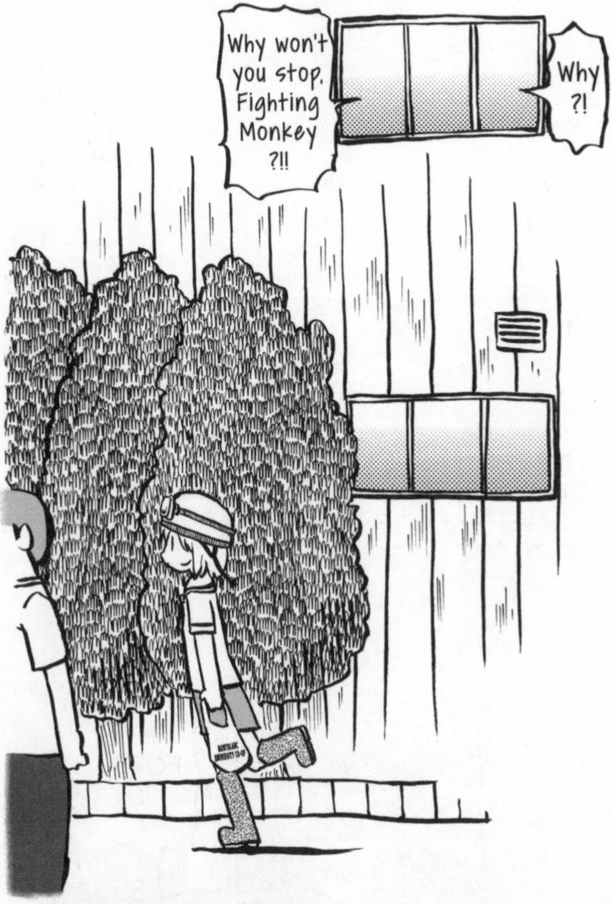
Why ?!
Why won't you stop, Fighting Monkey ?!!

CITY

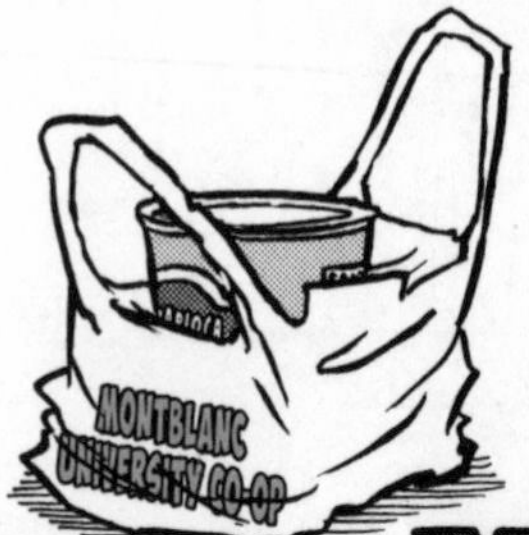
MONTBLANC
UNIVERSITY CO-OP

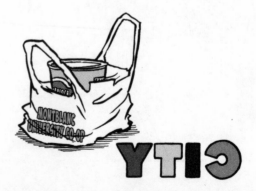

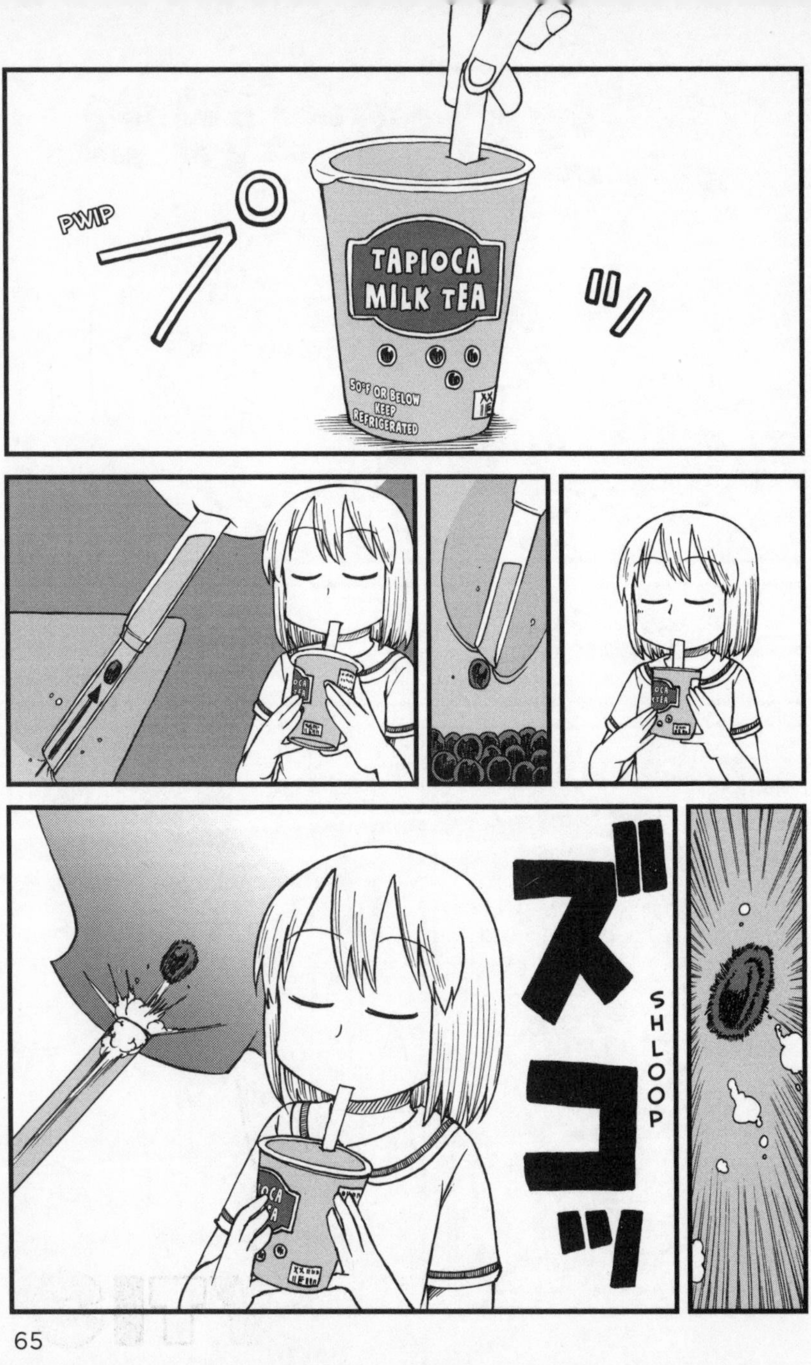
TAPIOCA
MILK TEA
50°F OR BELOW
KEEP
REFRIGERATED
プ
ッ
PWIP
ズゴッ
SHLOOP

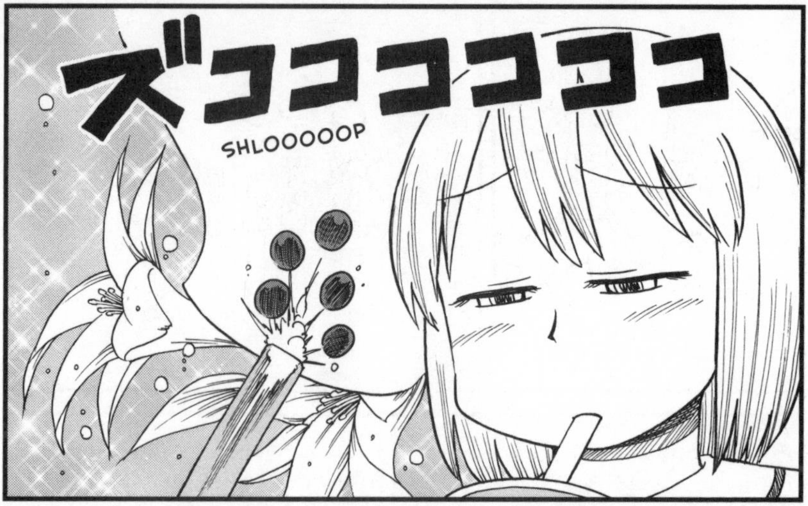
ズココココココ
SHLOOOOOP

Chapter 59 ◇ That Shlooping Feeling

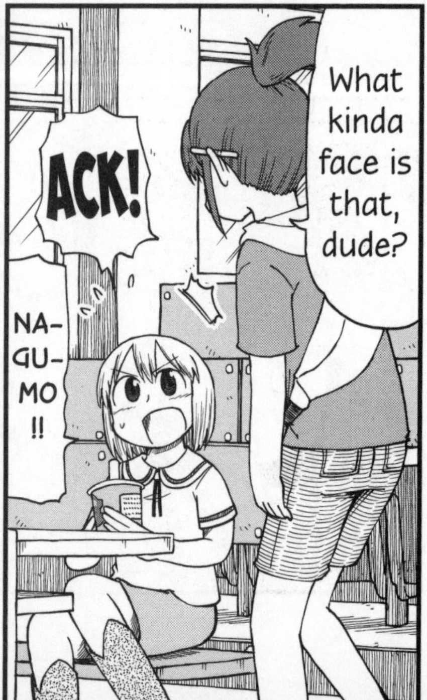
What kinda face is that, dude?
ACK!
NA-GU-MO !!

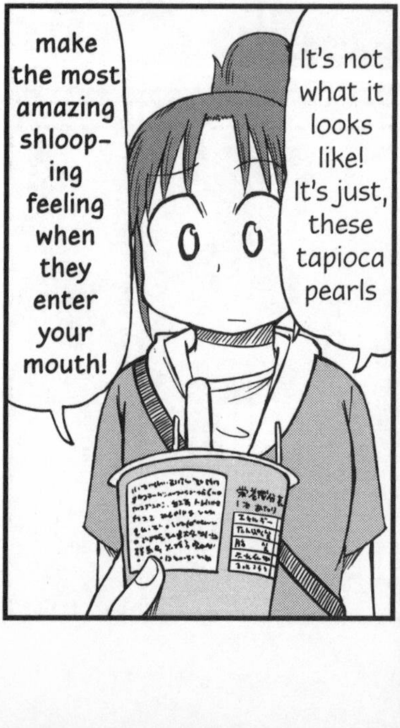
It's not what it looks like! It's just, these tapioca pearls
make the most amazing shlooping feeling when they enter your mouth!

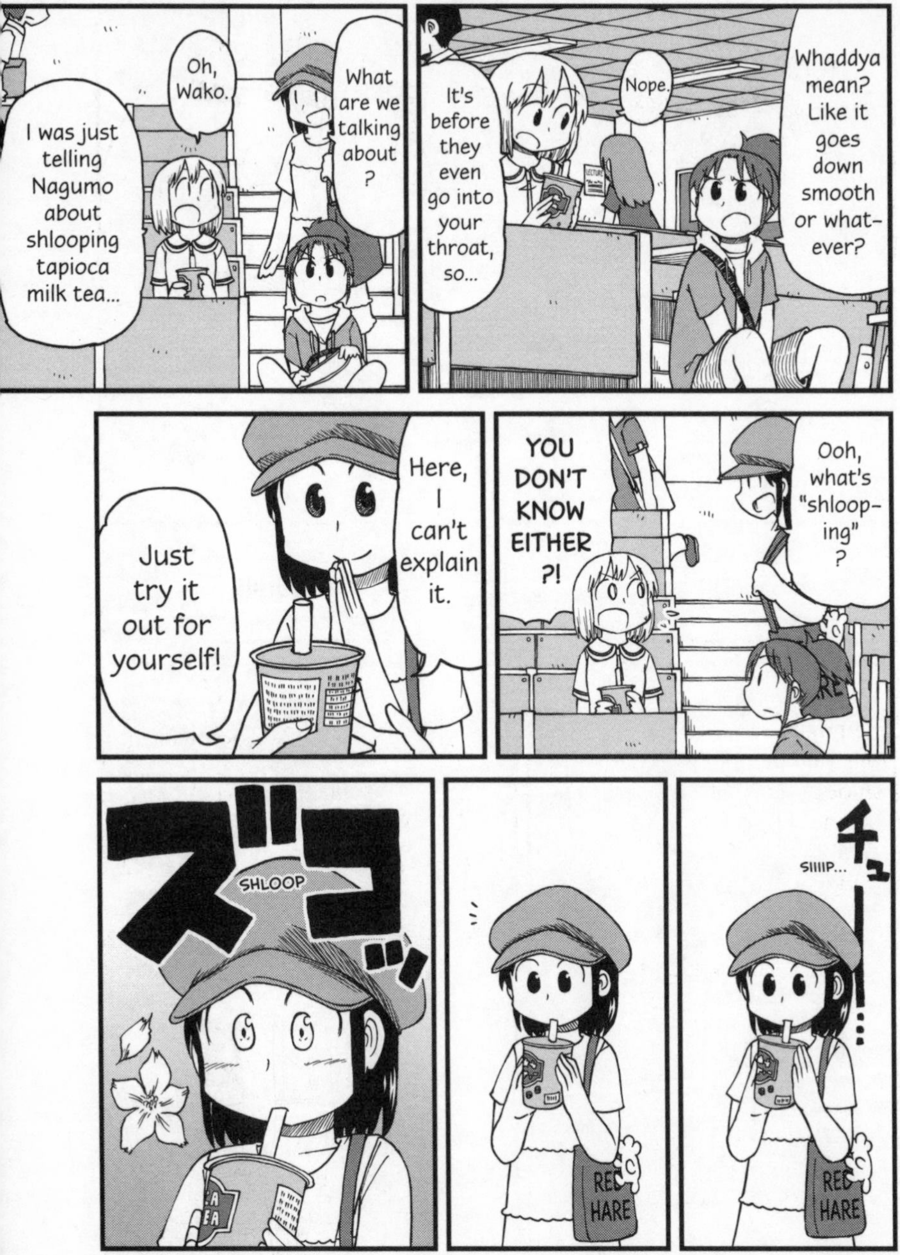
Whaddya mean? Like it goes down smooth or whatever?
Nope.
It's before they even go into your throat, so...
What are we talking about?
Oh, Wako.
I was just telling Nagumo about shlooping tapioca milk tea...
Ooh, what's "shlooping"?
YOU DON'T KNOW EITHER?!
Here, I can't explain it.
Just try it out for yourself!
チュー
SIIIP...
RED HARE
RED HARE
ズコ
SHLOOP

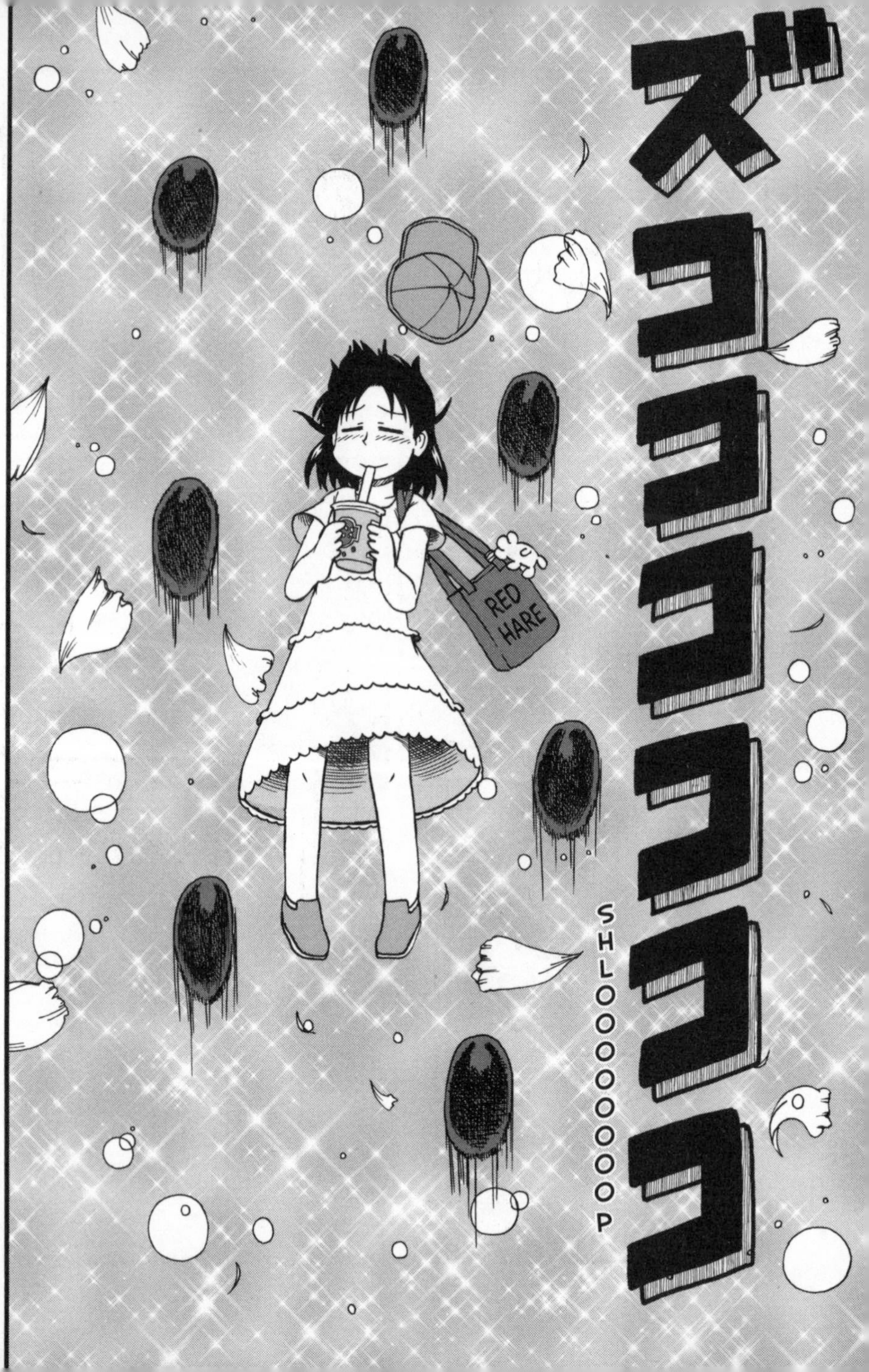
ズコココココココ
SHLOOOOOOOOP
RED HARE

WHAT ON EARTH IS THIS?!
AAAAAAH
TAPIOCA MILK TEA
IT'S SO, SO SHLOOPY!!
It's tapioca milk tea!
TAPIOCA MILK TEA!!
Here, Na-gu-mo.
Try it.
OK!
All right, here goes nothin'!!
PEEL

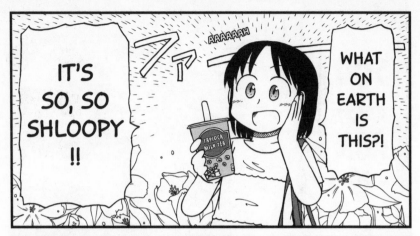

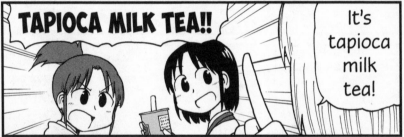

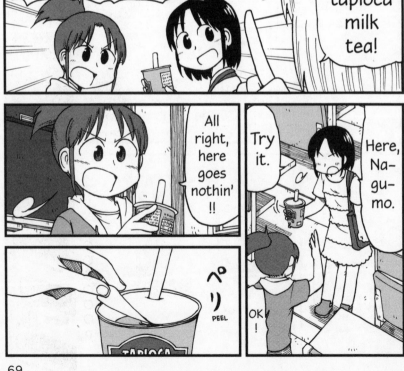

ゴク
GULP
ゴク
GULP
SWAAAKK
YOU MO-RON!!
MMM, NICE AND SWEET!!
baa ha ha
Why would you drink it straight from the cup?!
You need the straw to get the shloop!
Yeah, but you guys both used the straw, right?!
UH, WOW!!!
I can't believe you care about that kinda thing!
Here, use this straw, then.
プス
PWIP
TAPIOCA MILK TEA
50°F OR BELOW

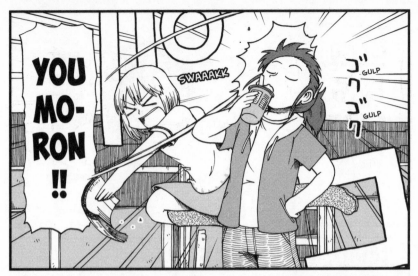

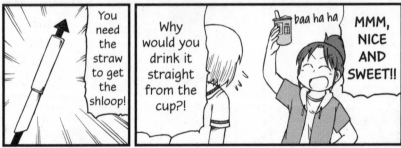

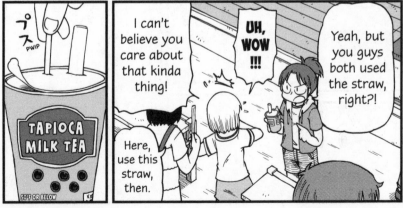

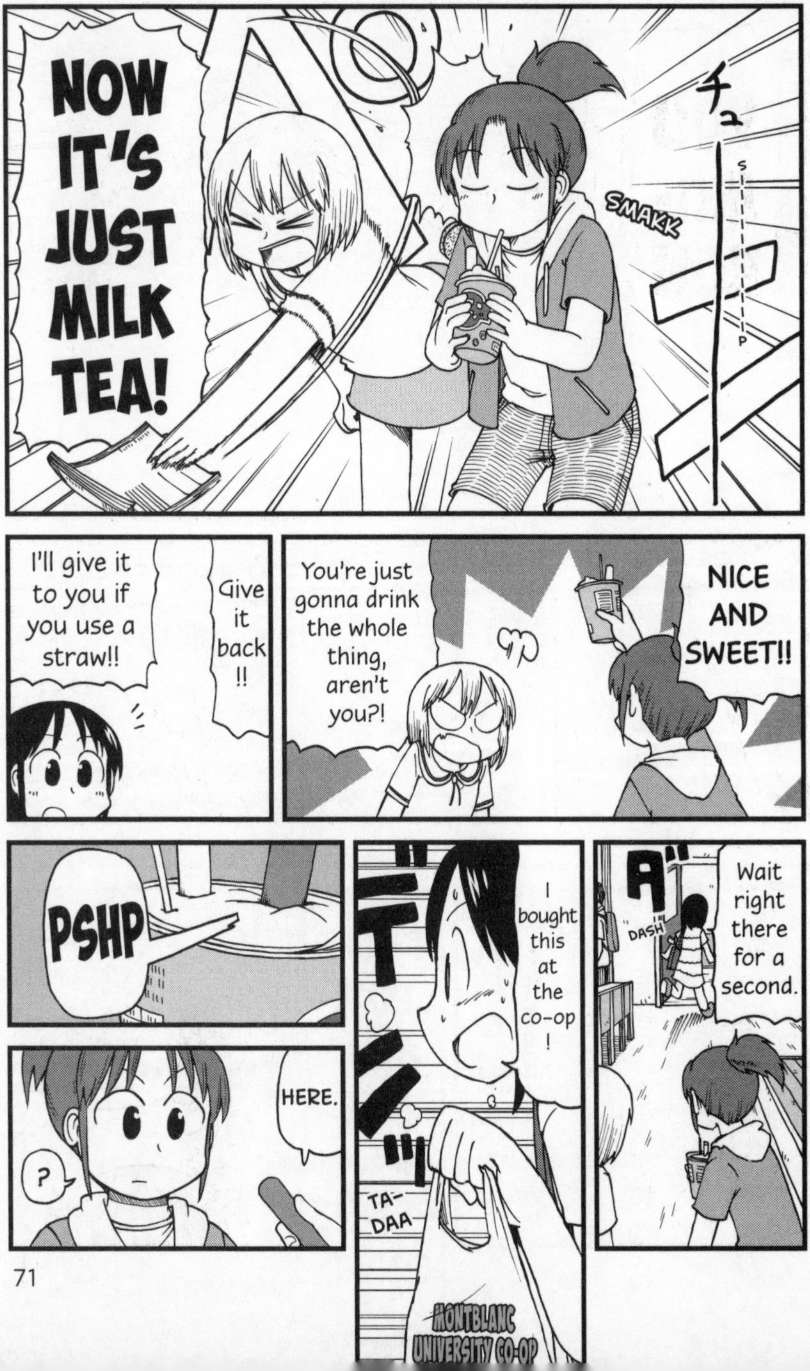
チュ
SMAKK
S P
NOW IT'S JUST MILK TEA!
NICE AND SWEET!!
You're just gonna drink the whole thing, aren't you?!
Give it back!!
I'll give it to you if you use a straw!!
Wait right there for a second.
DASH
I bought this at the co-op!
TA-DAA
MONTBLANC UNIVERSITY CO-OP
PSHP
HERE.
?

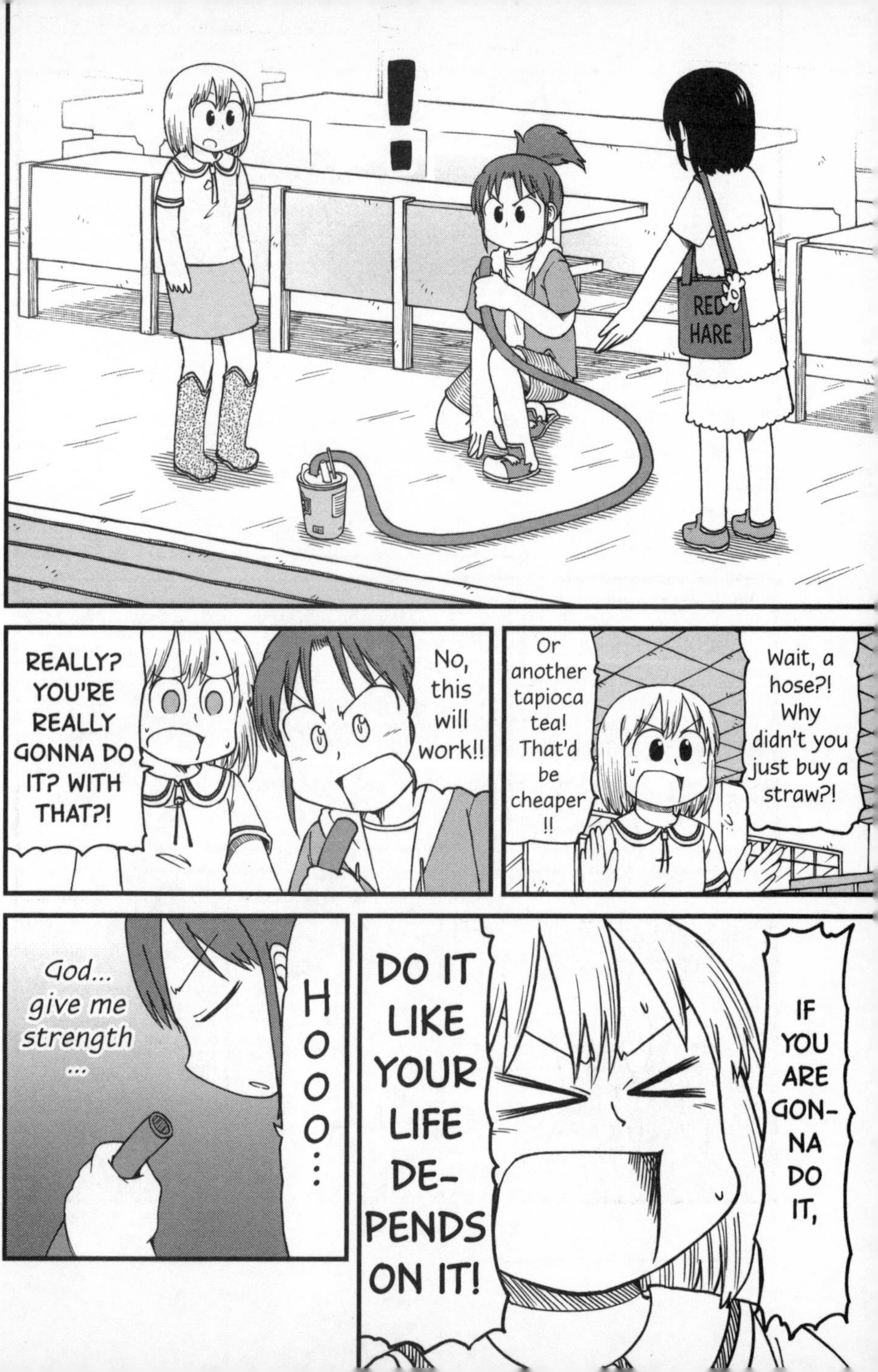
!
RED HARE
Wait, a hose?! Why didn't you just buy a straw?!
Or another tapioca tea! That'd be cheaper!!
No, this will work!!
REALLY? YOU'RE REALLY GONNA DO IT? WITH THAT?!
IF YOU ARE GON-NA DO IT,
DO IT LIKE YOUR LIFE DE-PENDS ON IT!
HOOOO...
God... give me strength...

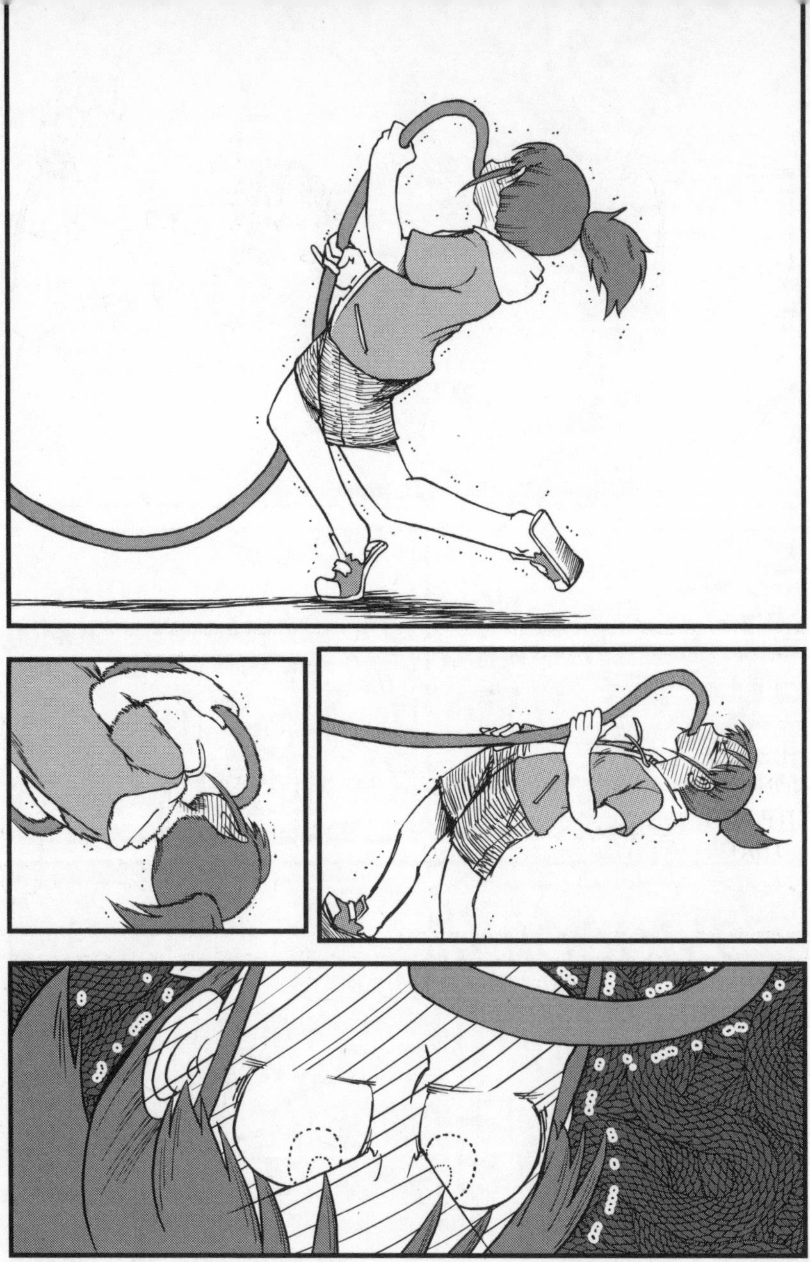

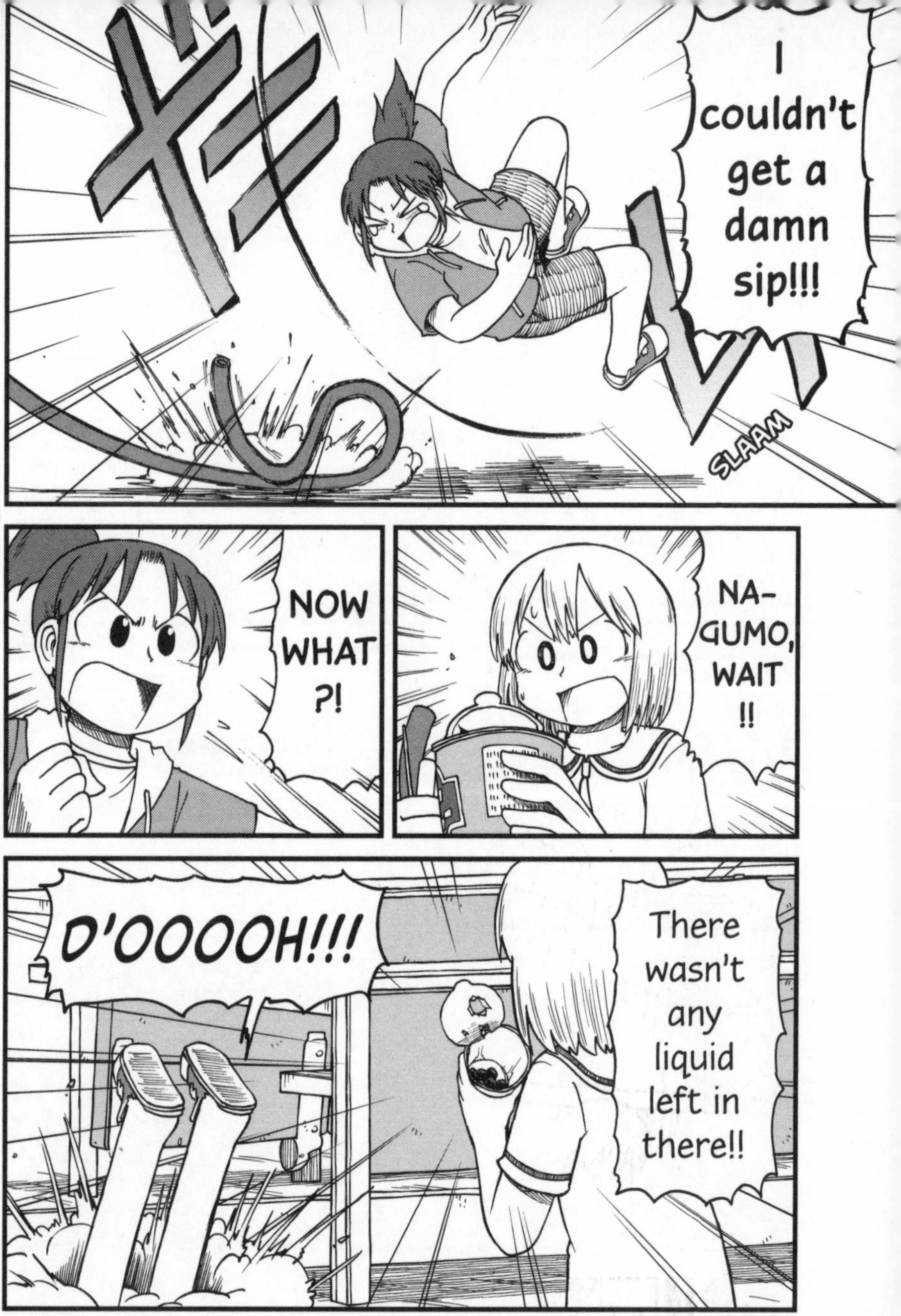
I couldn't get a damn sip!!!
SLAAM
NA-GUMO, WAIT !!
NOW WHAT ?!
There wasn't any liquid left in there!!
D'OOOOH!!!

CITY

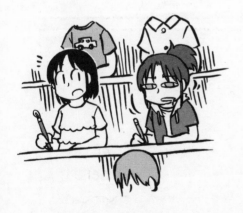

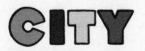

CITY

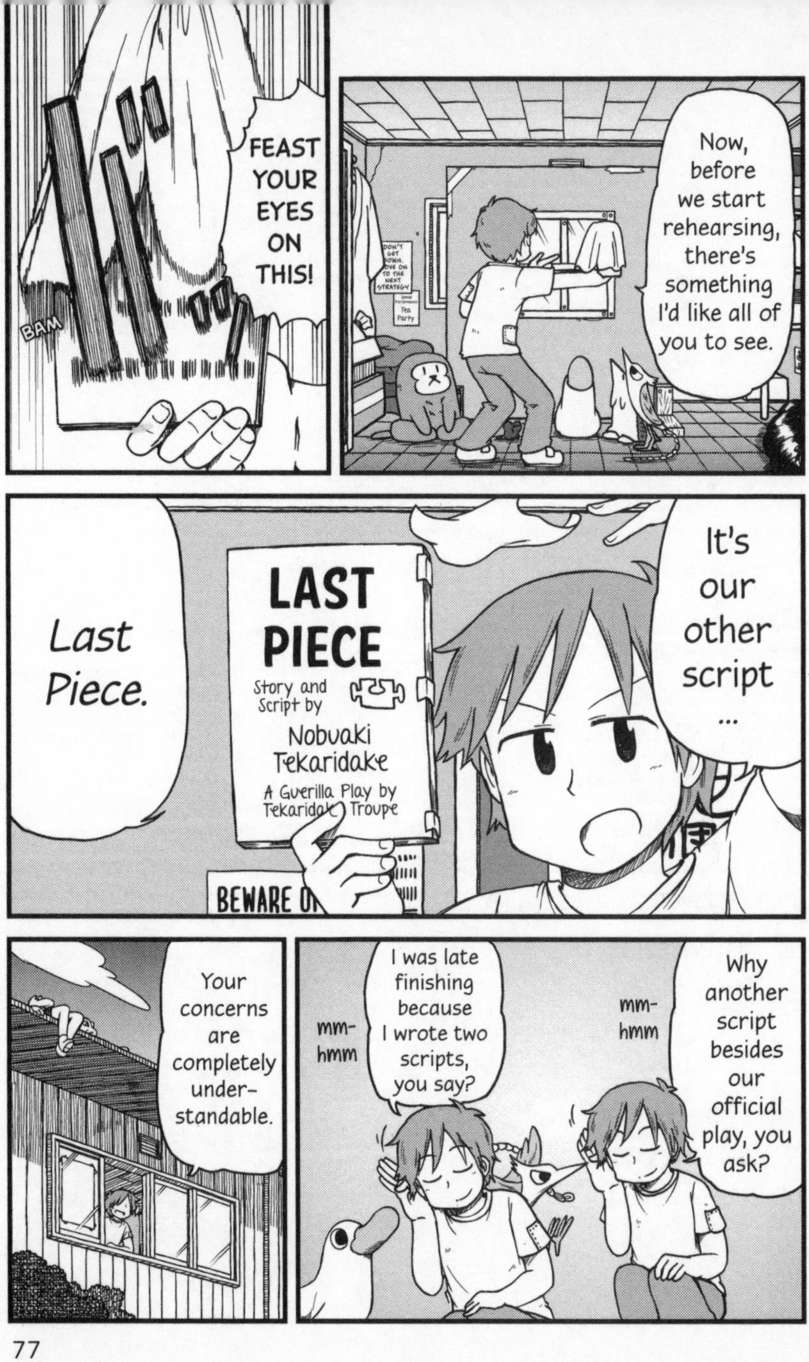
Now, before we start rehearsing, there's something I'd like all of you to see.
FEAST YOUR EYES ON THIS!
BAM
It's our other script...
Last Piece.
LAST PIECE
Story and Script by
Nobuaki Tekaridake
A Guerilla Play by
Why another script besides our official play, you ask?
mm-hmm
I was late finishing because I wrote two scripts, you say?
mm-hmm
Your concerns are completely under-standable.

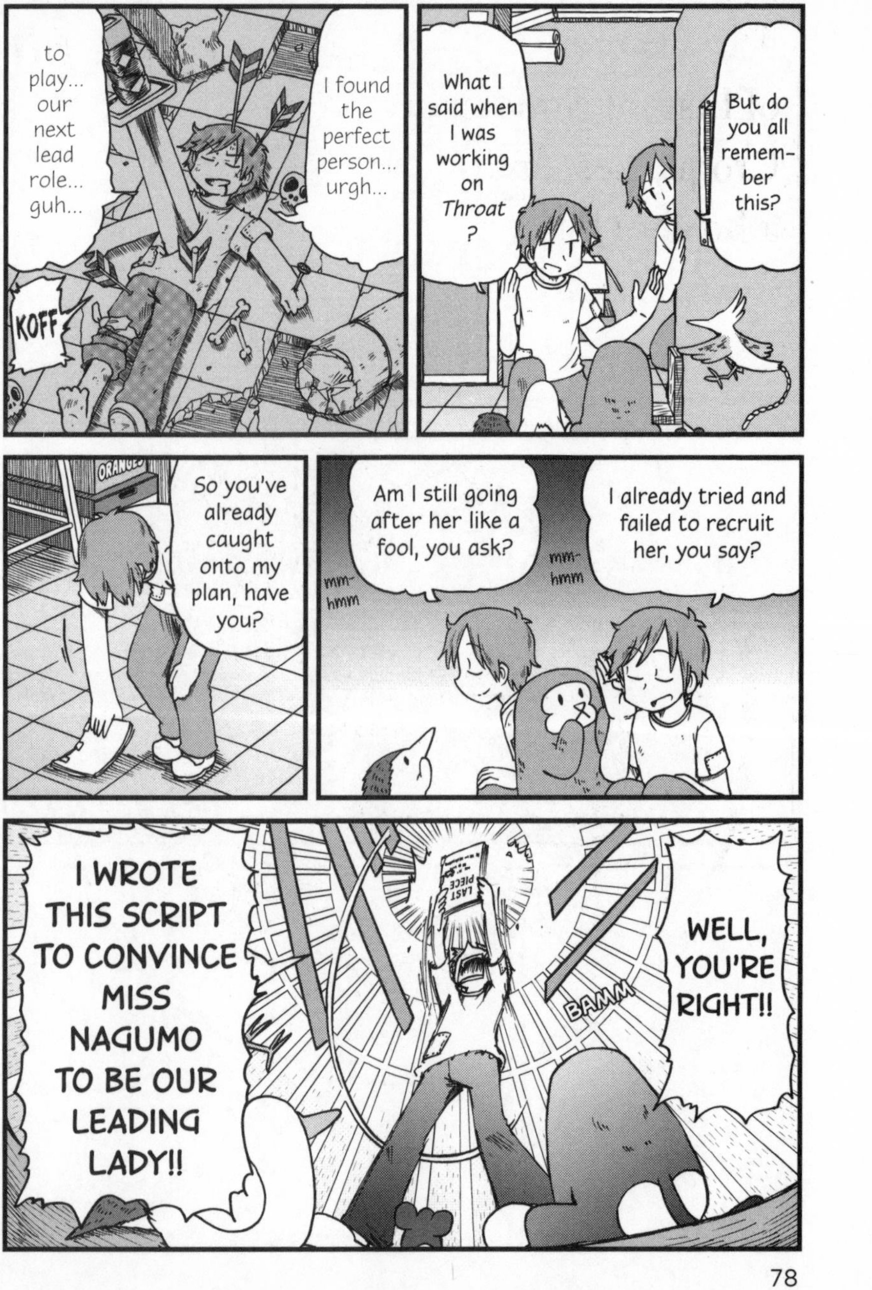
But do you all remember this?
What I said when I was working on *Throat*?
I found the perfect person... urgh...
to play... our next lead role... guh...
KOFF
I already tried and failed to recruit her, you say?
mm-hmm
Am I still going after her like a fool, you ask?
mm-hmm
So you've already caught onto my plan, have you?
WELL, YOU'RE RIGHT!!
LAST PIECE
BAMM
I WROTE THIS SCRIPT TO CONVINCE MISS NAGUMO TO BE OUR LEADING LADY!!

CHAPTER 60

The Legend of Instant Noodles, Croquettes, and a Bowl of Ramen for Assets!

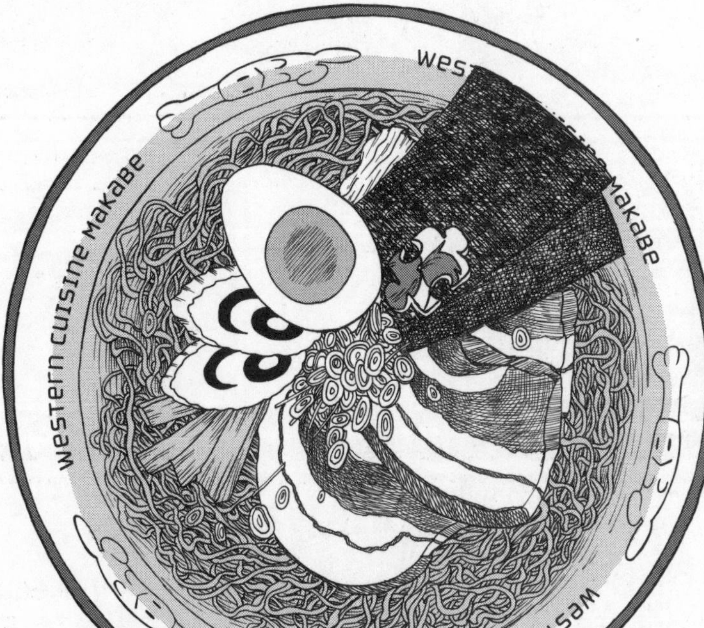
Western cuisine Makabe
Western cuisine Makabe

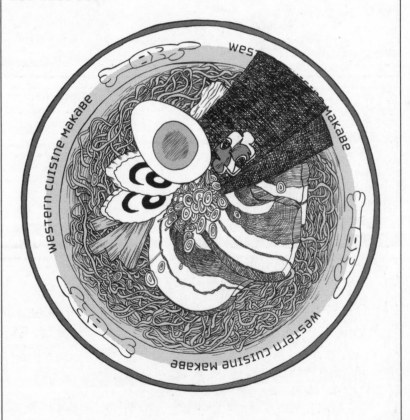

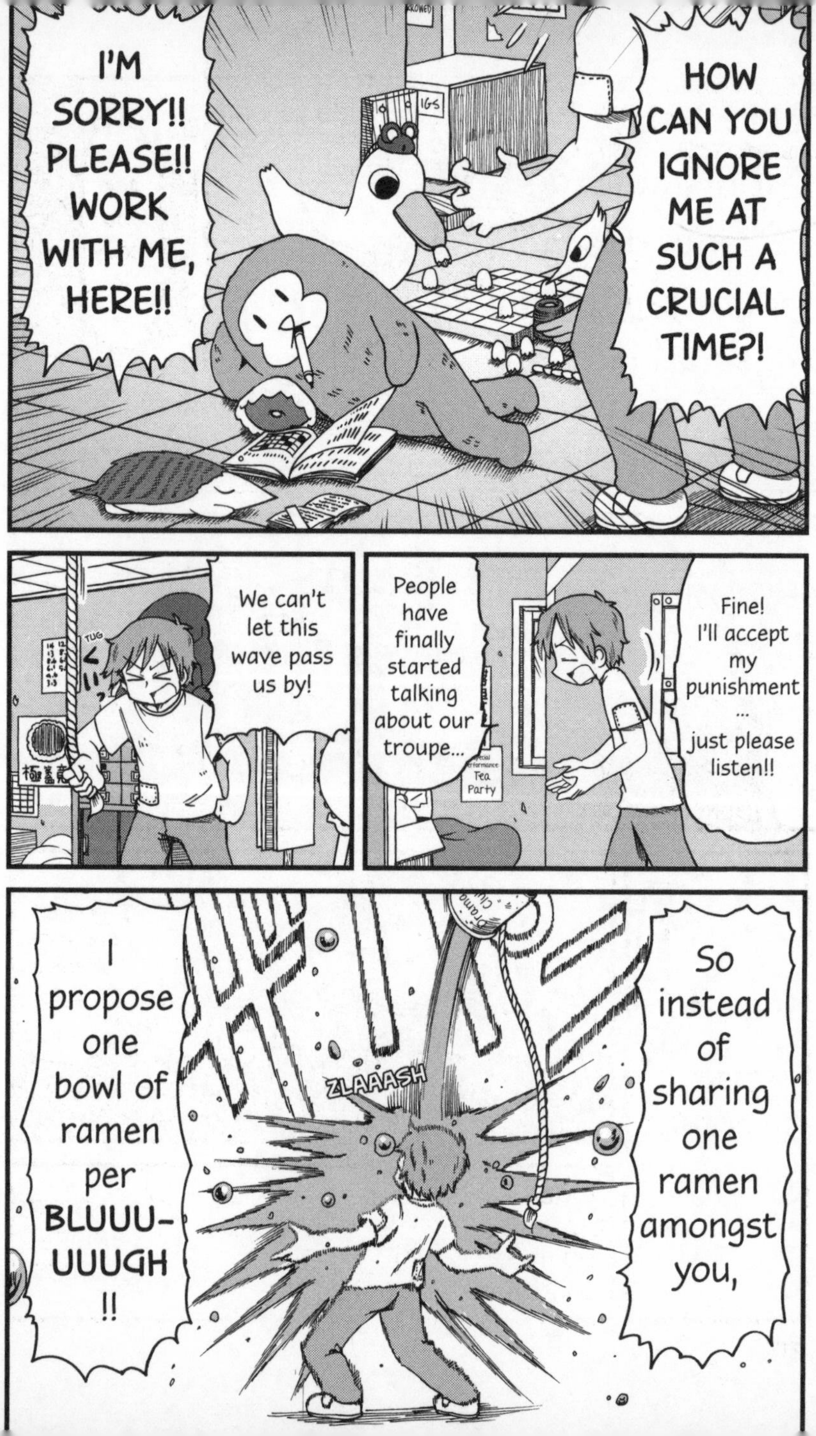
HOW CAN YOU IGNORE ME AT SUCH A CRUCIAL TIME?!
I'M SORRY!! PLEASE!! WORK WITH ME, HERE!!
Fine! I'll accept my punishment ... just please listen!!
People have finally started talking about our troupe...
Tea Party
TUG
We can't let this wave pass us by!
So instead of sharing one ramen amongst you,
ZLAAASH
I propose one bowl of ramen per BLUUU-UUUGH !!

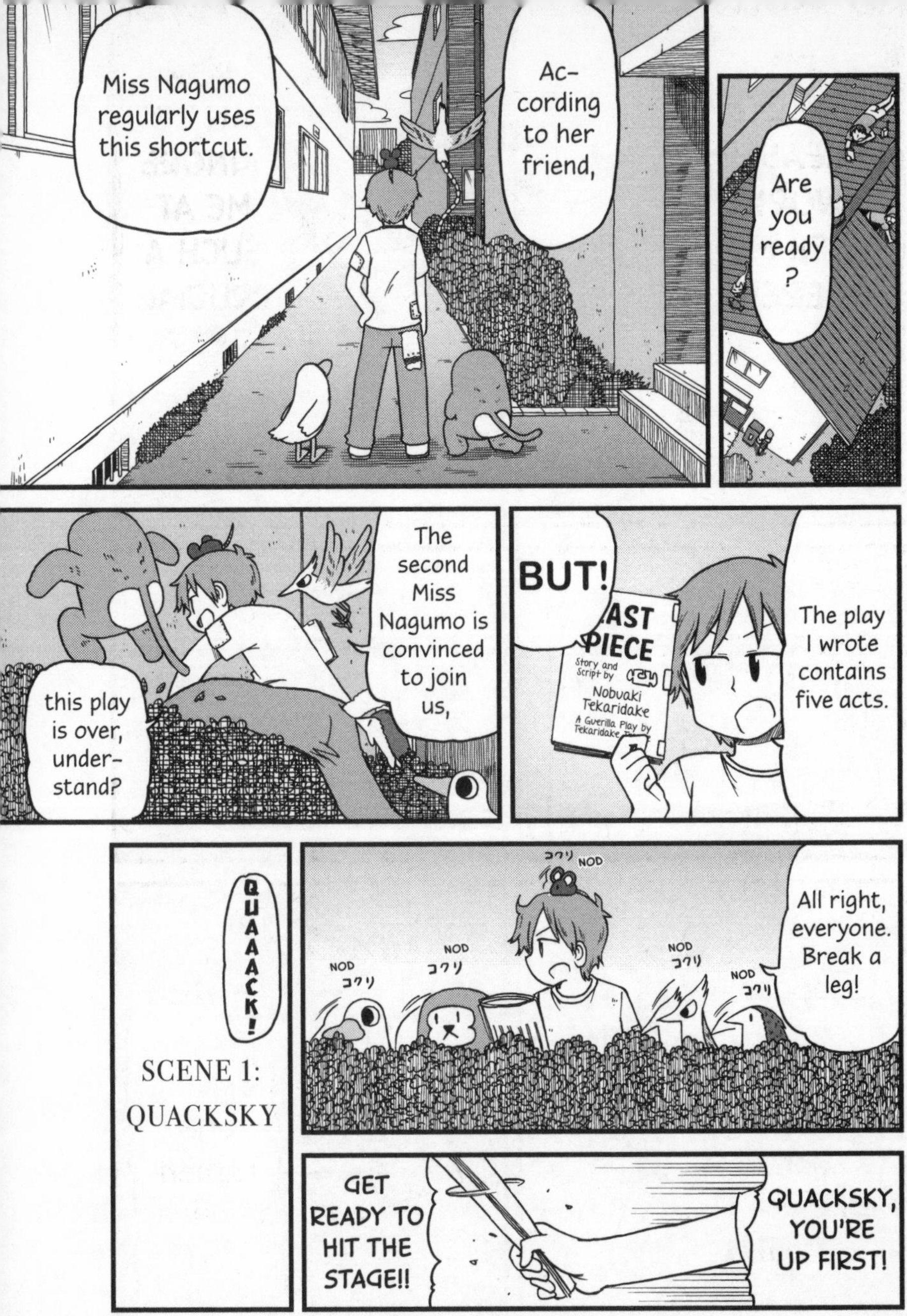
Are you ready?
Ac-cording to her friend,
Miss Nagumo regularly uses this shortcut.
The play I wrote contains five acts.
BUT!
AST PIECE
Story and Script by
Nobuaki Tekaridake
A Guerilla Play by Tekaridake
The second Miss Nagumo is convinced to join us,
this play is over, under-stand?
All right, everyone. Break a leg!
NOD コクリ
NOD コクリ
NOD コクリ
NOD コクリ
NOD コクリ
QUACKSKY, YOU'RE UP FIRST!
GET READY TO HIT THE STAGE!!
QUAAAACK!
SCENE 1: QUACKSKY

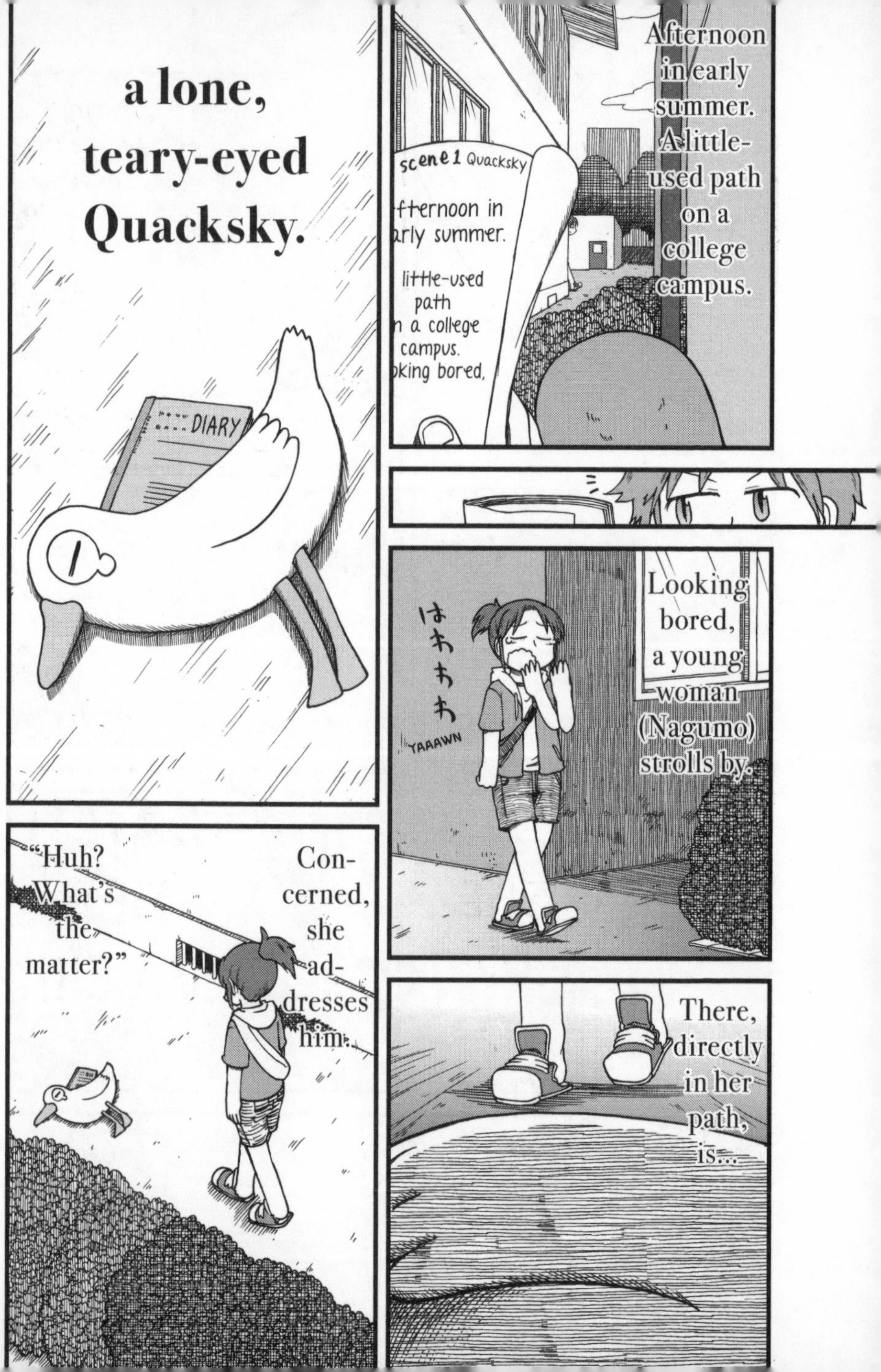

Afternoon in early summer. A little-used path on a college campus.
scene 1 Quacksky
fternoon in arly summer.
little-used path n a college campus. oking bored,
Looking bored, a young woman (Nagumo) strolls by.
はあああ
YAAAWN
There, directly in her path, is...
a lone, teary-eyed Quacksky.
DIARY
Concerned, she addresses him.
"Huh? What's the matter?"

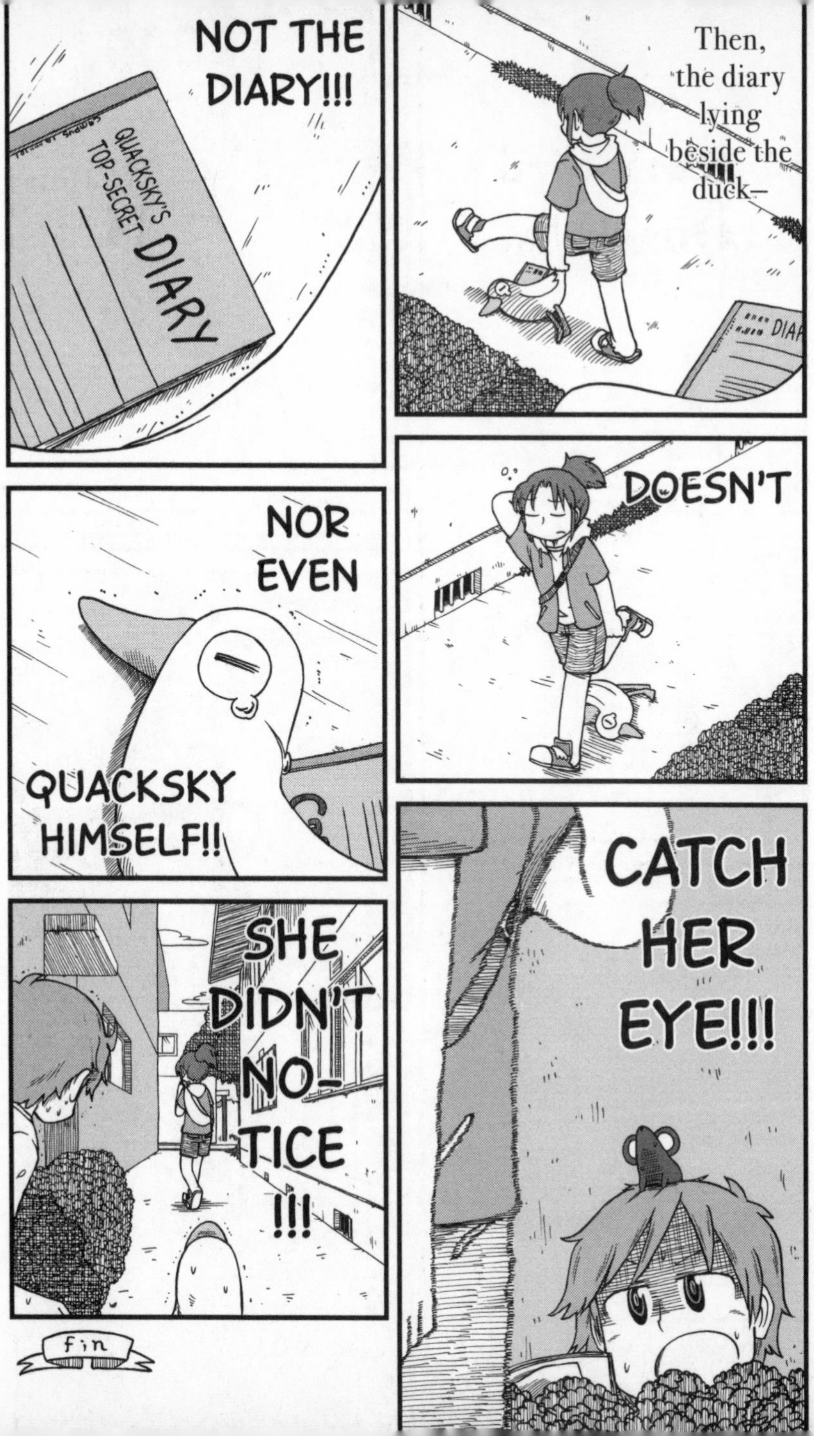
Then, the diary lying beside the duck—
NOT THE DIARY!!!
QUACKSKY'S TOP-SECRET DIARY
DOESN'T
NOR EVEN QUACKSKY HIMSELF!!
CATCH HER EYE!!!
SHE DIDN'T NO-TICE !!!
fin

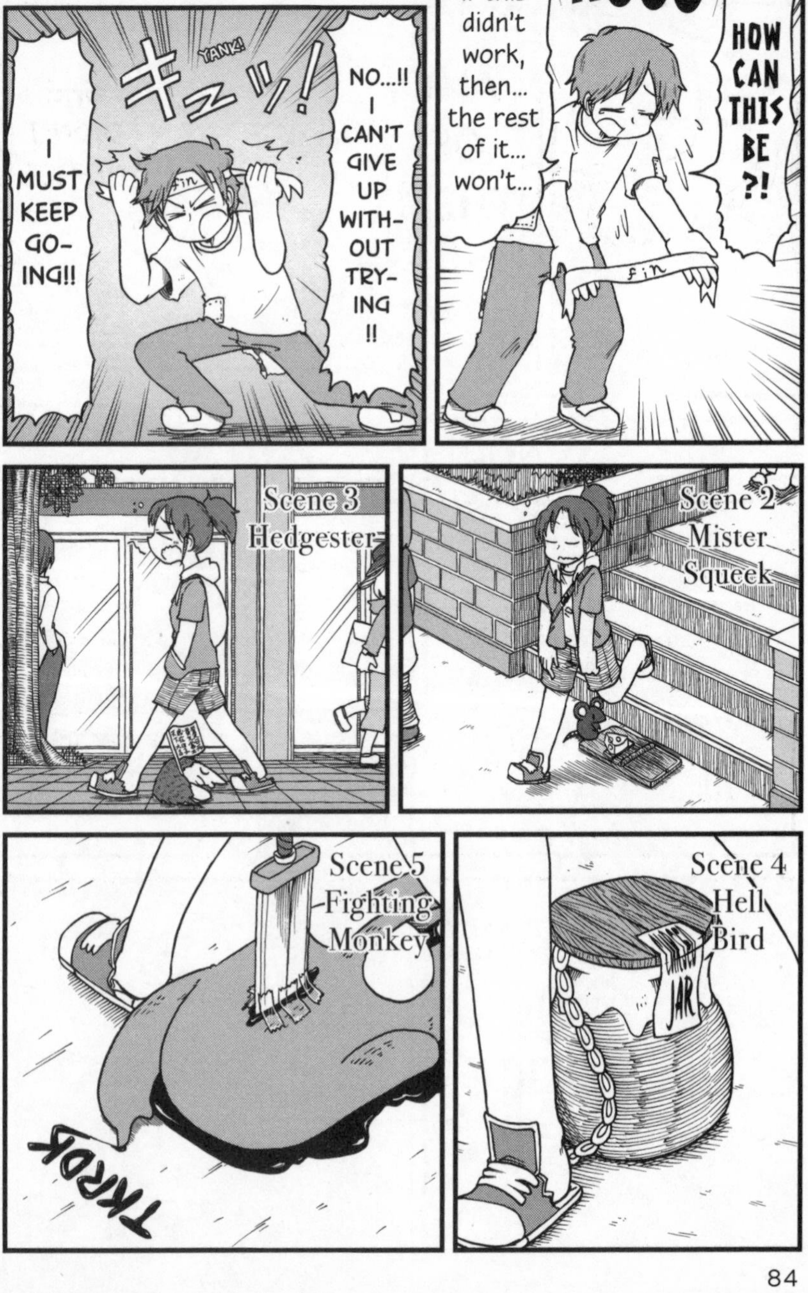
NOOO
HOW CAN THIS BE?!
If this didn't work, then... the rest of it... won't...
NO...!! I CAN'T GIVE UP WITHOUT TRYING!!
キュッ!
YANK!
I MUST KEEP GOING!!
fin
Scene 2 Mister Squeek
Scene 3 Hedgester
Scene 4 Hell Bird
JAR
Scene 5 Fighting Monkey
TKROK

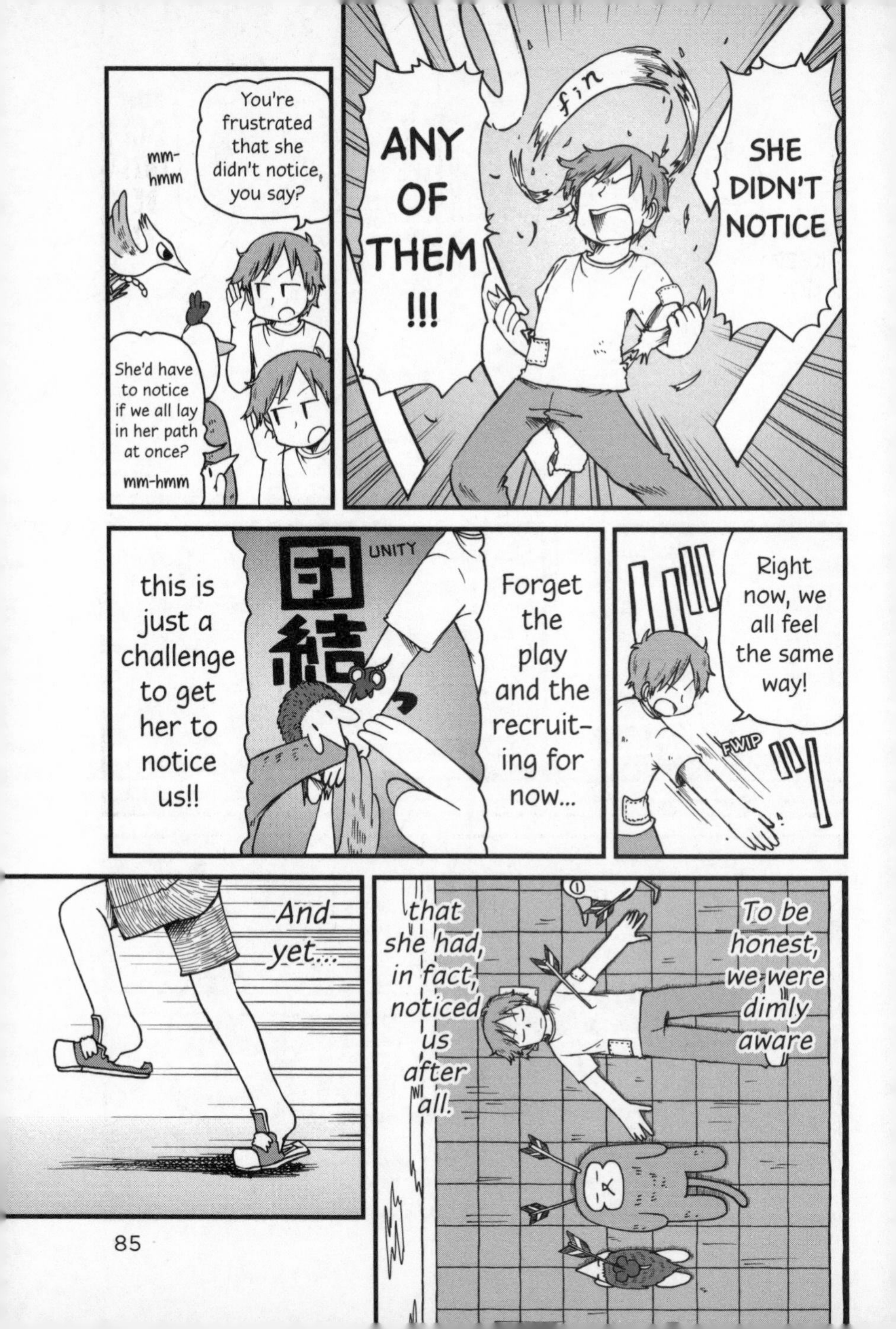
SHE DIDN'T NOTICE
fin
ANY OF THEM !!!
You're frustrated that she didn't notice, you say?
mm-hmm
She'd have to notice if we all lay in her path at once?
mm-hmm
Right now, we all feel the same way!
FWIP
Forget the play and the recruit-ing for now...
団結
UNITY
this is just a challenge to get her to notice us!!
To be honest, we were dimly aware
that she had, in fact, noticed us after all.
And yet...

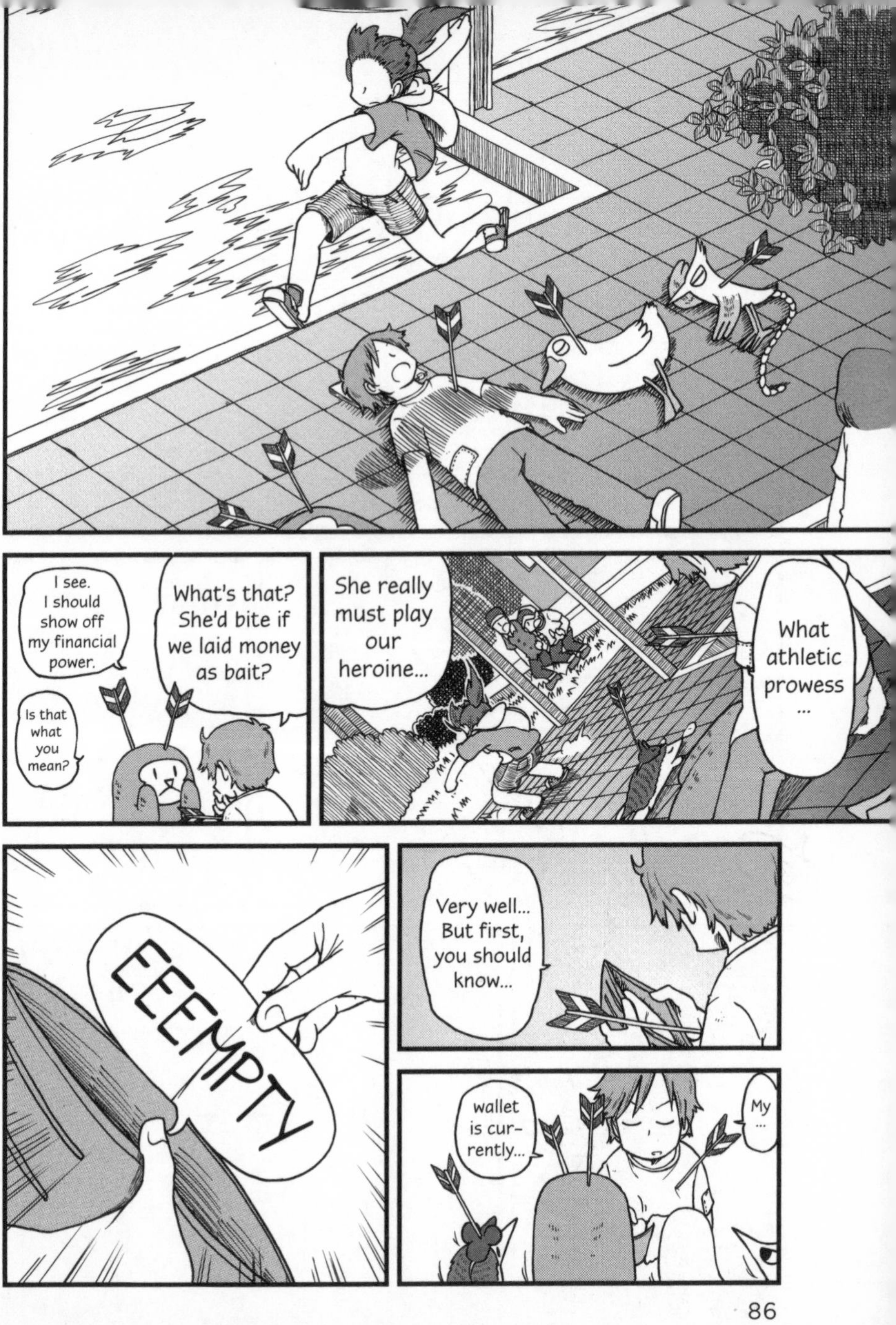
What athletic prowess ...
She really must play our heroine...
What's that? She'd bite if we laid money as bait?
I see. I should show off my financial power.
Is that what you mean?
Very well... But first, you should know...
My ...
wallet is cur-rently...
EEEMPTY

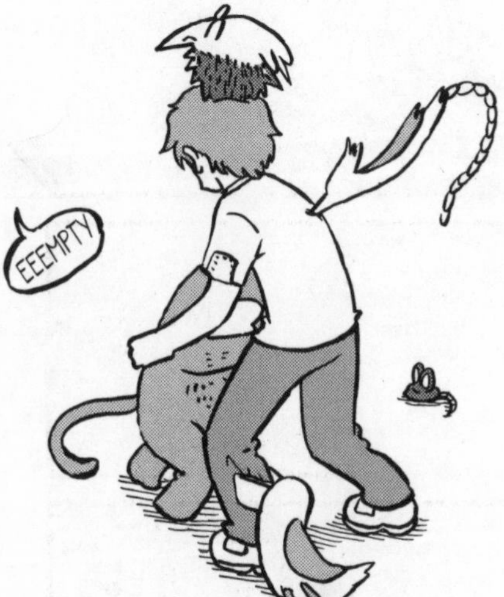
EEEMPTY

CITY

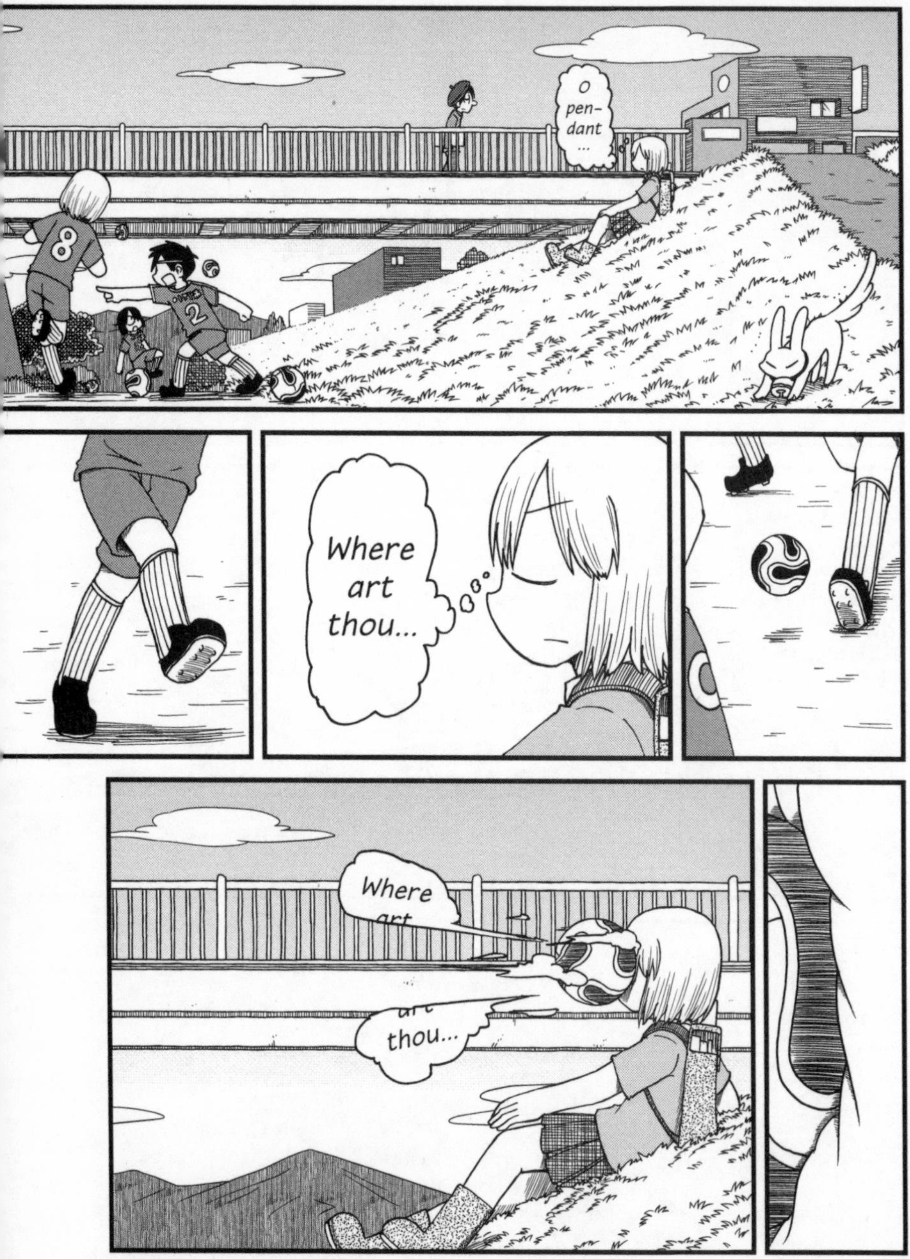
O pen-dant ...
Where art thou...
Where
thou...

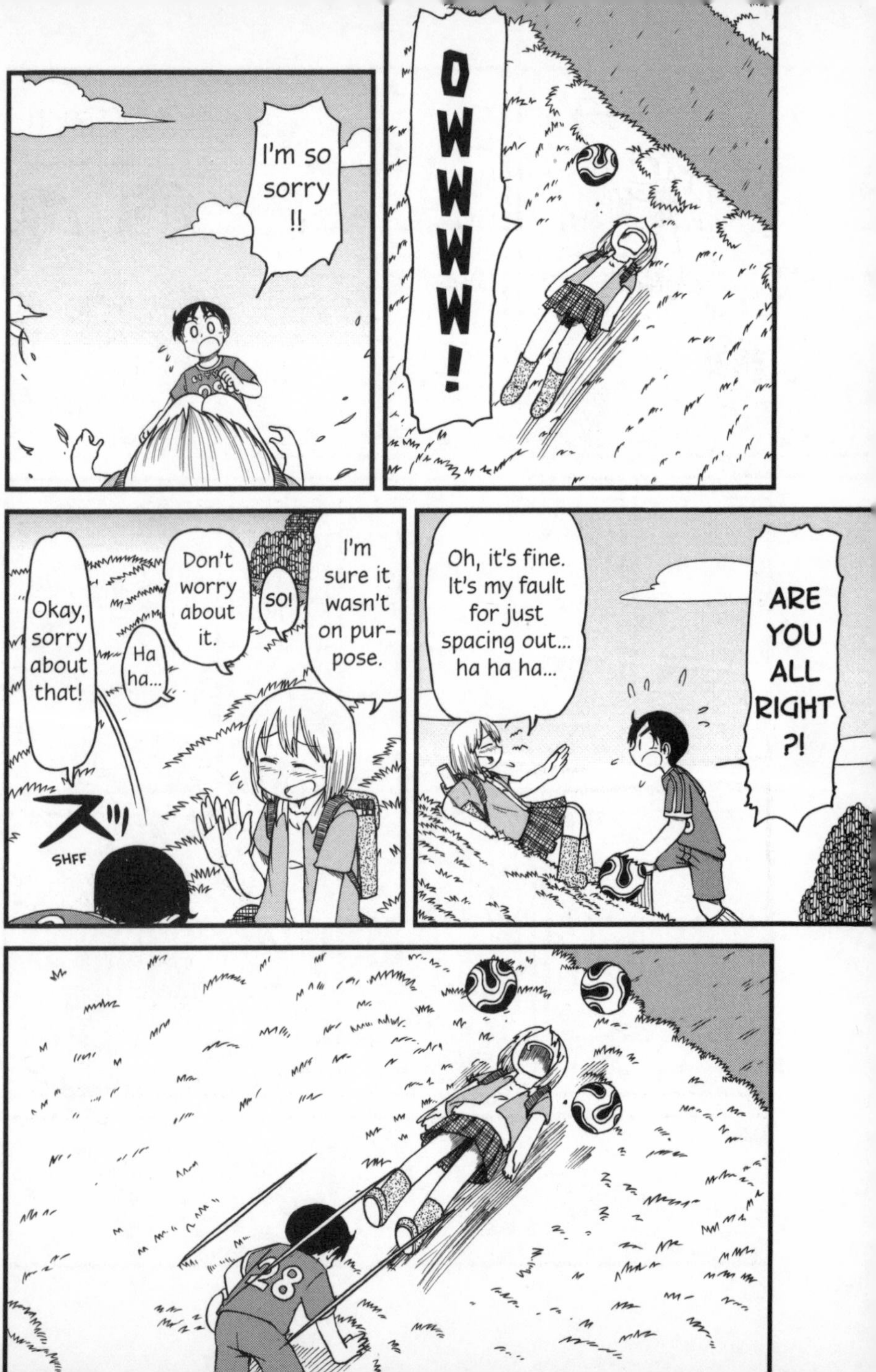
OWWWWW!
I'm so sorry !!
ARE YOU ALL RIGHT ?!
Oh, it's fine. It's my fault for just spacing out... ha ha ha...
I'm sure it wasn't on pur-pose.
SO!
Don't worry about it.
Ha ha...
Okay, sorry about that!
ズッ
SHFF
28

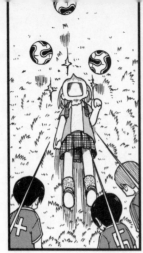

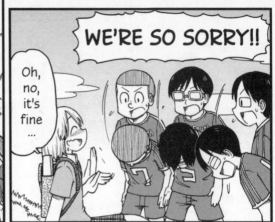

WE'RE SO SORRY!!
Oh, no, it's fine ...
ARE YOU ALL RIGHT?!
Ha ha ha, don't worry about—
I'M SO SORRY!!
SO SORRY!!
SORRY!!

Chapter 61 Niikura vs. the Soccer Team

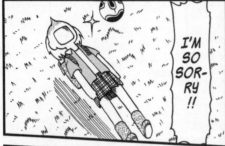

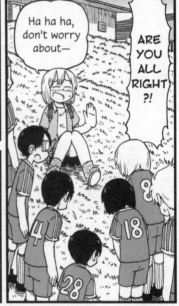

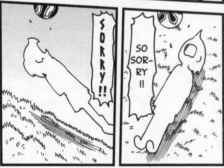

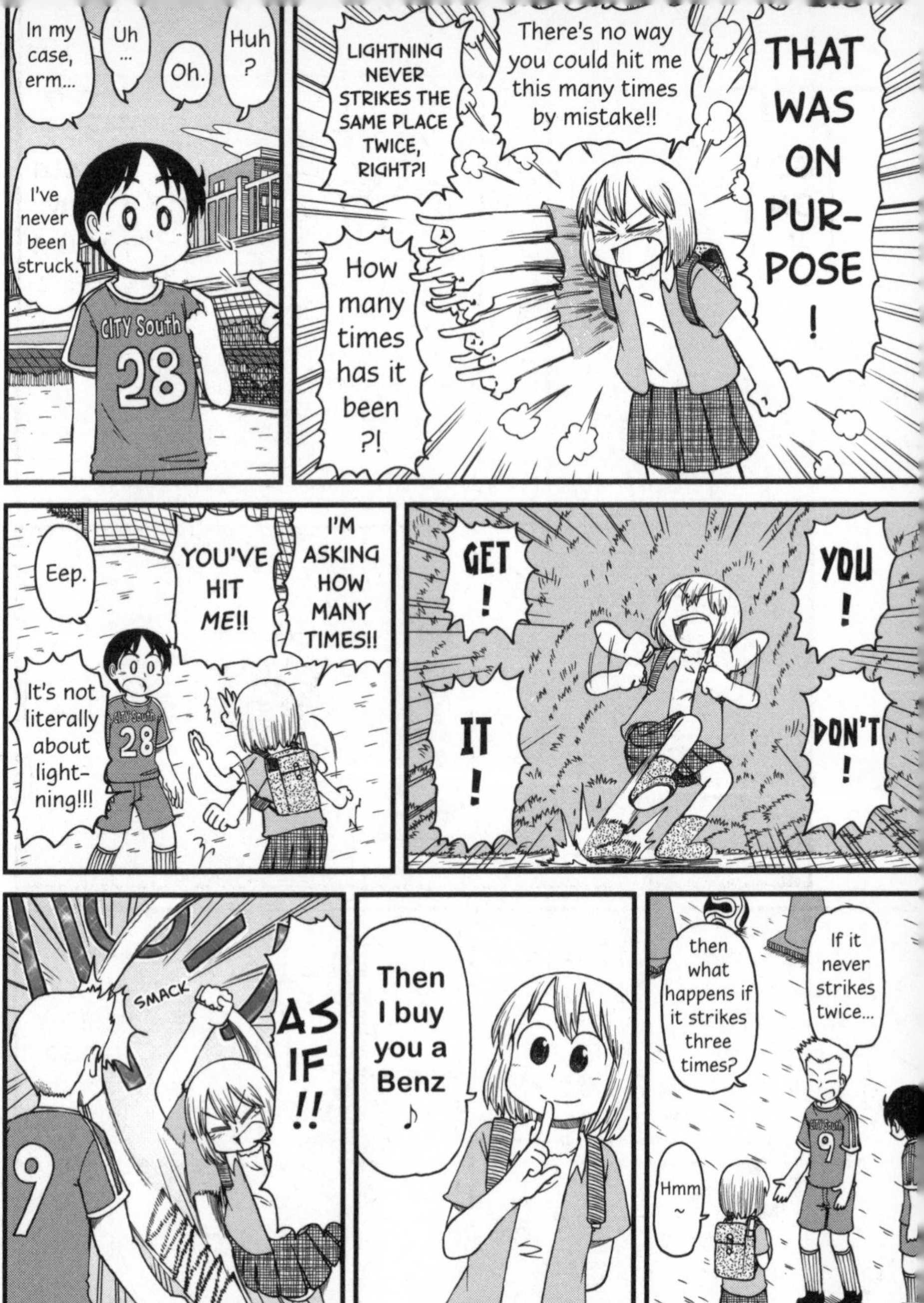
THAT WAS ON PUR-POSE!
There's no way you could hit me this many times by mistake!!
LIGHTNING NEVER STRIKES THE SAME PLACE TWICE, RIGHT?!
How many times has it been?!
Huh?
Oh.
Uh ...
In my case, erm...
I've never been struck.
YOU!
DON'T!
GET!
IT!
I'M ASKING HOW MANY TIMES!!
YOU'VE HIT ME!!
Eep.
It's not literally about light-ning!!!
If it never strikes twice...
then what happens if it strikes three times?
Hmm~
Then I buy you a Benz ♪
AS IF!!
SMACK

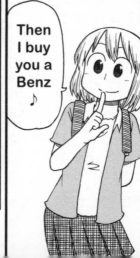

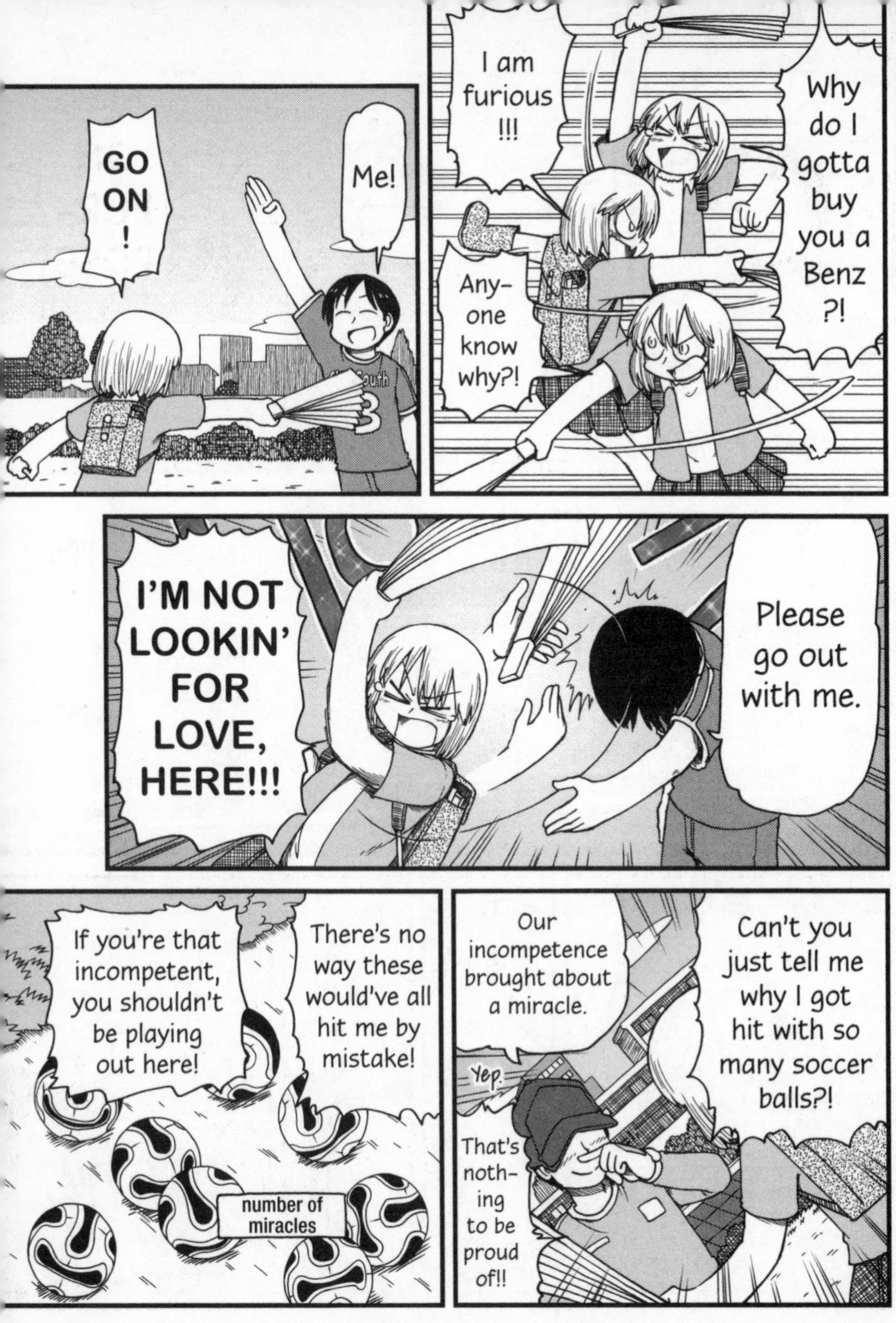
Why do I gotta buy you a Benz?!
I am furious!!!
Anyone know why?!
Me!
GO ON!
Please go out with me.
I'M NOT LOOKIN' FOR LOVE, HERE!!!
Can't you just tell me why I got hit with so many soccer balls?!
Our incompetence brought about a miracle.
Yep.
That's nothing to be proud of!!
There's no way these would've all hit me by mistake!
If you're that incompetent, you shouldn't be playing out here!
number of miracles

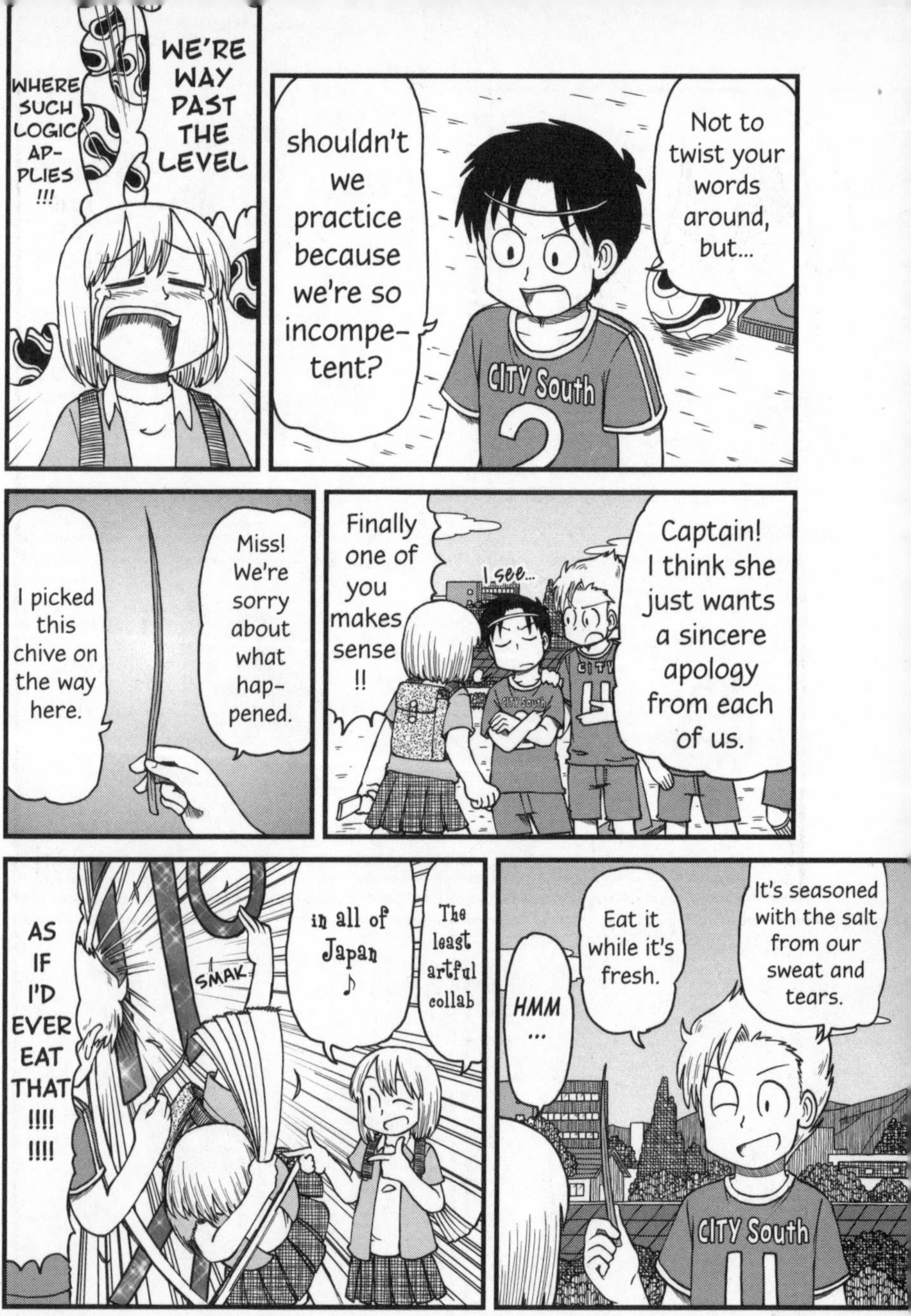
Not to twist your words around, but...
shouldn't we practice because we're so incompetent?
WE'RE WAY PAST THE LEVEL
WHERE SUCH LOGIC APPLIES !!!
Captain! I think she just wants a sincere apology from each of us.
I see...
Finally one of you makes sense !!
Miss! We're sorry about what happened.
I picked this chive on the way here.
It's seasoned with the salt from our sweat and tears.
Eat it while it's fresh.
HMM ...
The least artful collab
in all of Japan ♪
SMAK
AS IF I'D EVER EAT THAT !!!! !!!!

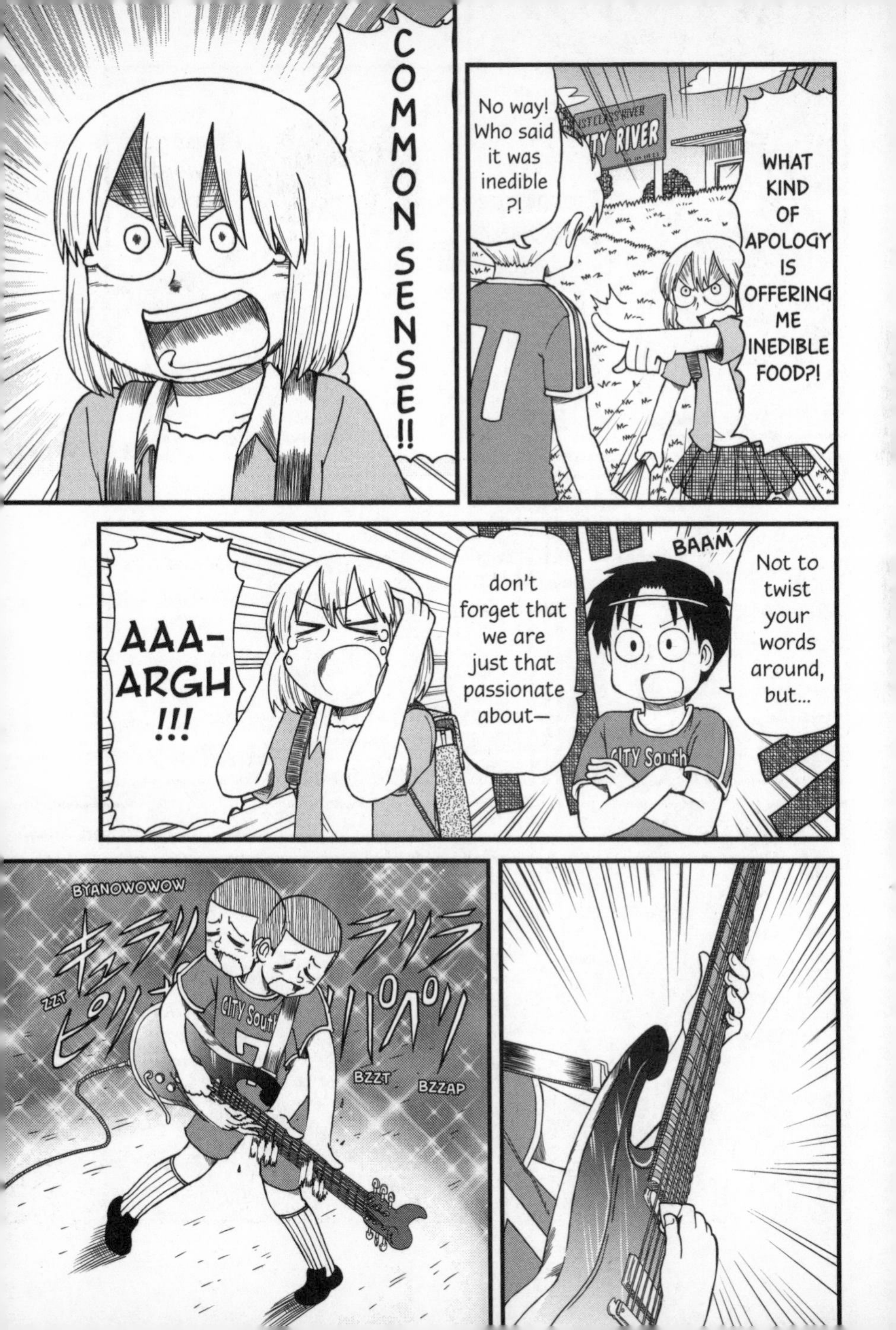
WHAT KIND OF APOLOGY IS OFFERING ME INEDIBLE FOOD?!
No way! Who said it was inedible ?!
COMMON SENSE!!
Not to twist your words around, but...
BAAM
don't forget that we are just that passionate about—
CITY South
AAA-ARGH !!!
BYANOWOWOW
ZZT
CITY South
BZZT
BZZAP

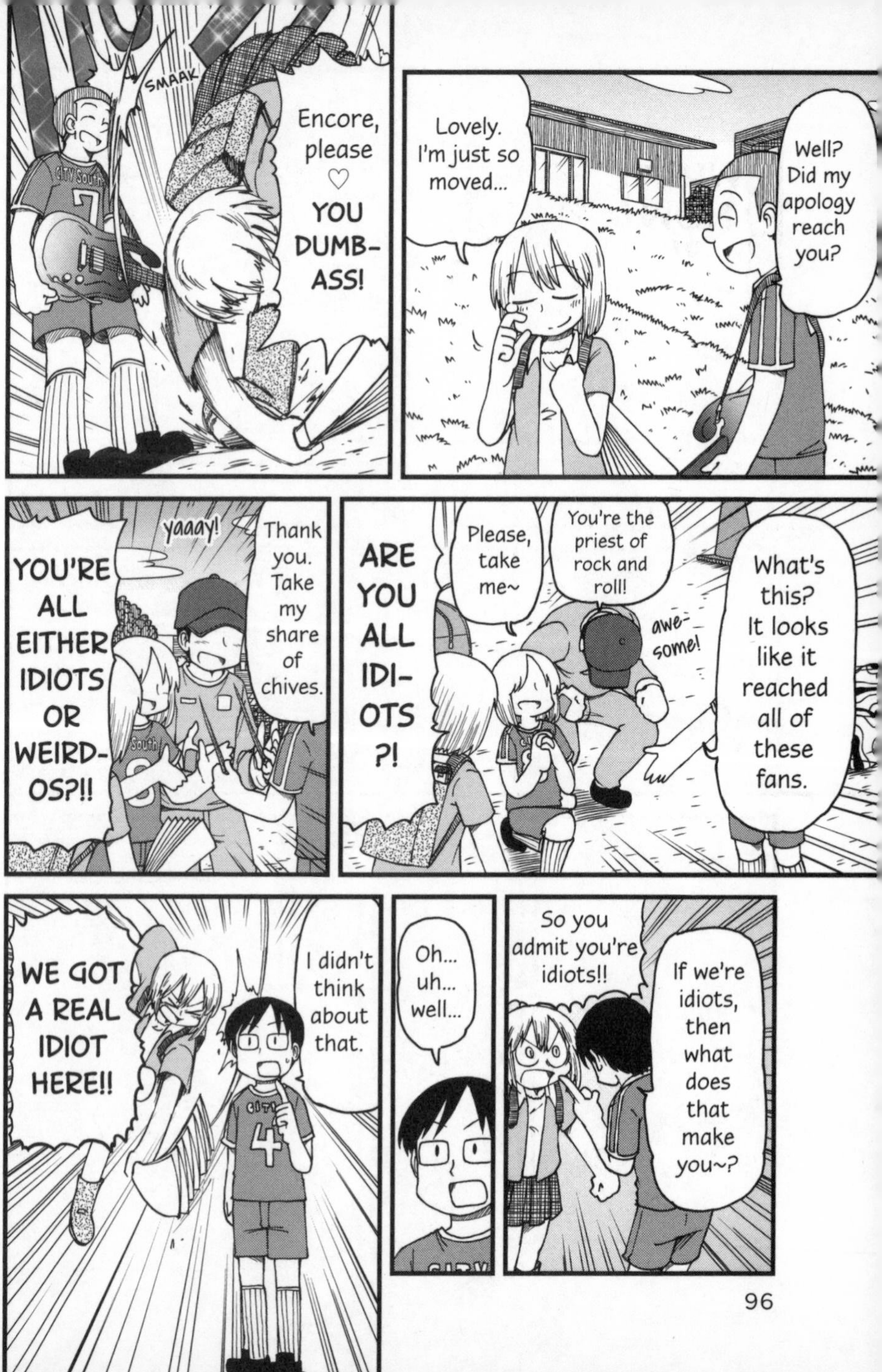
Well? Did my apology reach you?
Lovely. I'm just so moved...
Encore, please ♡
SMAAK
YOU DUMB-ASS!
What's this? It looks like it reached all of these fans.
You're the priest of rock and roll!
Please, take me~
awe-some!
ARE YOU ALL IDI-OTS?!
Thank you. Take my share of chives.
yaaay!
YOU'RE ALL EITHER IDIOTS OR WEIRD-OS?!!
If we're idiots, then what does that make you~?
So you admit you're idiots!!
Oh... uh... well...
I didn't think about that.
WE GOT A REAL IDIOT HERE!!

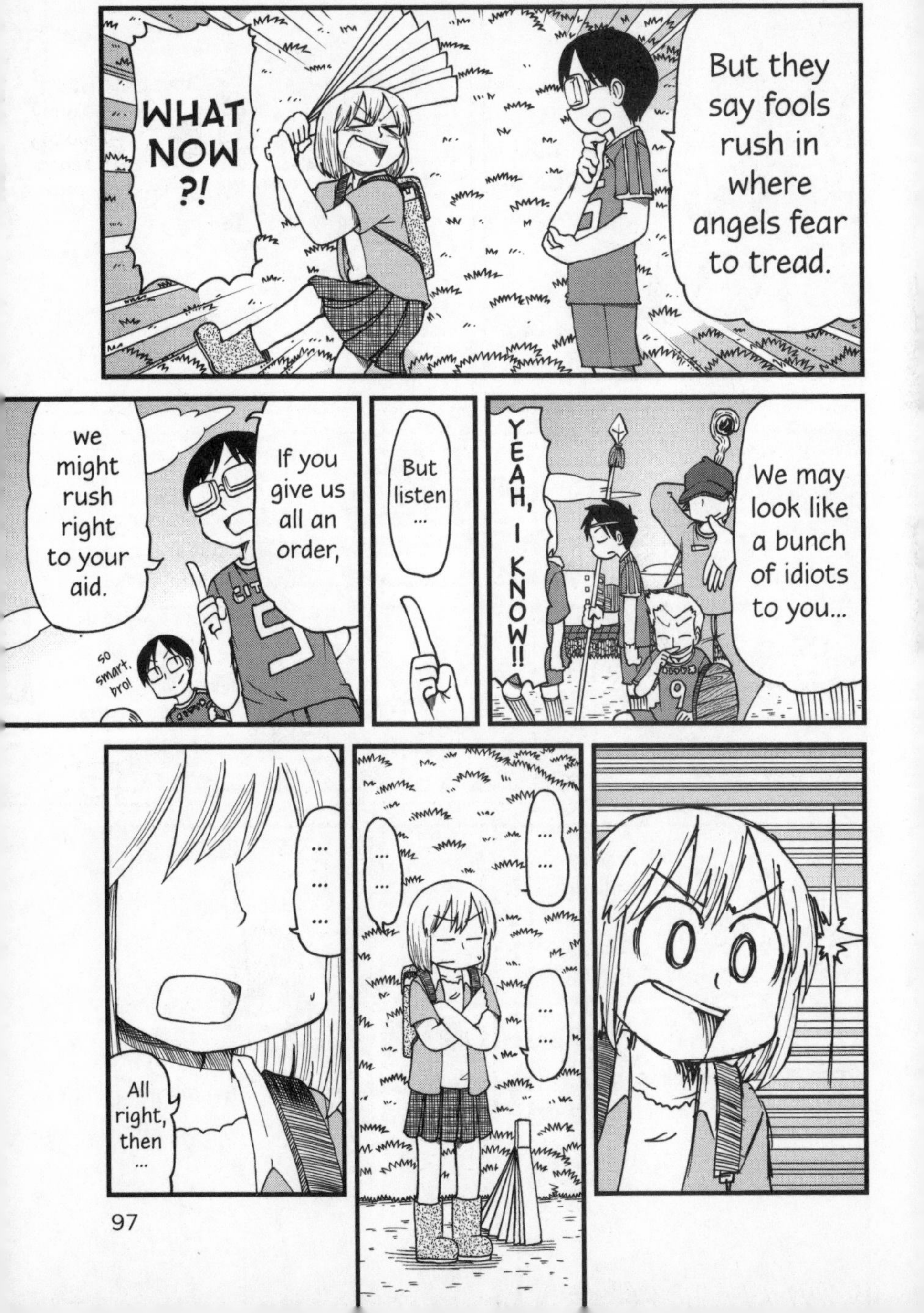

But they say fools rush in where angels fear to tread.
WHAT NOW ?!
We may look like a bunch of idiots to you...
YEAH, I KNOW!!
But listen ...
If you give us all an order,
we might rush right to your aid.
So smart, bro!
... ...
... ...
... ...
... ...
All right, then ...

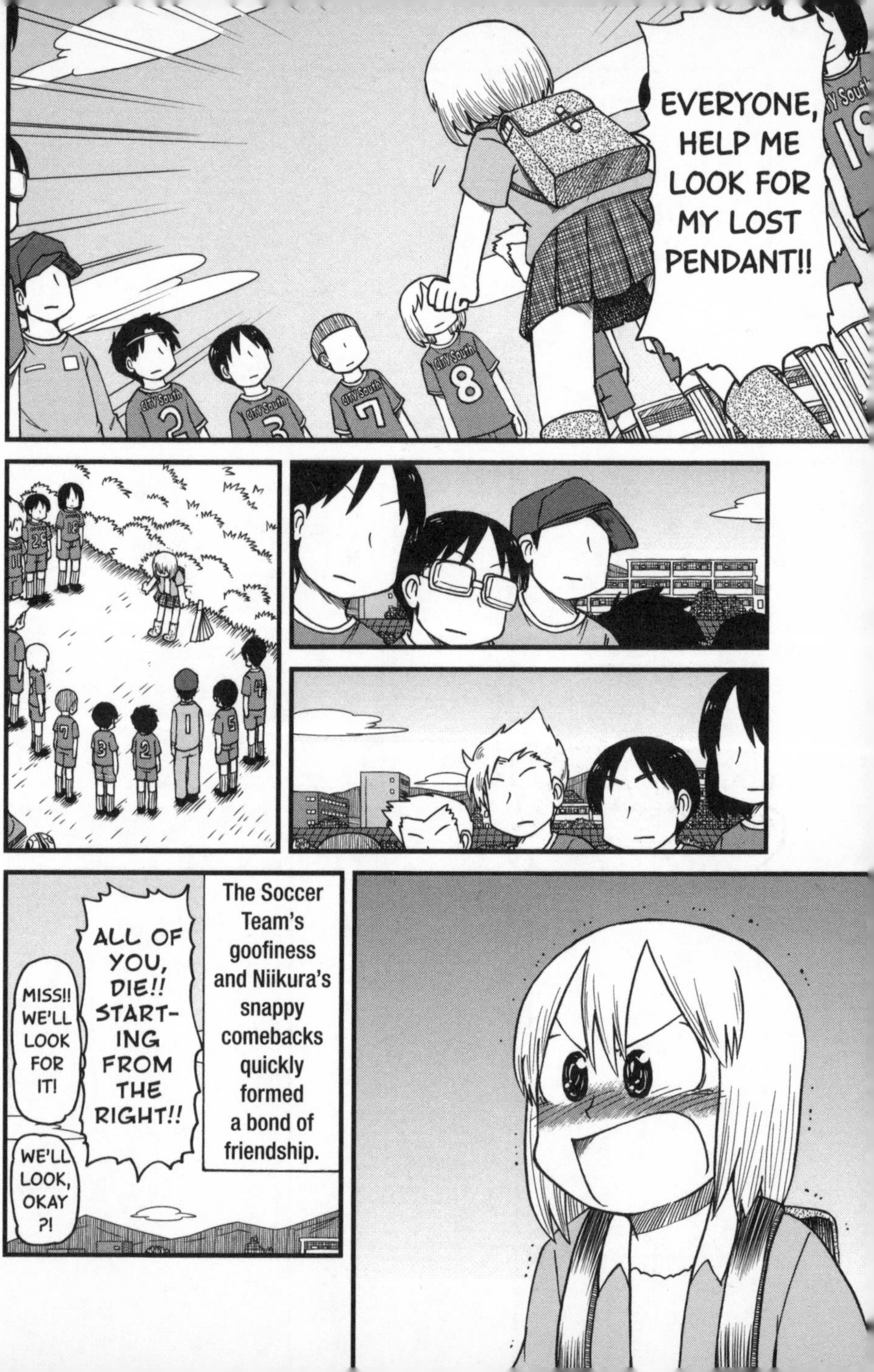
EVERYONE, HELP ME LOOK FOR MY LOST PENDANT!!
The Soccer Team's goofiness and Niikura's snappy comebacks quickly formed a bond of friendship.
ALL OF YOU, DIE!! START-ING FROM THE RIGHT!!
MISS!! WE'LL LOOK FOR IT!
WE'LL LOOK, OKAY?!

ALL
¥100

CITY

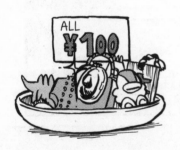

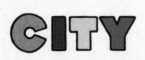

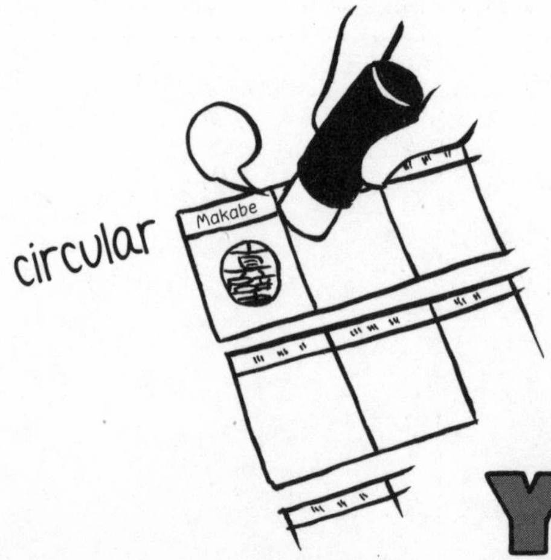
circular
Makabe

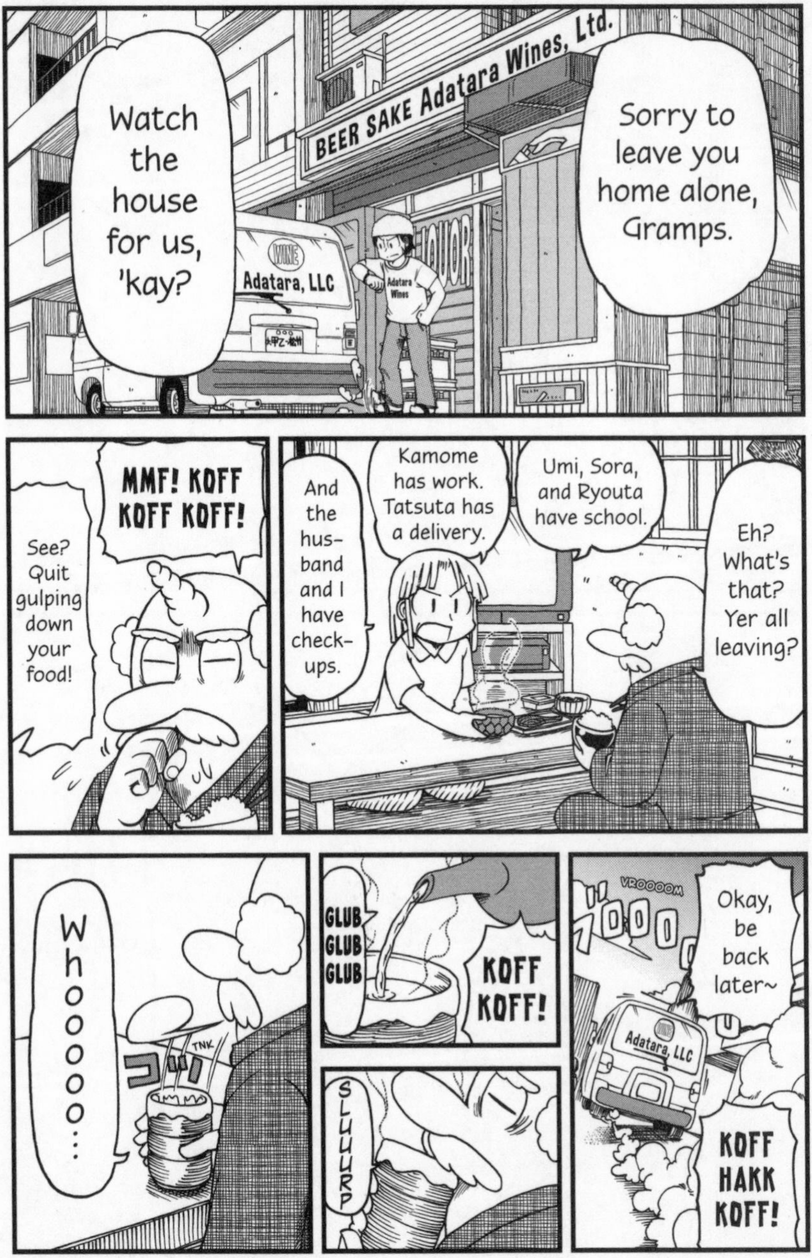
Sorry to leave you home alone, Gramps.
BEER SAKE Adatara Wines, Ltd.
Adatara, LLC
Adatara Wines
Watch the house for us, 'kay?
Eh? What's that? Yer all leaving?
Umi, Sora, and Ryouta have school.
Kamome has work. Tatsuta has a delivery.
And the hus-band and I have check-ups.
MMF! KOFF KOFF KOFF!
See? Quit gulping down your food!
VROOOOM
Okay, be back later~
Adatara, LLC
KOFF HAKK KOFF!
GLUB GLUB GLUB
KOFF KOFF!
SLUURP
TNK
Whoooooo...

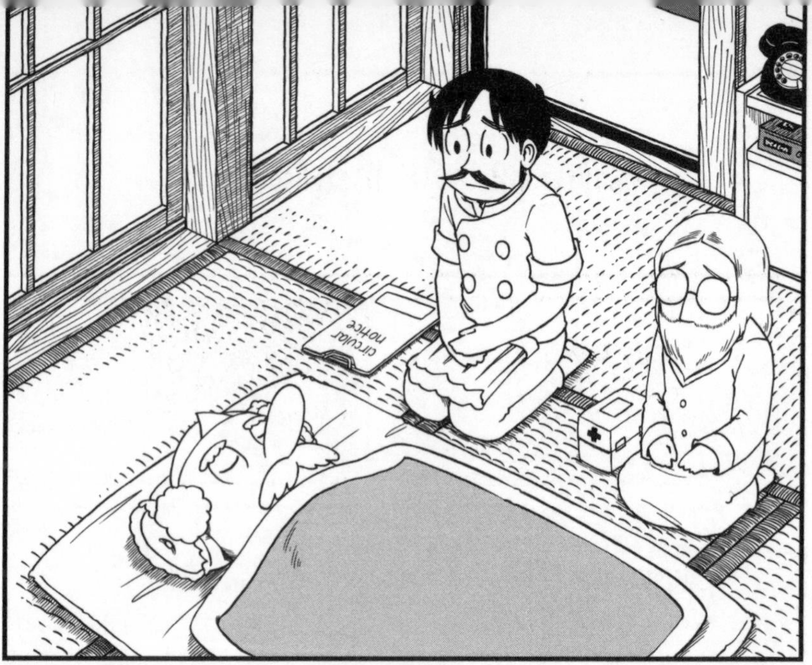
circular notice
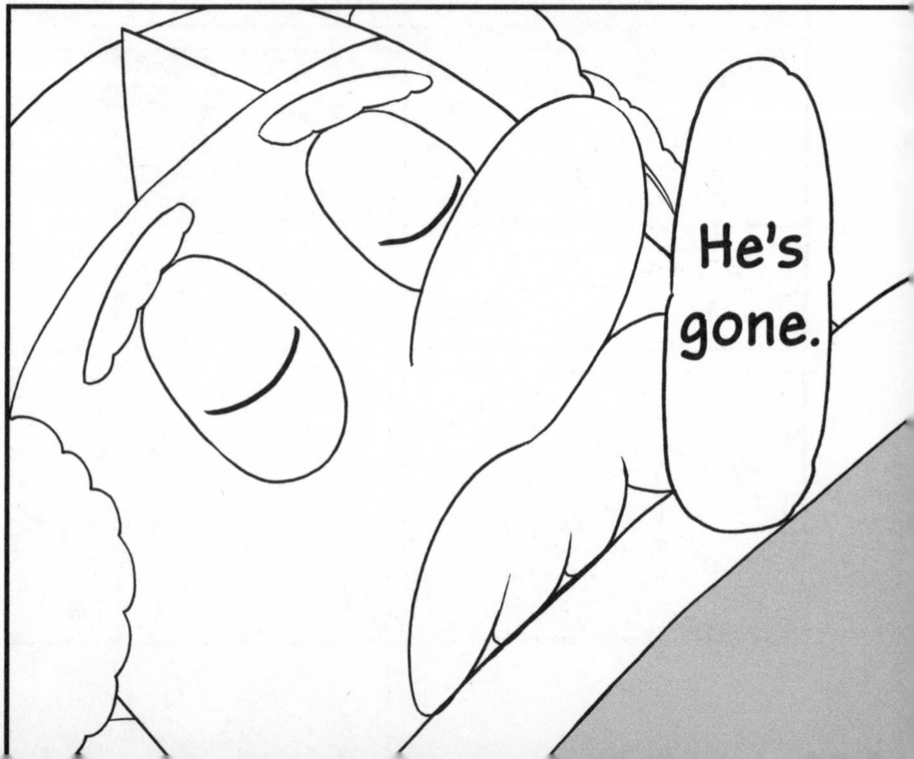
He's gone.

Chapter 62 ◇ Deathbed March

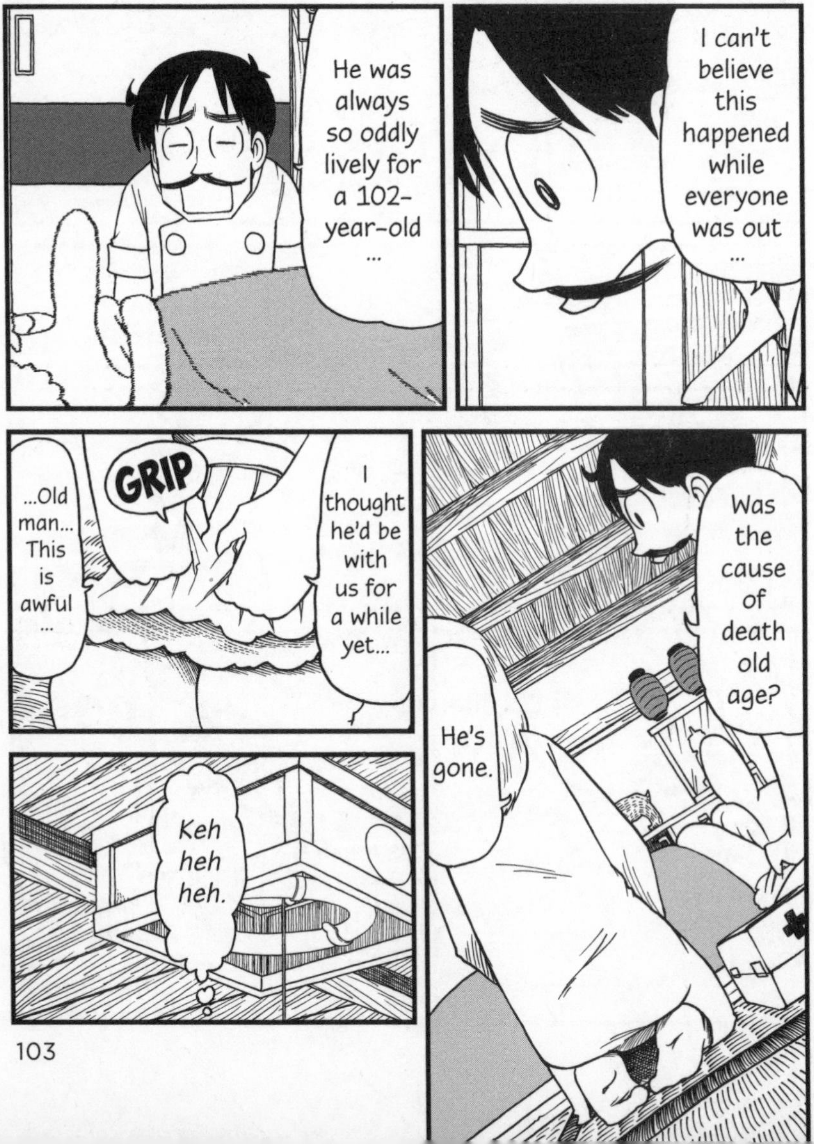
I can't believe this happened while everyone was out ...
He was always so oddly lively for a 102-year-old ...
Was the cause of death old age?
He's gone.
I thought he'd be with us for a while yet...
GRIP
...Old man... This is awful ...
Keh heh heh.

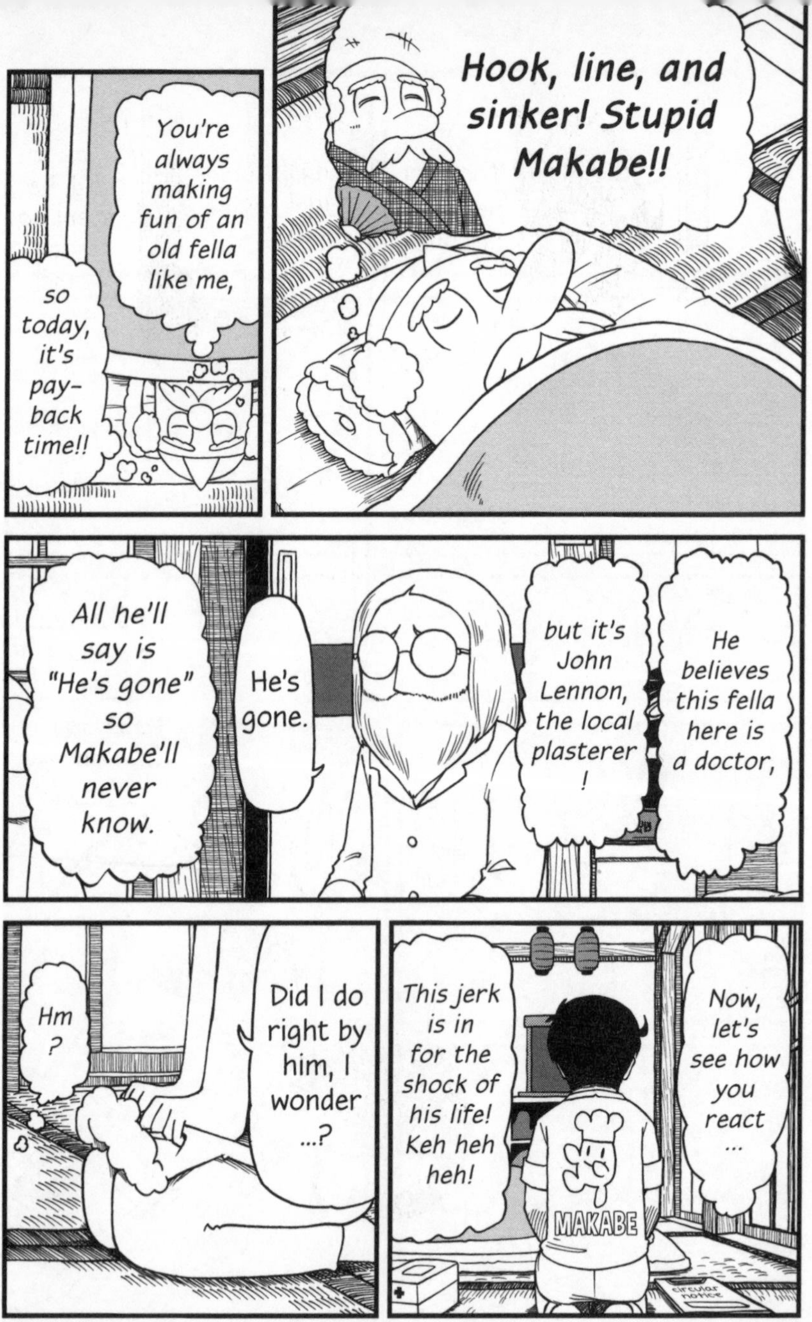
Hook, line, and sinker! Stupid Makabe!!
You're always making fun of an old fella like me,
so today, it's pay-back time!!
He believes this fella here is a doctor,
but it's John Lennon, the local plasterer!
He's gone.
All he'll say is "He's gone" so Makabe'll never know.
Now, let's see how you react...
This jerk is in for the shock of his life! Keh heh heh!
MAKABE
circular notice
Did I do right by him, I wonder...?
Hm?

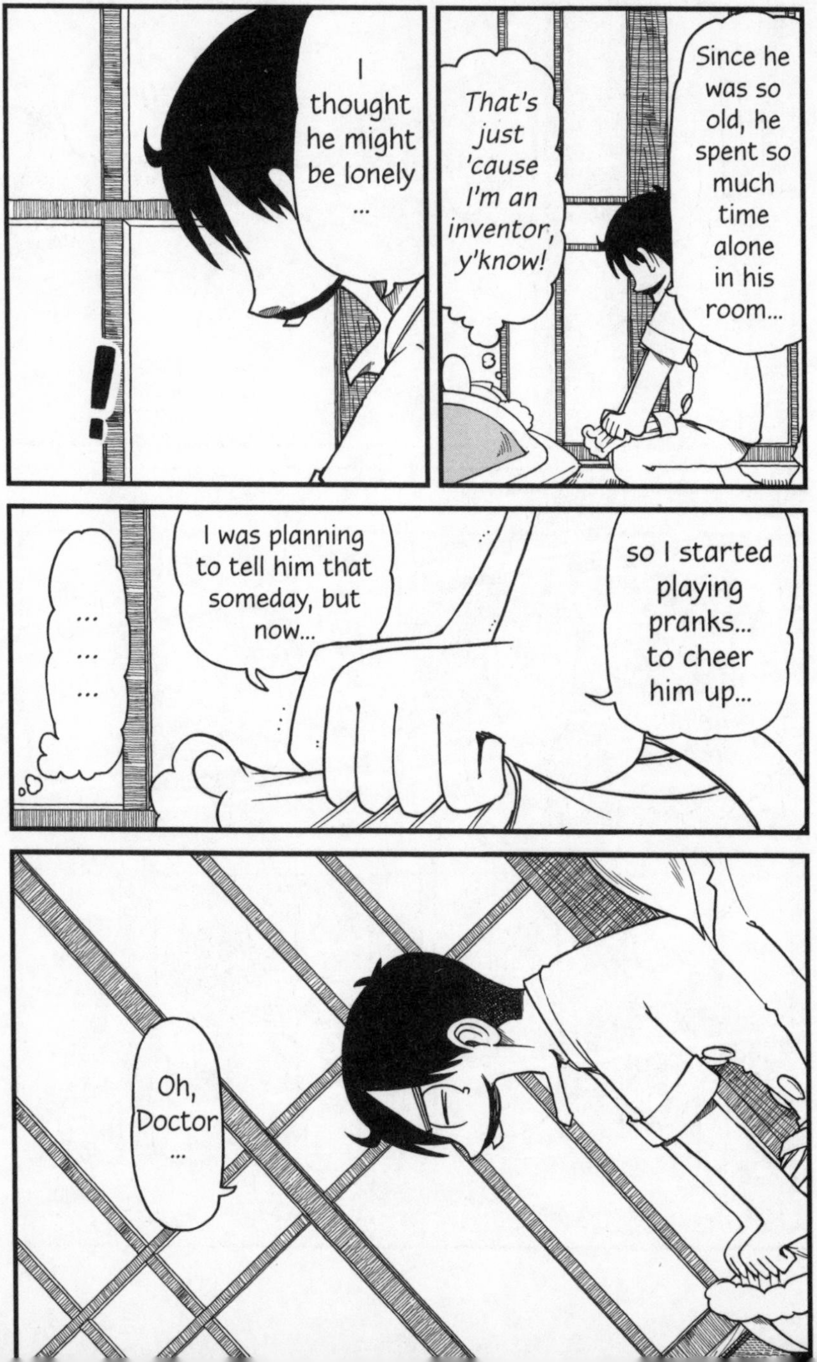
Since he was so old, he spent so much time alone in his room...
That's just 'cause I'm an inventor, y'know!
I thought he might be lonely ...
!
so I started playing pranks... to cheer him up...
I was planning to tell him that someday, but now...
... ...
Oh, Doctor ...

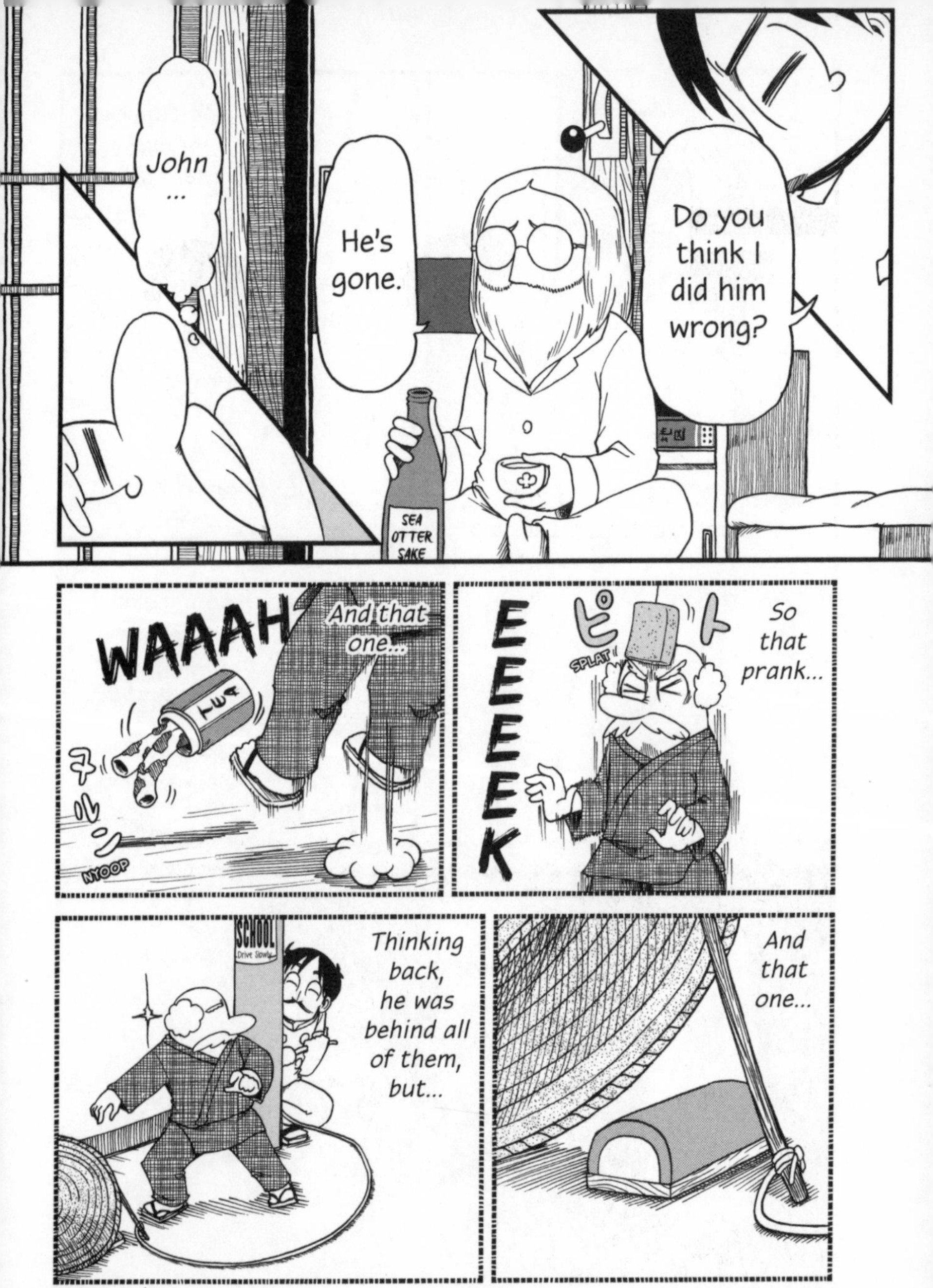
Do you think I did him wrong?
He's gone.
SEA OTTER SAKE
John ...
So that prank...
ピト
SPLAT
EEEEEEK
And that one...
WAAAH
TEA
ヌルン
NYOOP
And that one...
Thinking back, he was behind all of them, but...
SCHOOL
Drive Slowly

And yet, I've only thought of revenge...

just for my sake...

To think he did them all...

This is the end of my revenge, then.

I'm sorry, young Tsuru.

It is I who must apologize to you.

Three, two, one...

Here we go!!

SFF

Now to give him a happy surprise!!

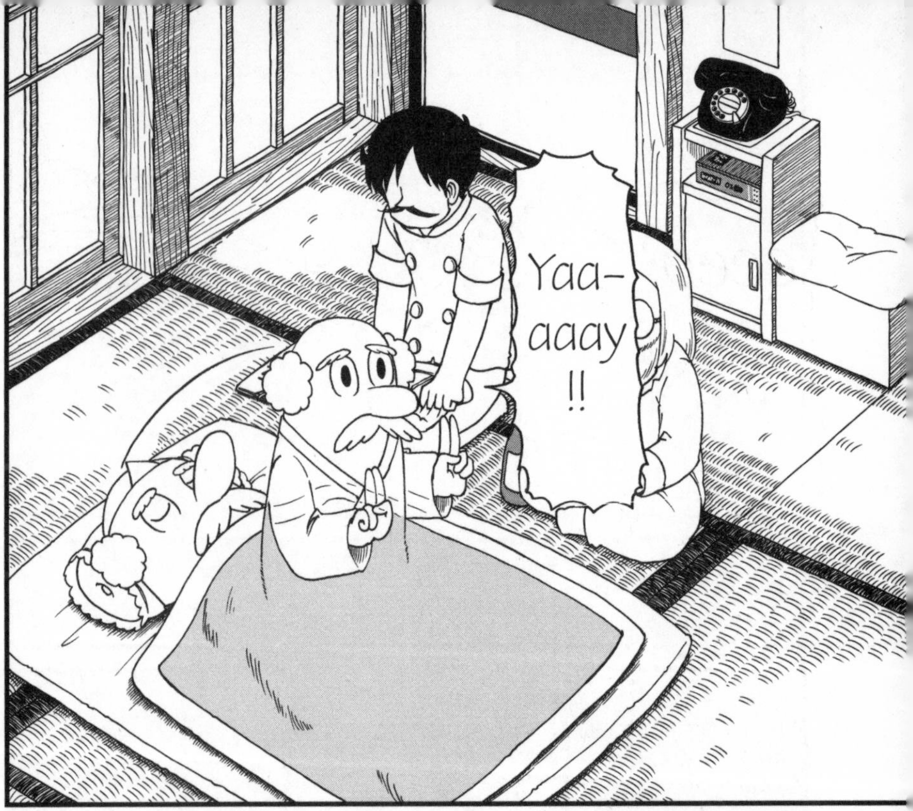
Yaa-aaay !!
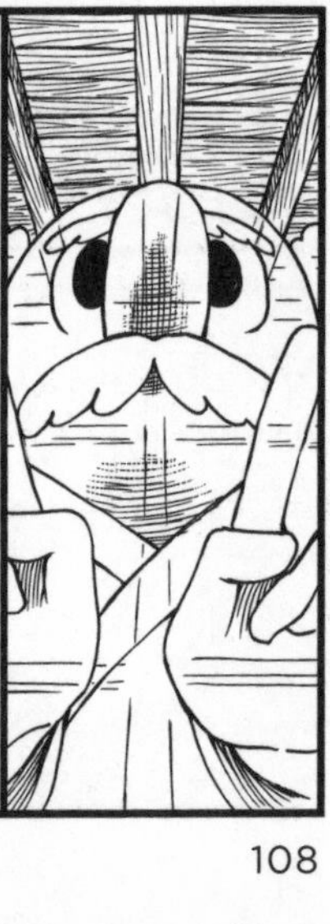
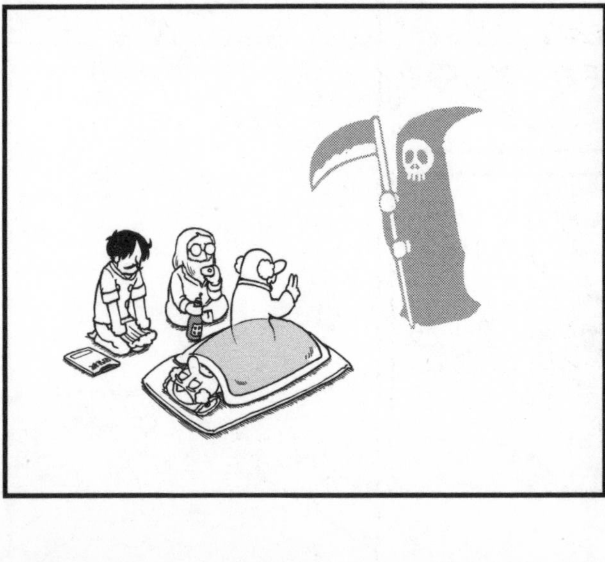

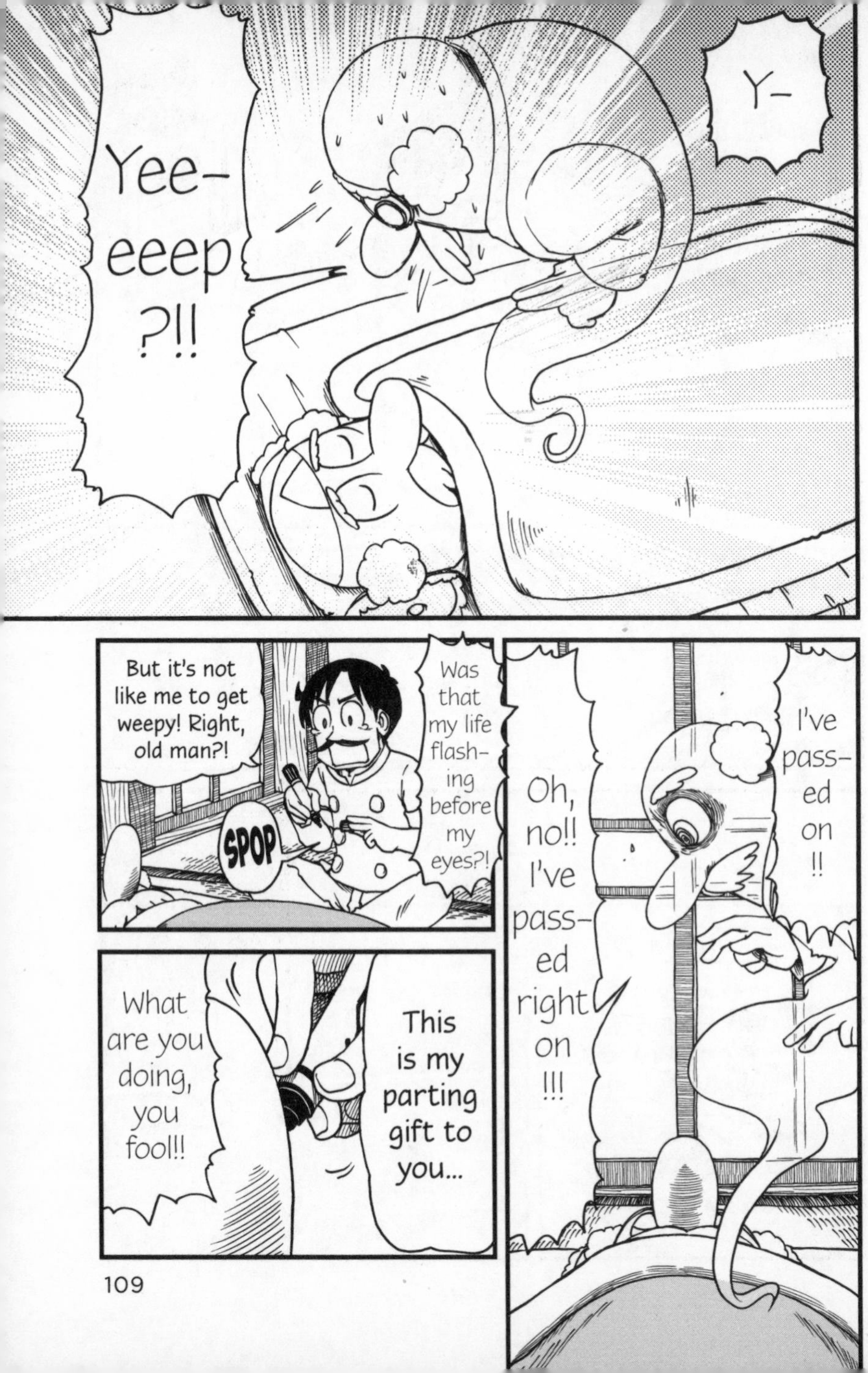
Y–
Yee–eeep?!!
I've pass–ed on!!
Oh, no!! I've pass–ed right on!!!
Was that my life flash–ing before my eyes?!
But it's not like me to get weepy! Right, old man?!
SPOP
This is my parting gift to you...
What are you doing, you fool!!

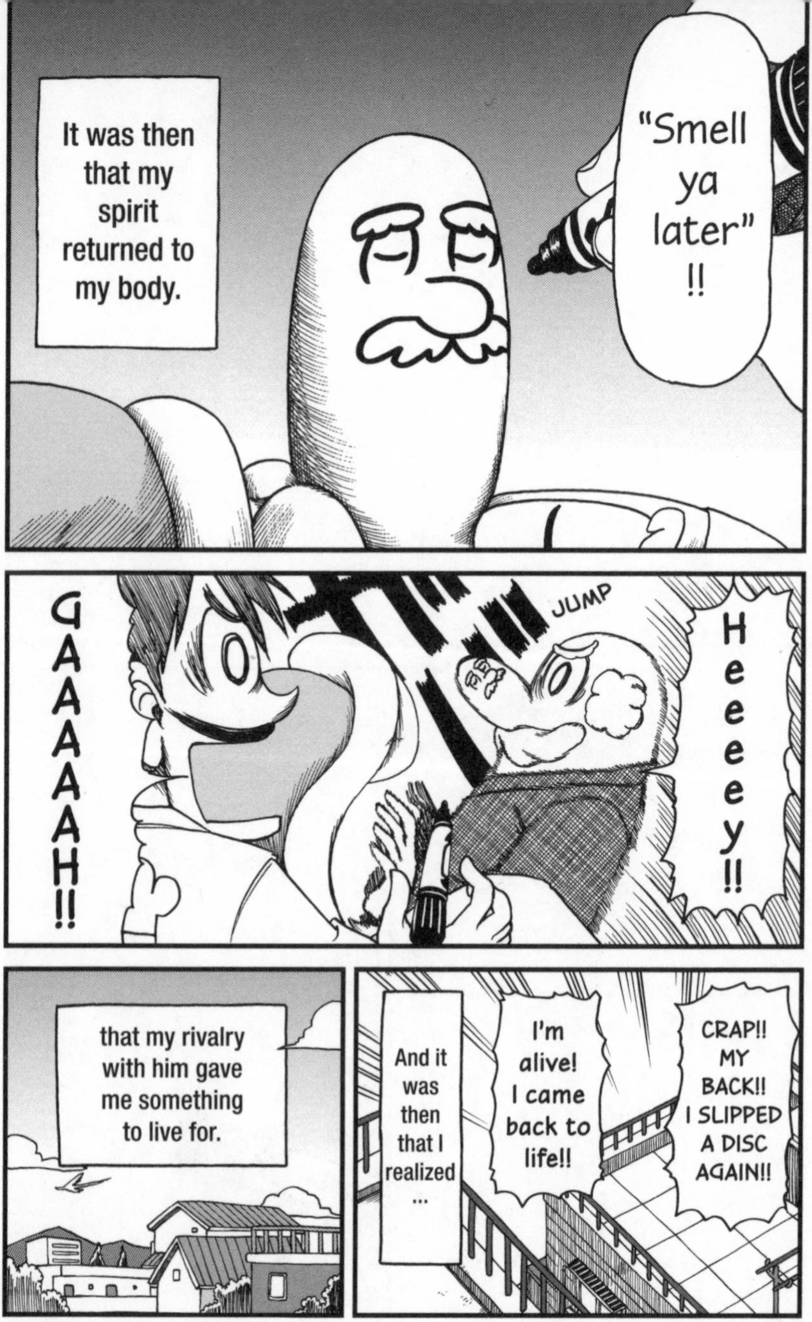
"Smell ya later" !!
It was then that my spirit returned to my body.
Heeeey!!
JUMP
GAAAAAAH!!
CRAP!! MY BACK!! I SLIPPED A DISC AGAIN!!
I'm alive! I came back to life!!
And it was then that I realized ...
that my rivalry with him gave me something to live for.

PERMANENT

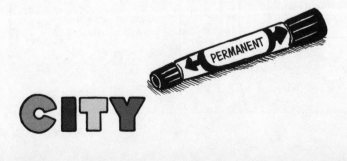

CITY

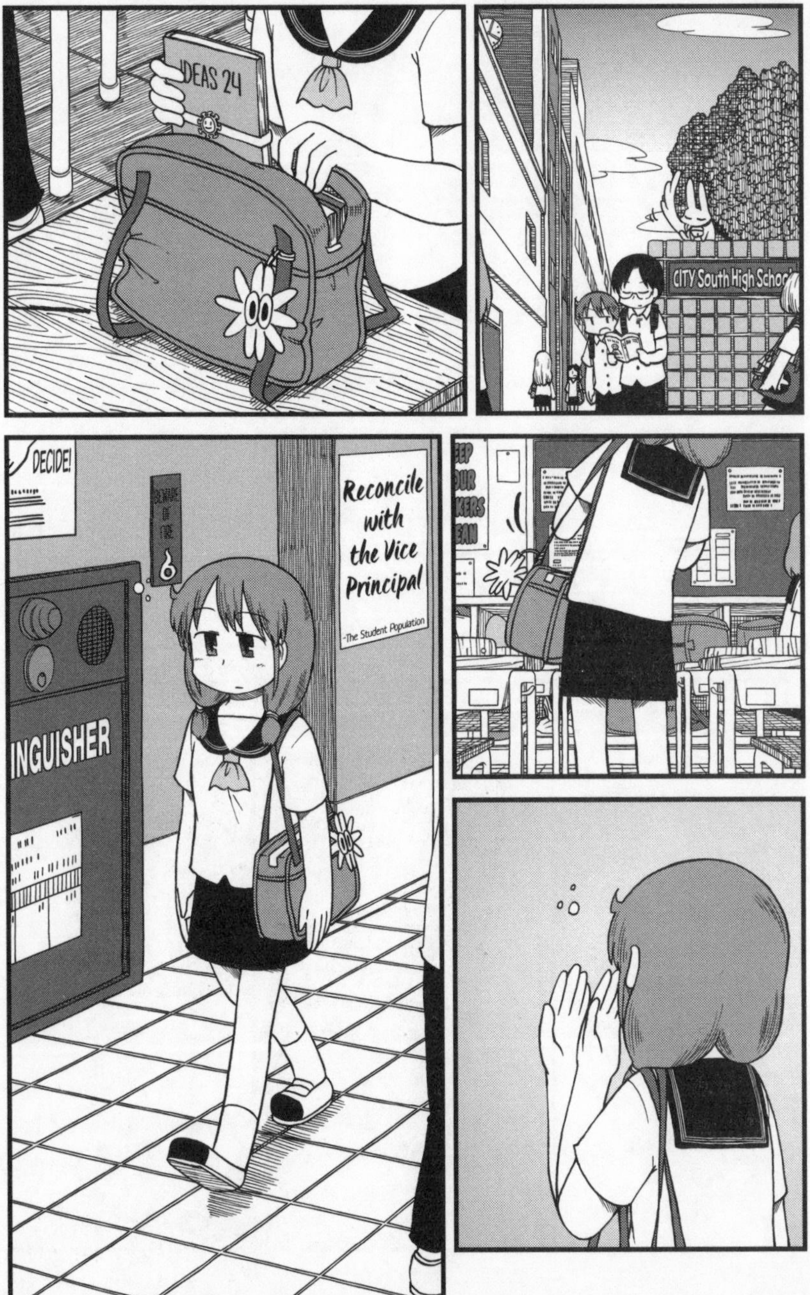
CITY South High Schoo
IDEAS 24
DECIDE!
BEWARE OF FIRE
Reconcile with the Vice Principal
-The Student Population
INGUISHER

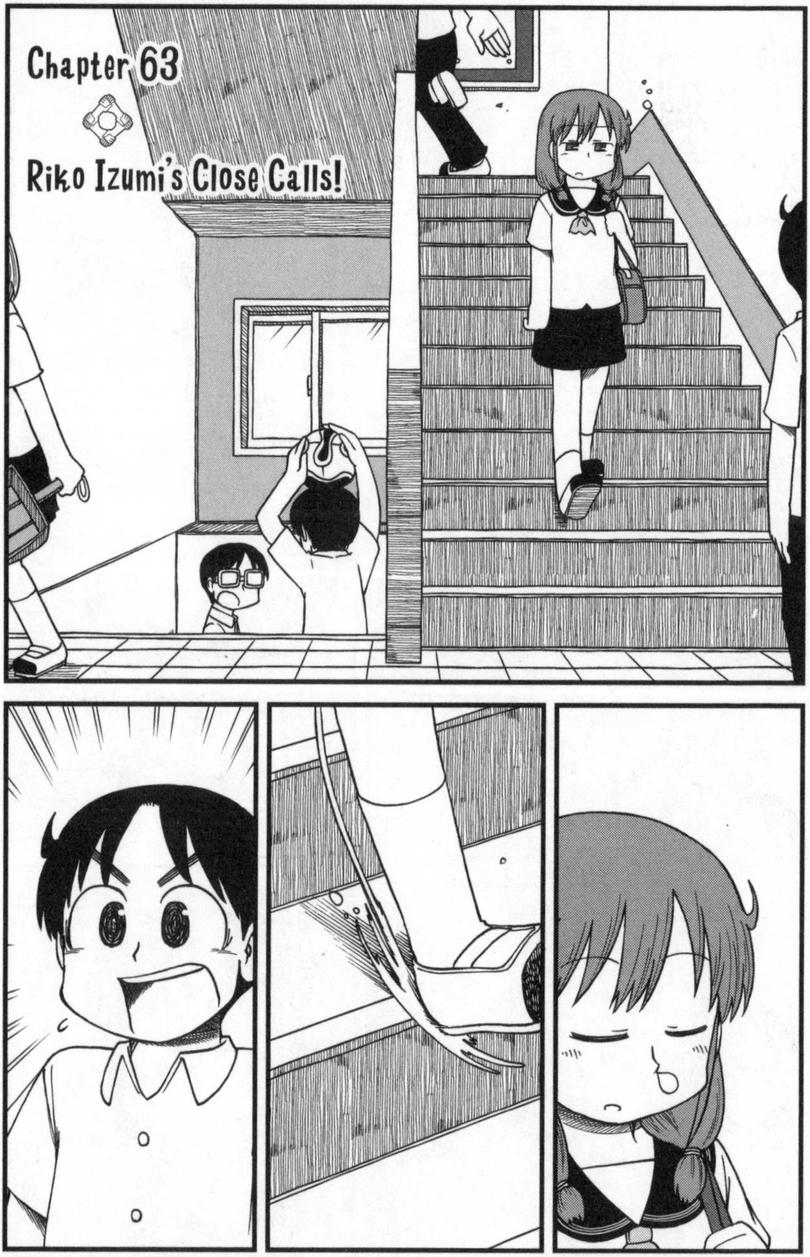
Chapter 63
Riko Izumi's Close Calls!

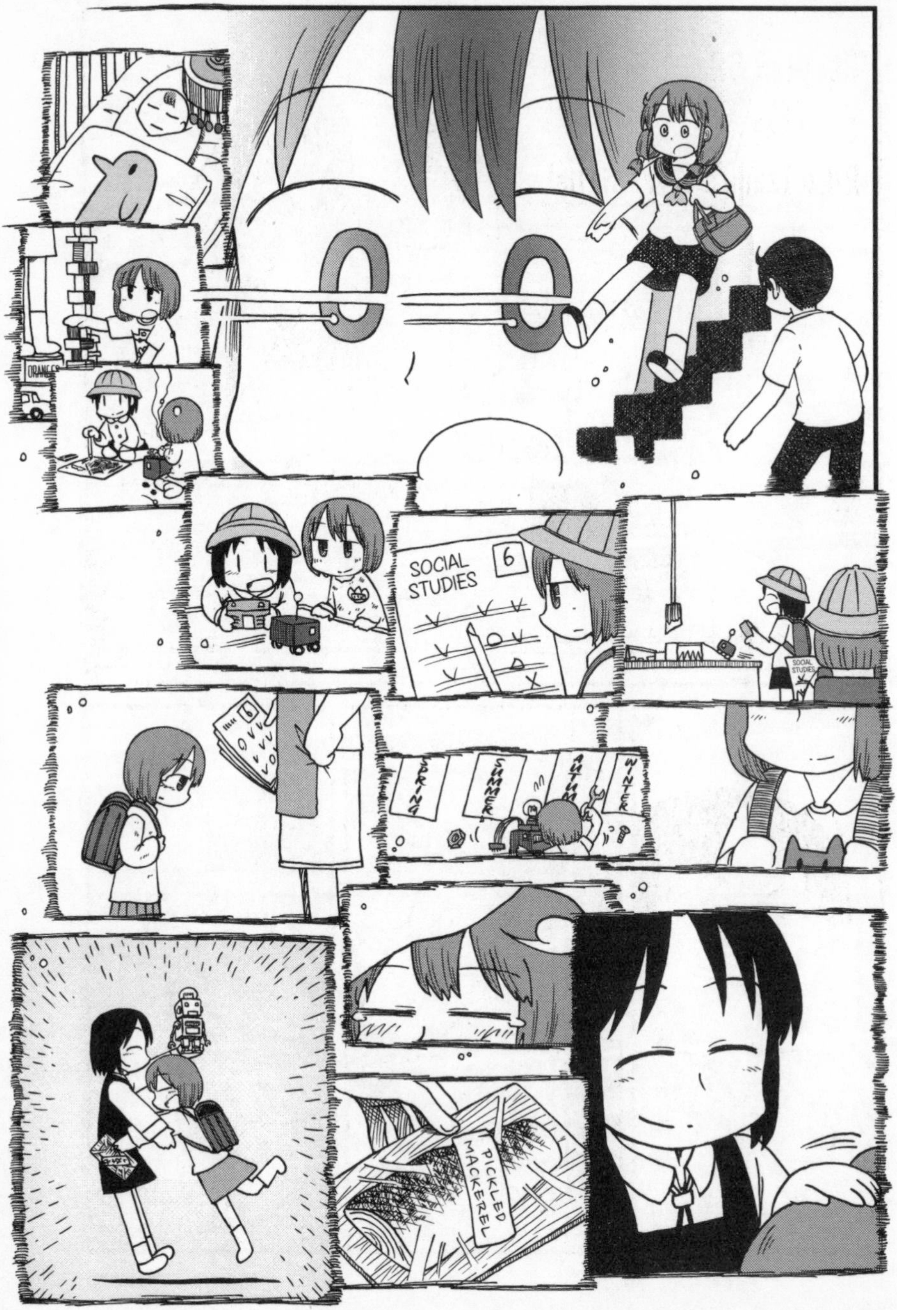
SOCIAL STUDIES
SOCIAL STUDIES
6
SPRING
SUMMER
AUTUMN
WINTER
PICKLED MACKEREL

IZUMI
to Miss Izumi

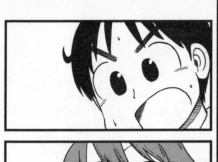

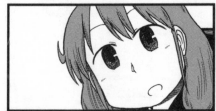

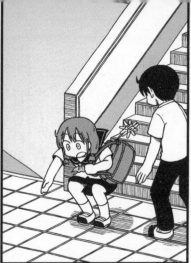

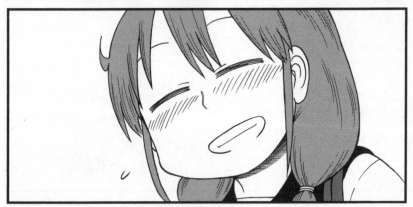

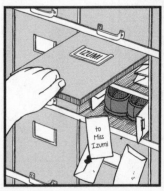

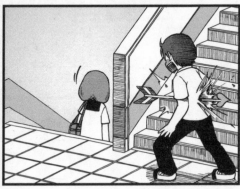

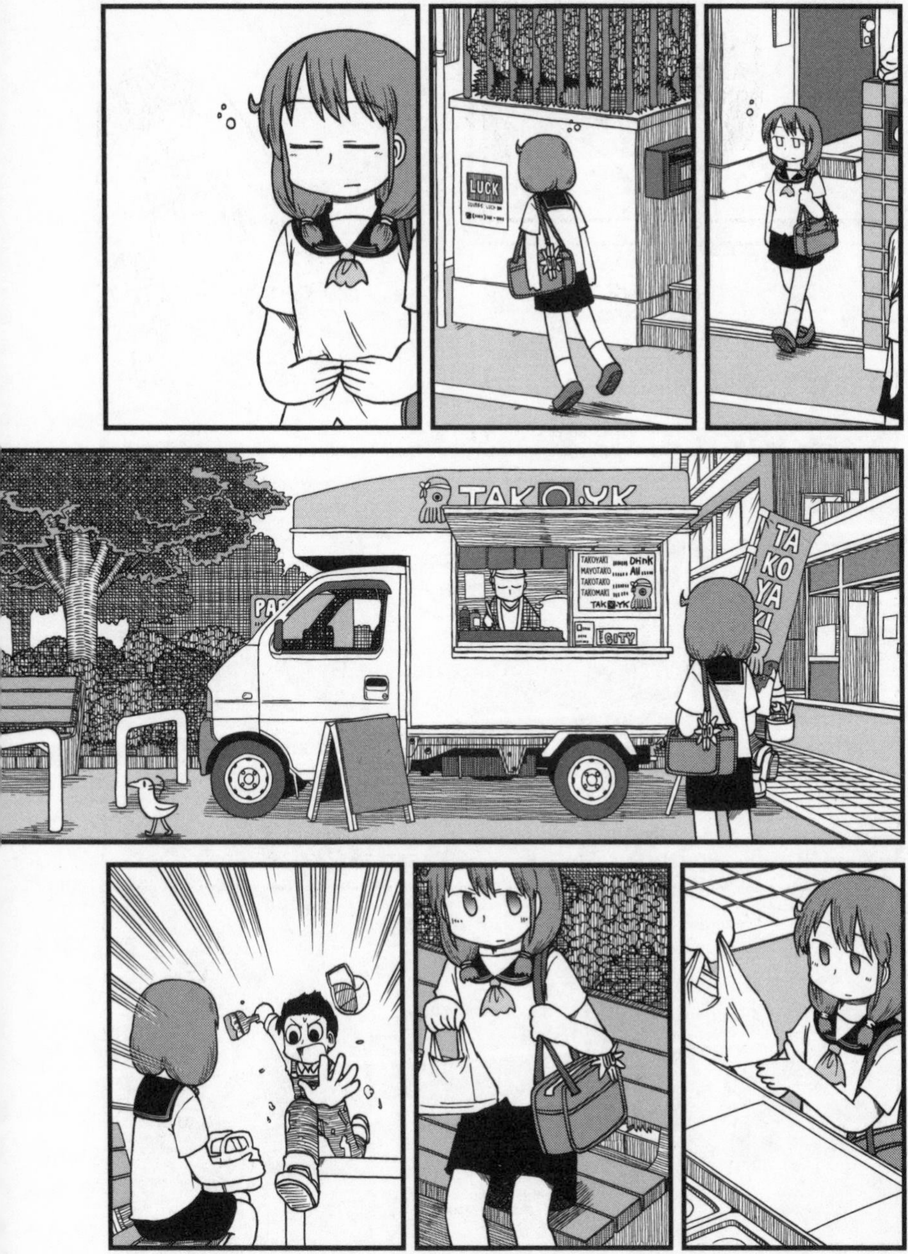
LUCK
TAKO YK
TAKOYAKI
MAYOTAKO
TAKOTAKO
TAKOMAKI
Drink
All
TAKO YK
CITY
TA
KO
YA
KI

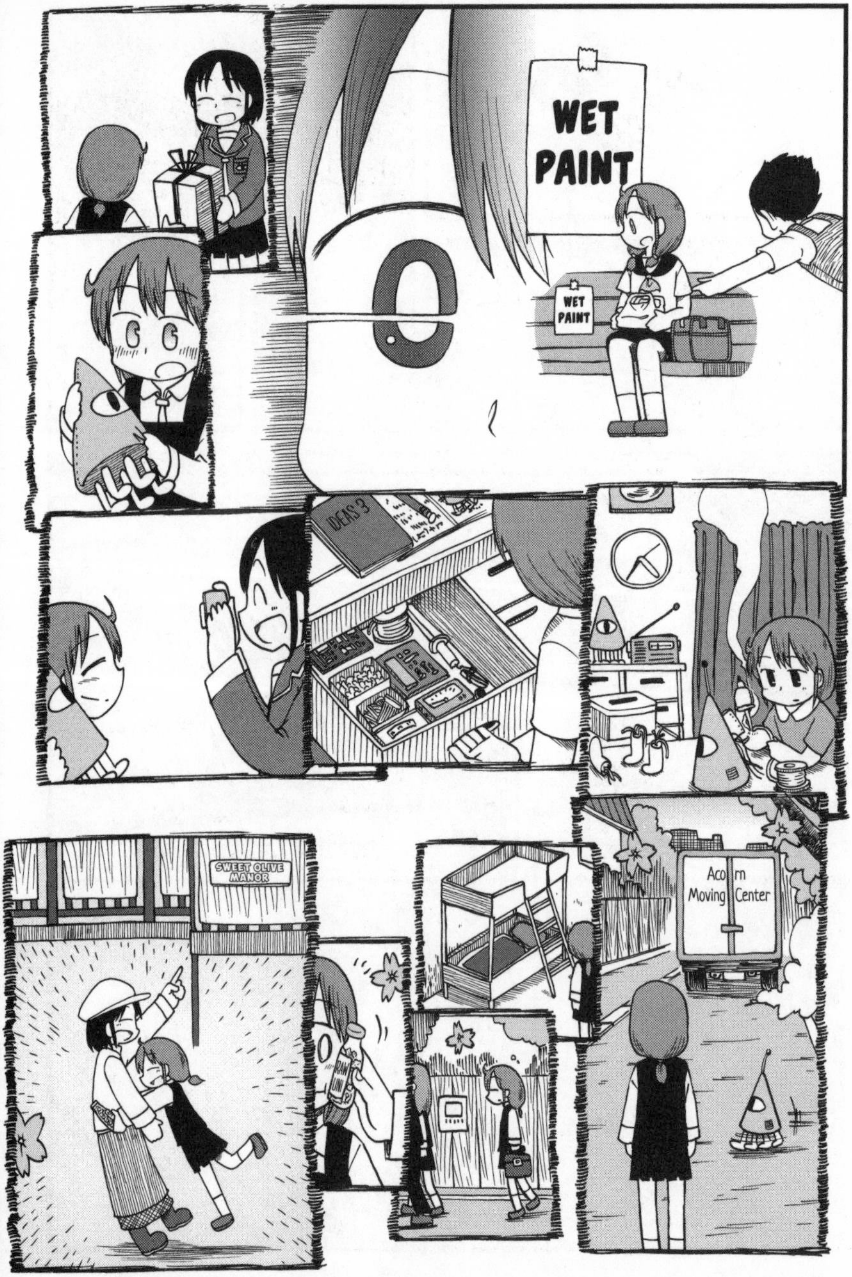
WET PAINT
WET PAINT
IDEAS 3
Acorn
Moving Center
SWEET OLIVE MANOR

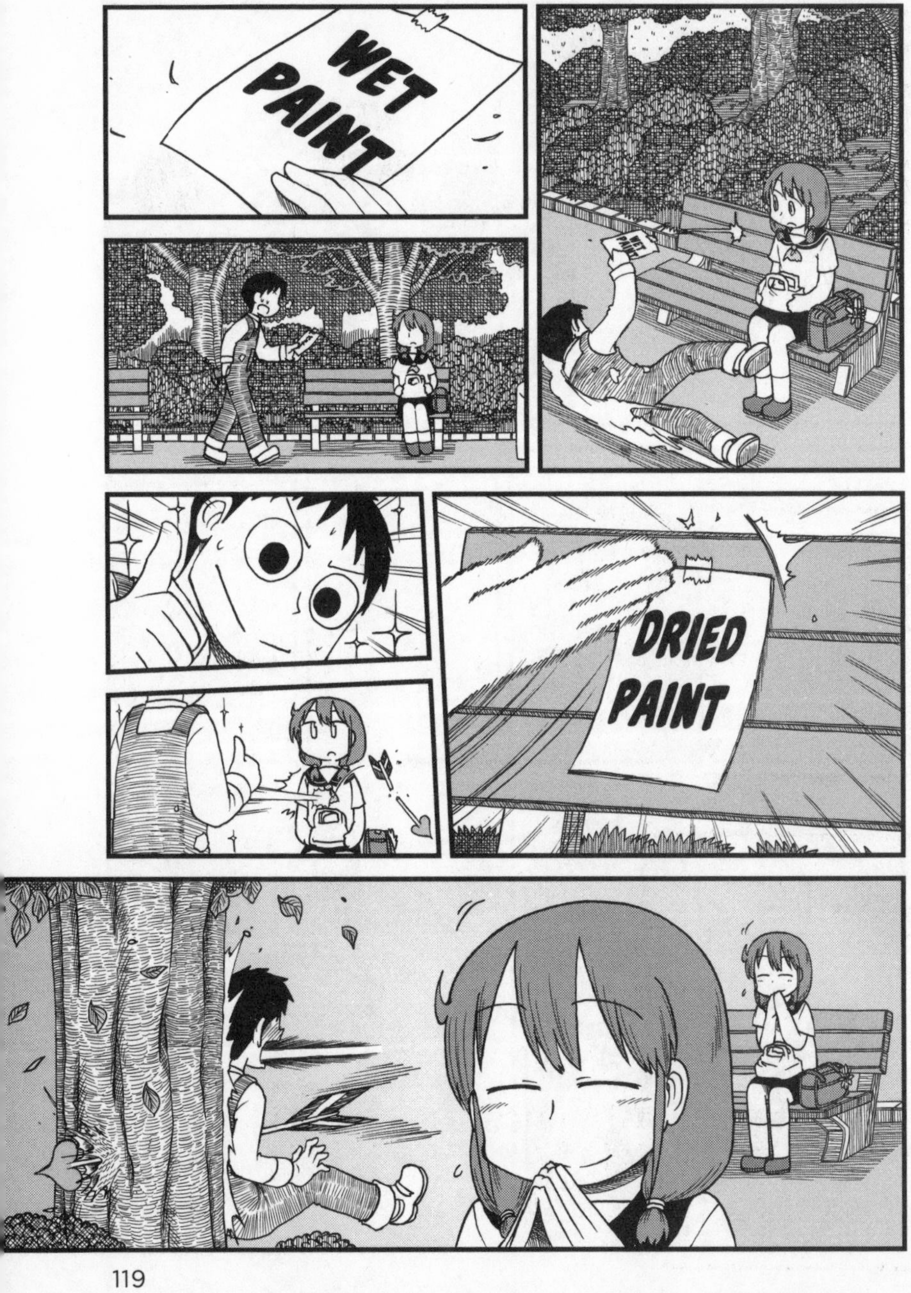
WET PAINT
DRIED PAINT

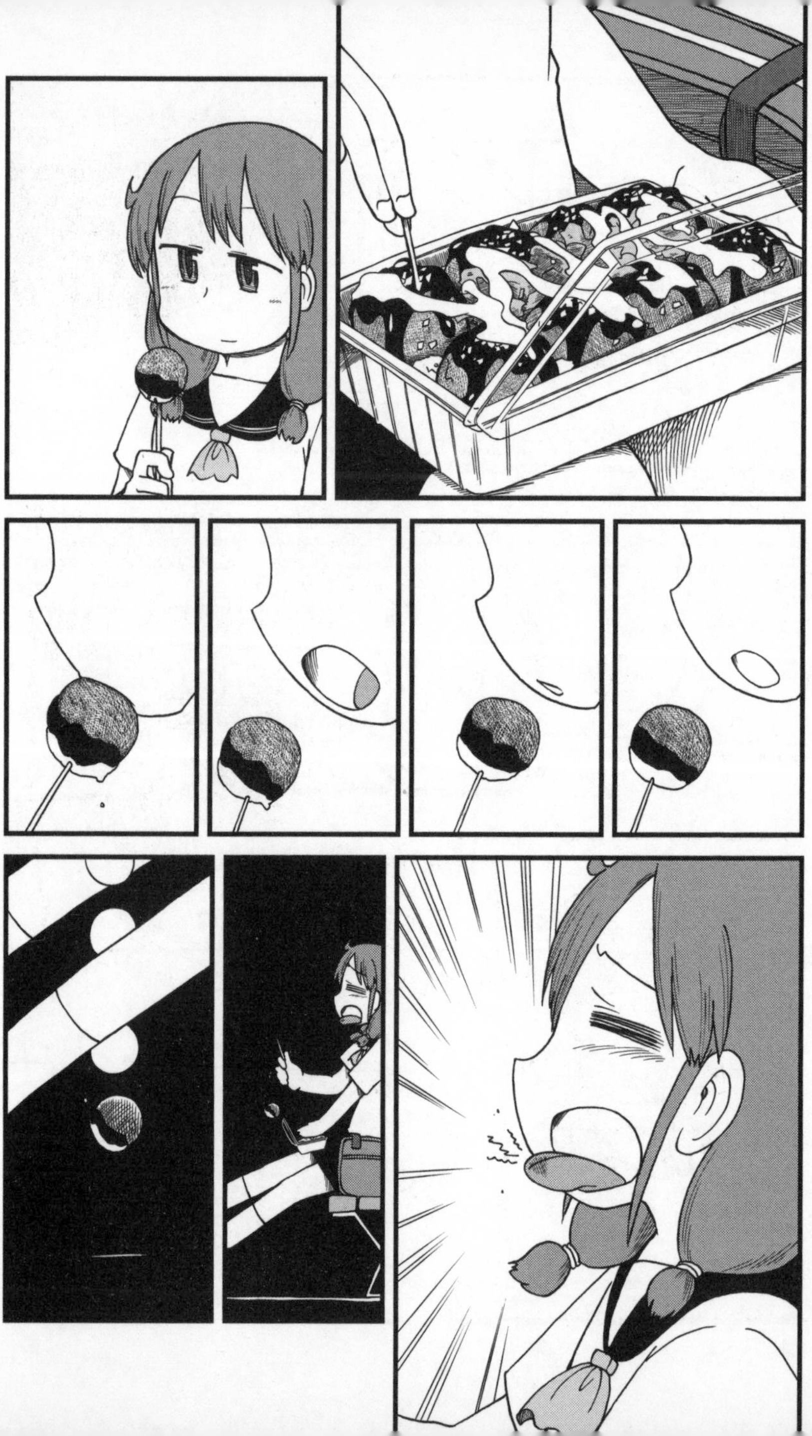

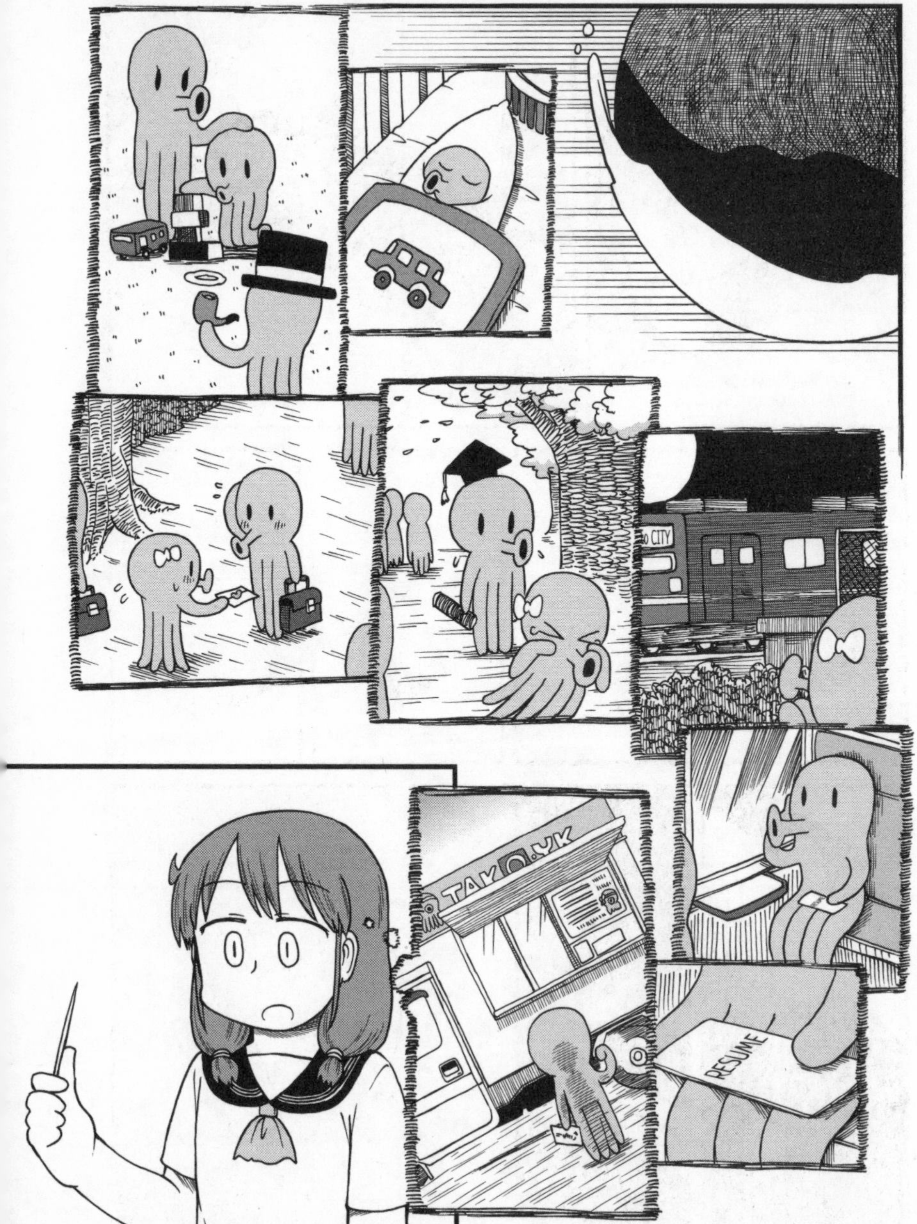
CITY
RESUME

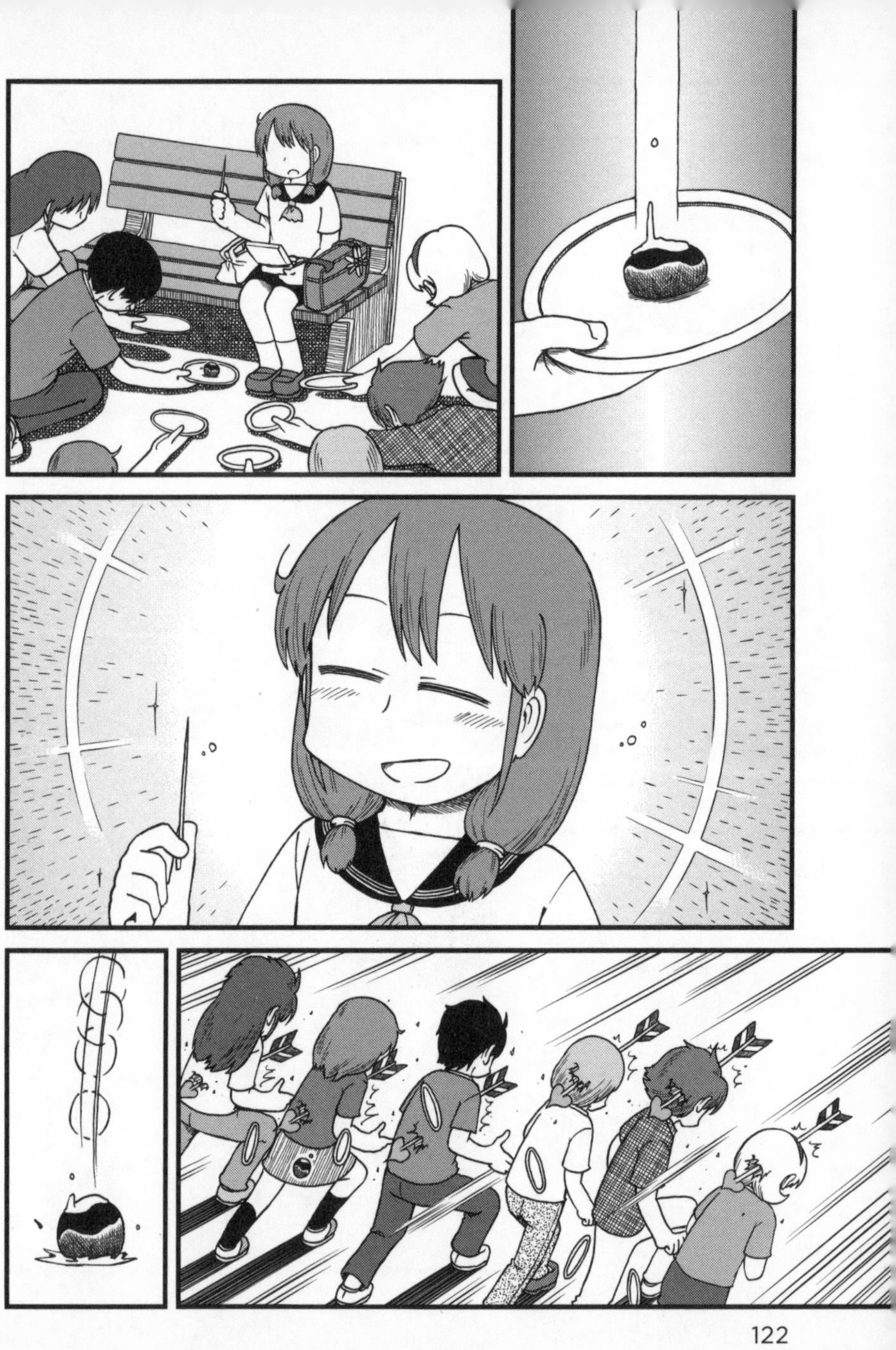

CITY

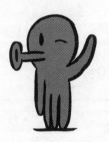

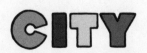

CITY

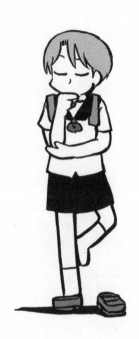

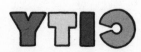

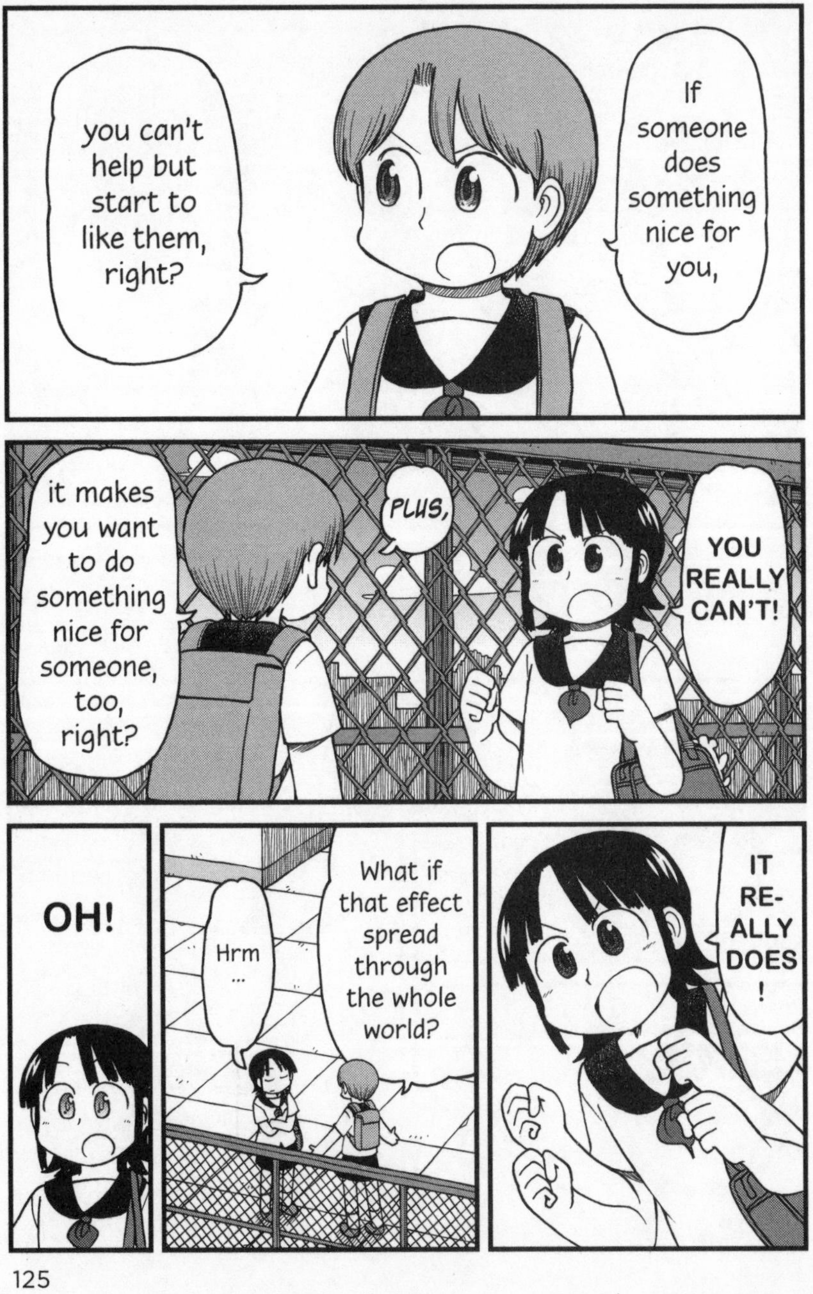
If someone does something nice for you,
you can't help but start to like them, right?
YOU REALLY CAN'T!
PLUS,
it makes you want to do something nice for someone, too, right?
IT RE-ALLY DOES!
What if that effect spread through the whole world?
Hrm ...
OH!

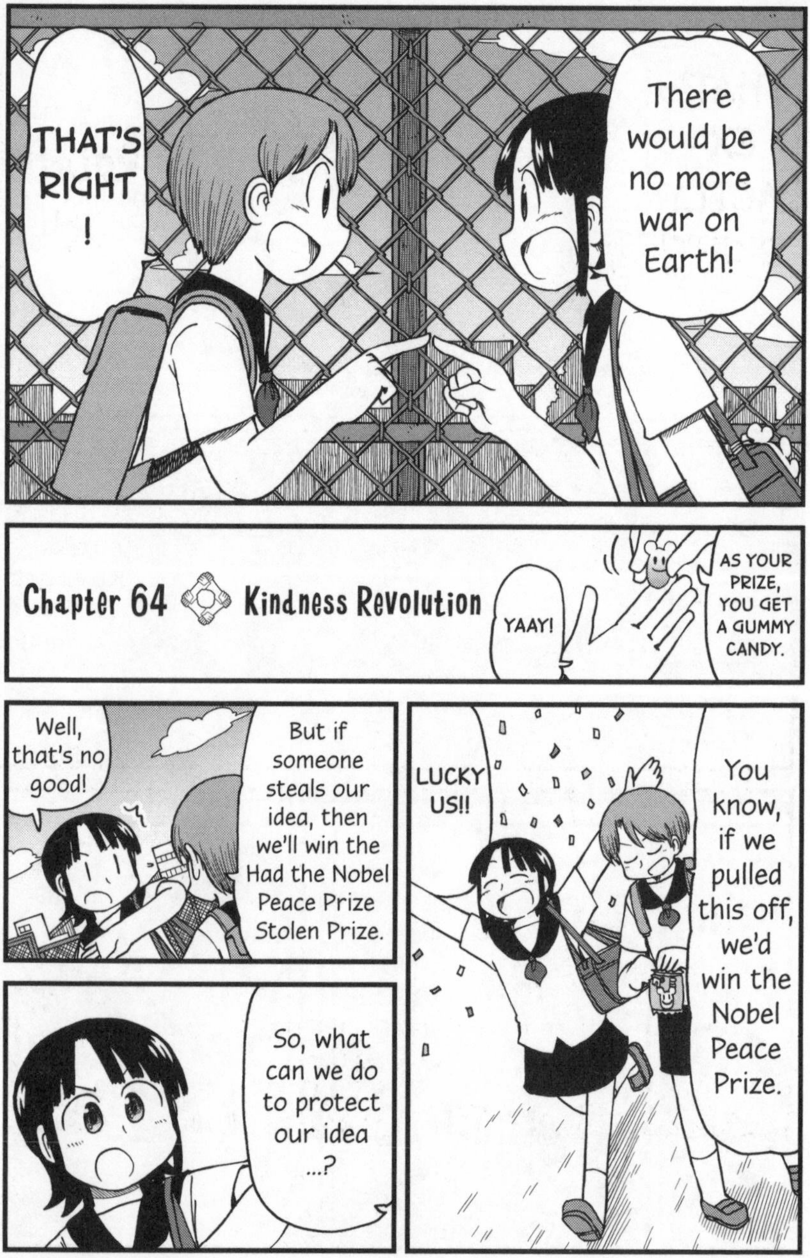
There would be no more war on Earth!
THAT'S RIGHT !
AS YOUR PRIZE, YOU GET A GUMMY CANDY.
YAAY!
Chapter 64 Kindness Revolution
You know, if we pulled this off, we'd win the Nobel Peace Prize.
LUCKY US!!
But if someone steals our idea, then we'll win the Had the Nobel Peace Prize Stolen Prize.
Well, that's no good!
So, what can we do to protect our idea ...?

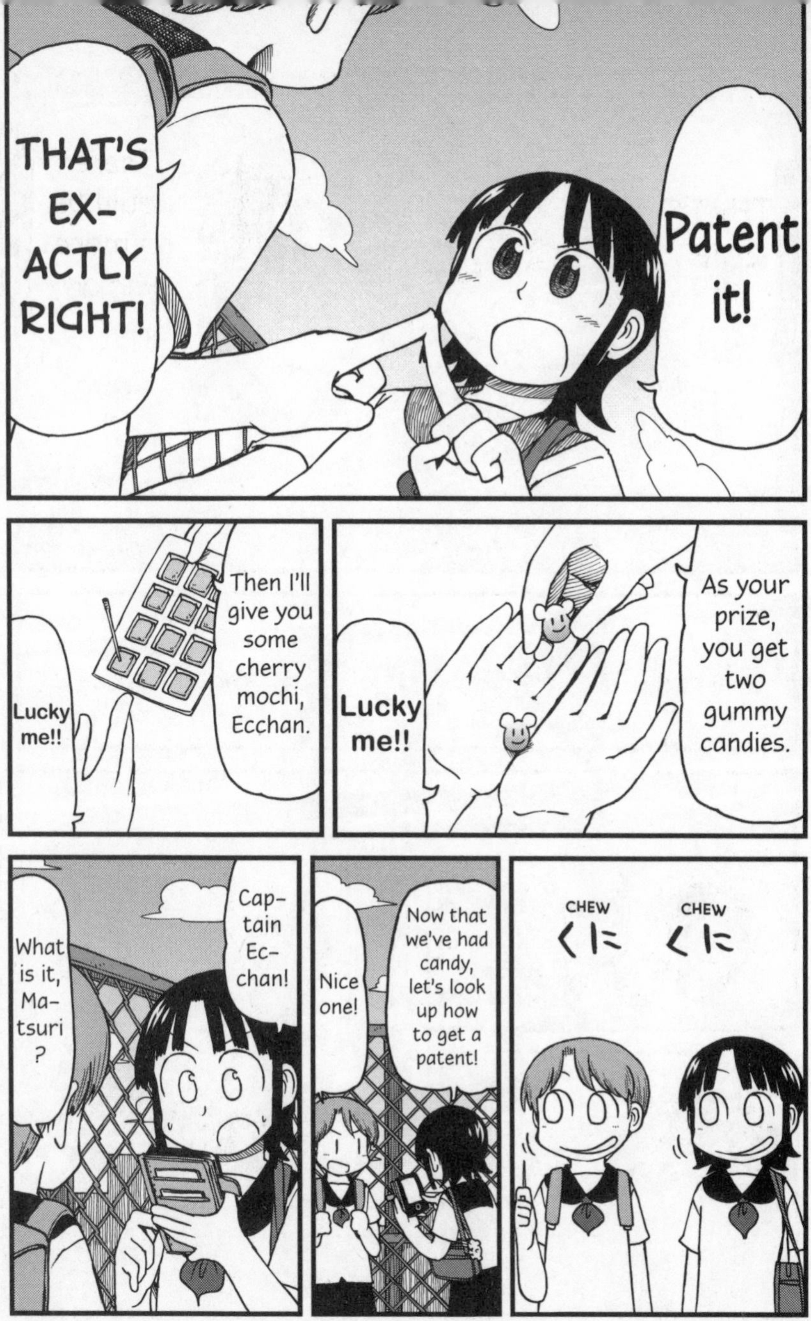
Patent it!
THAT'S EX-ACTLY RIGHT!
As your prize, you get two gummy candies.
Lucky me!!
Then I'll give you some cherry mochi, Ecchan.
Lucky me!!
CHEW くに
CHEW くに
Now that we've had candy, let's look up how to get a patent!
Nice one!
Cap-tain Ec-chan!
What is it, Ma-tsuri?

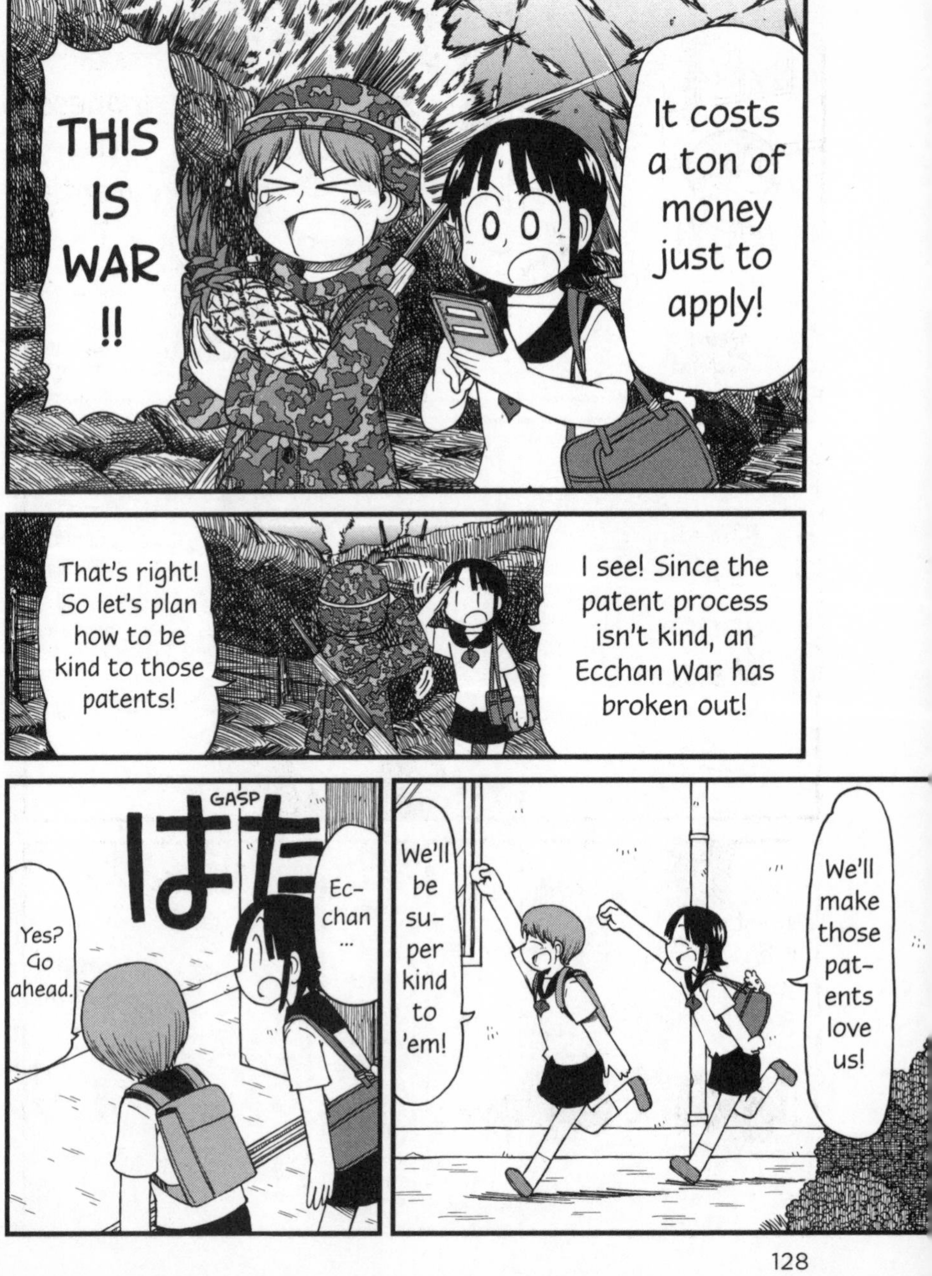
It costs a ton of money just to apply!
THIS IS WAR!!
I see! Since the patent process isn't kind, an Ecchan War has broken out!
That's right! So let's plan how to be kind to those patents!
We'll make those patents love us!
We'll be super kind to 'em!
Ec-chan...
GASP
はた
Yes? Go ahead.

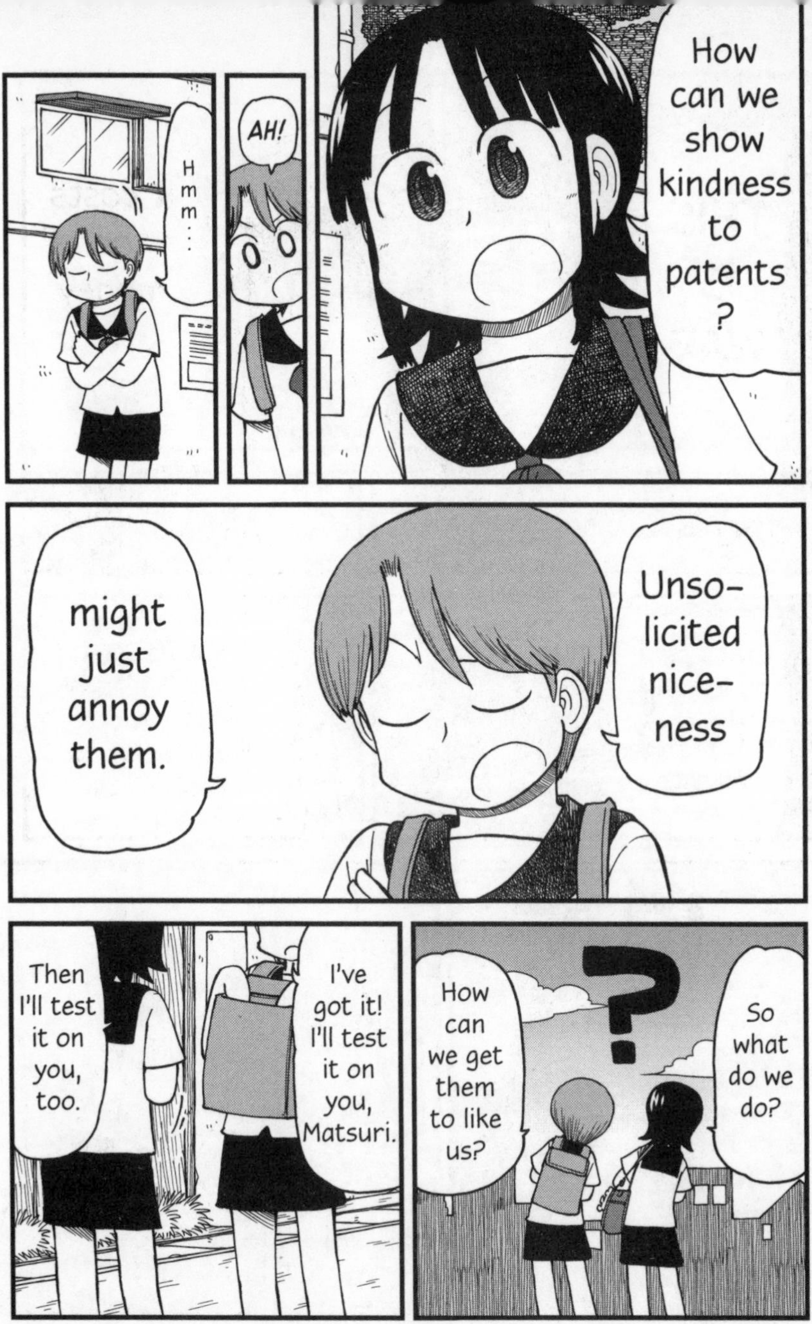
How can we show kindness to patents?
AH!
Hmm...
Unsolicited niceness
might just annoy them.
So what do we do?
How can we get them to like us?
I've got it! I'll test it on you, Matsuri.
Then I'll test it on you, too.

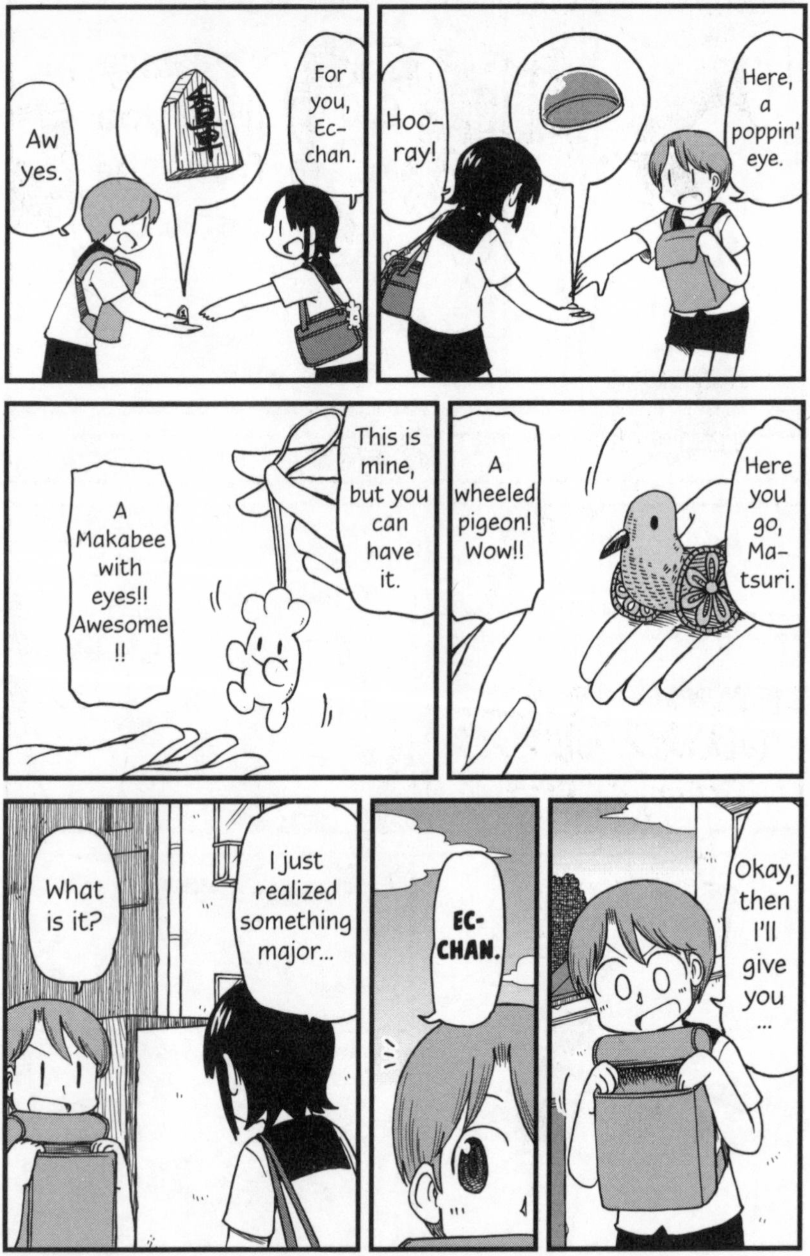
Here, a poppin' eye.
Hoo-ray!
For you, Ec-chan.
Aw yes.
Here you go, Ma-tsuri.
A wheeled pigeon! Wow!!
This is mine, but you can have it.
A Makabee with eyes!! Awesome !!
Okay, then I'll give you ...
EC-CHAN.
I just realized something major...
What is it?

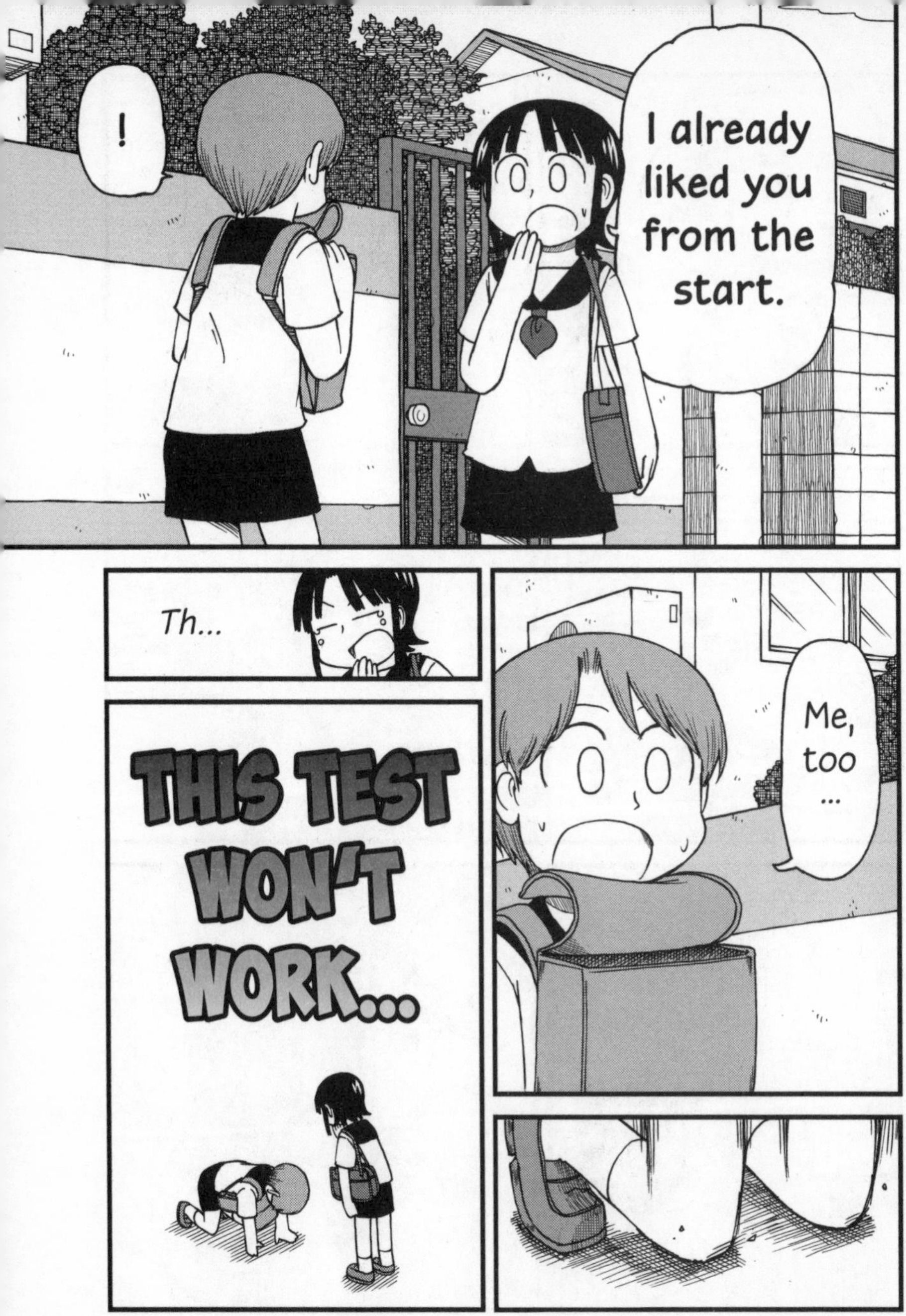
I already liked you from the start.
!
Me, too ...
Th...
THIS TEST WON'T WORK...

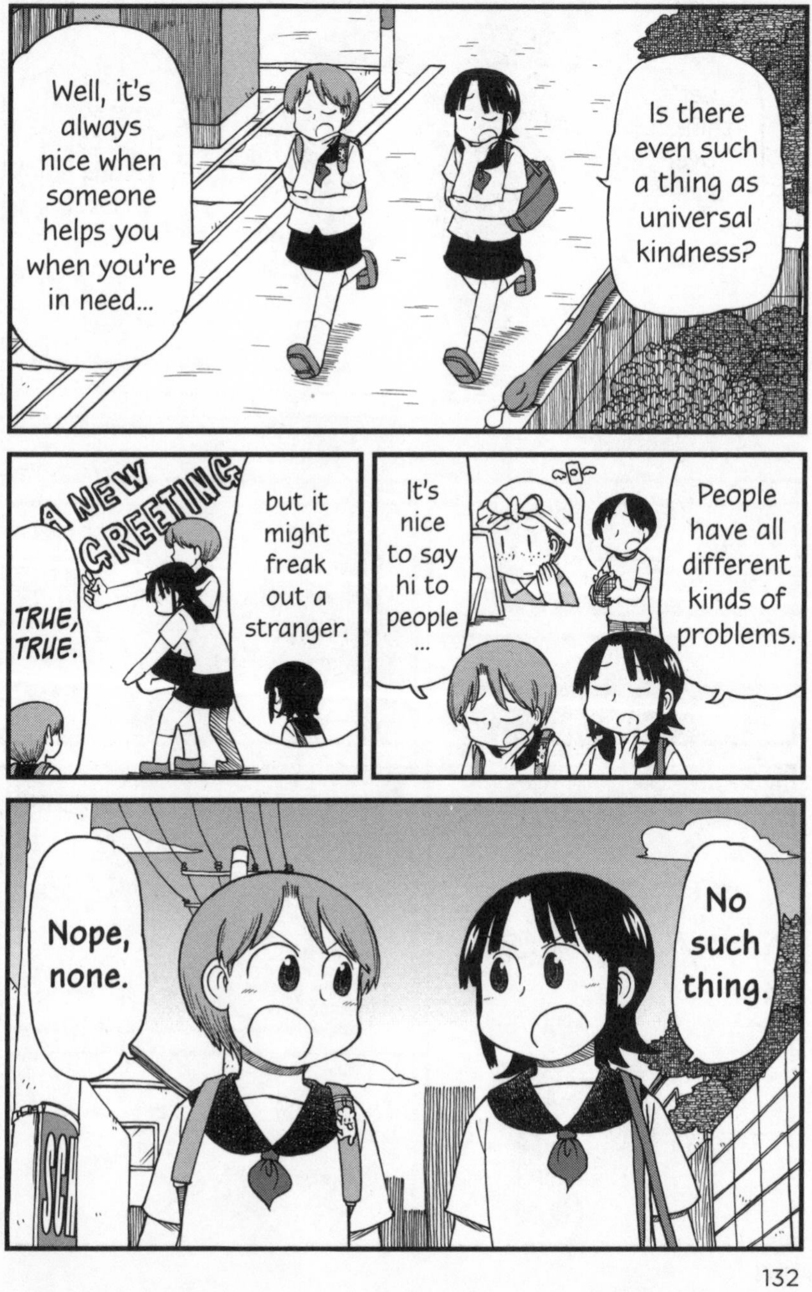
Is there even such a thing as universal kindness?
Well, it's always nice when someone helps you when you're in need...
People have all different kinds of problems.
It's nice to say hi to people ...
but it might freak out a stranger.
A NEW GREETING
TRUE, TRUE.
No such thing.
Nope, none.

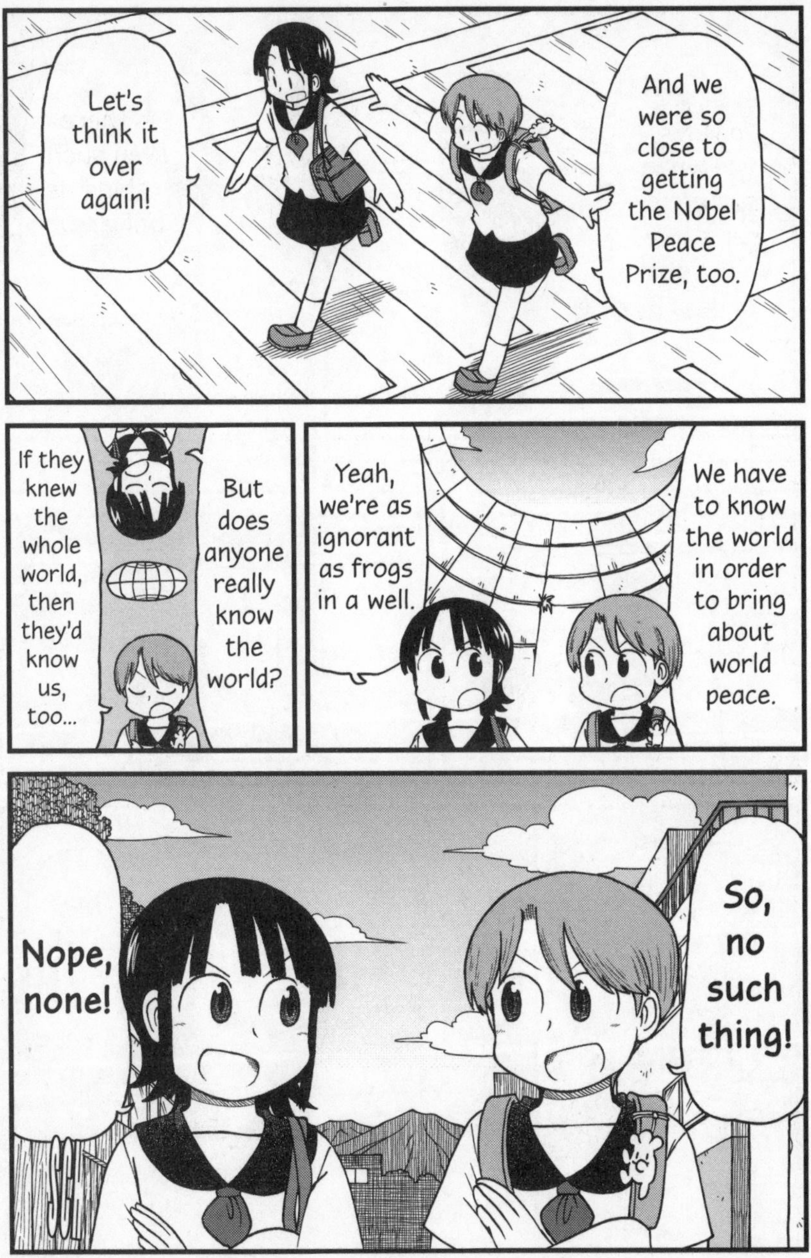
And we were so close to getting the Nobel Peace Prize, too.
Let's think it over again!
We have to know the world in order to bring about world peace.
Yeah, we're as ignorant as frogs in a well.
But does anyone really know the world?
If they knew the whole world, then they'd know us, too...
So, no such thing!
Nope, none!

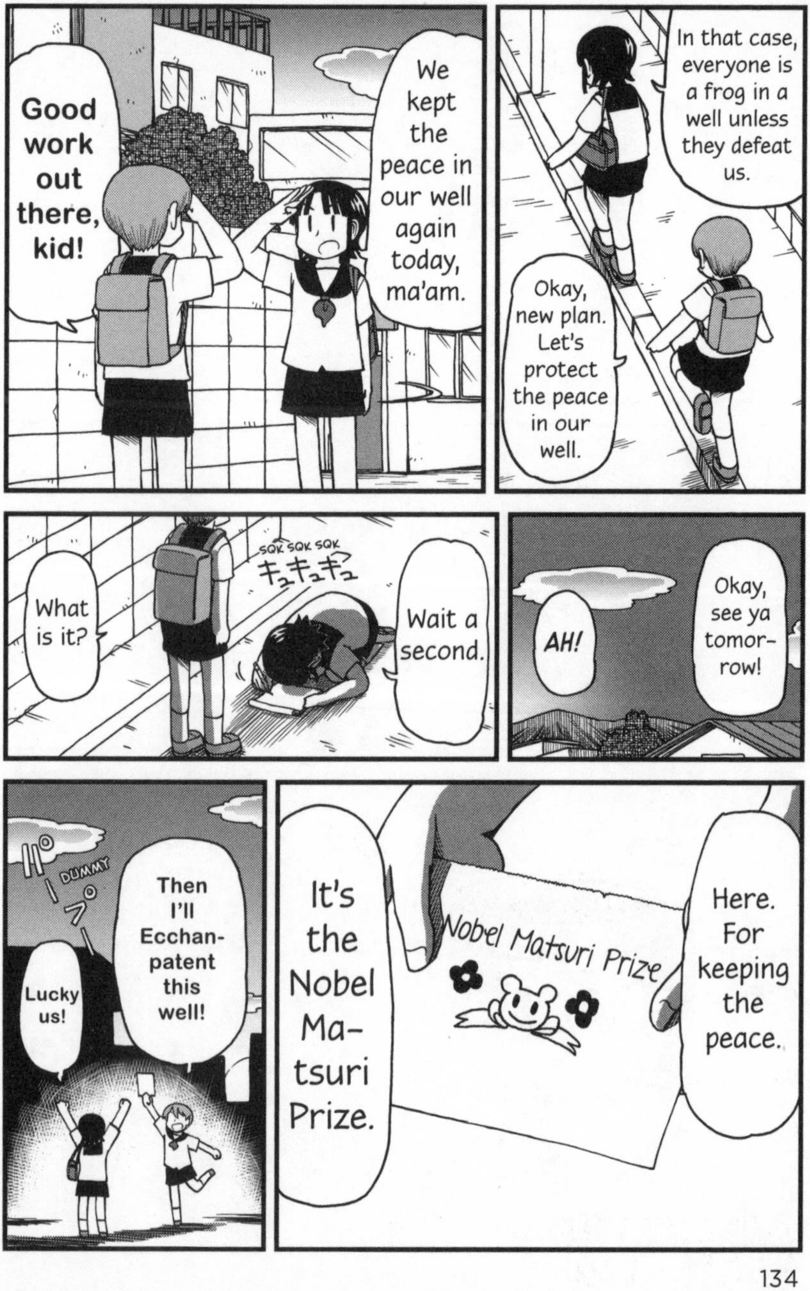
In that case, everyone is a frog in a well unless they defeat us.
Okay, new plan. Let's protect the peace in our well.
We kept the peace in our well again today, ma'am.
Good work out there, kid!
Okay, see ya tomor-row!
AH!
Wait a second.
SQK SQK SQK
キュキュキュ
What is it?
Here. For keeping the peace.
Nobel Matsuri Prize
It's the Nobel Ma-tsuri Prize.
Then I'll Ecchan-patent this well!
DUMMY
Lucky us!

CITY

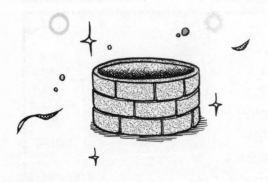

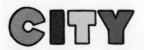

CITY

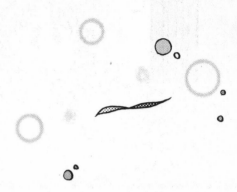

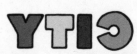

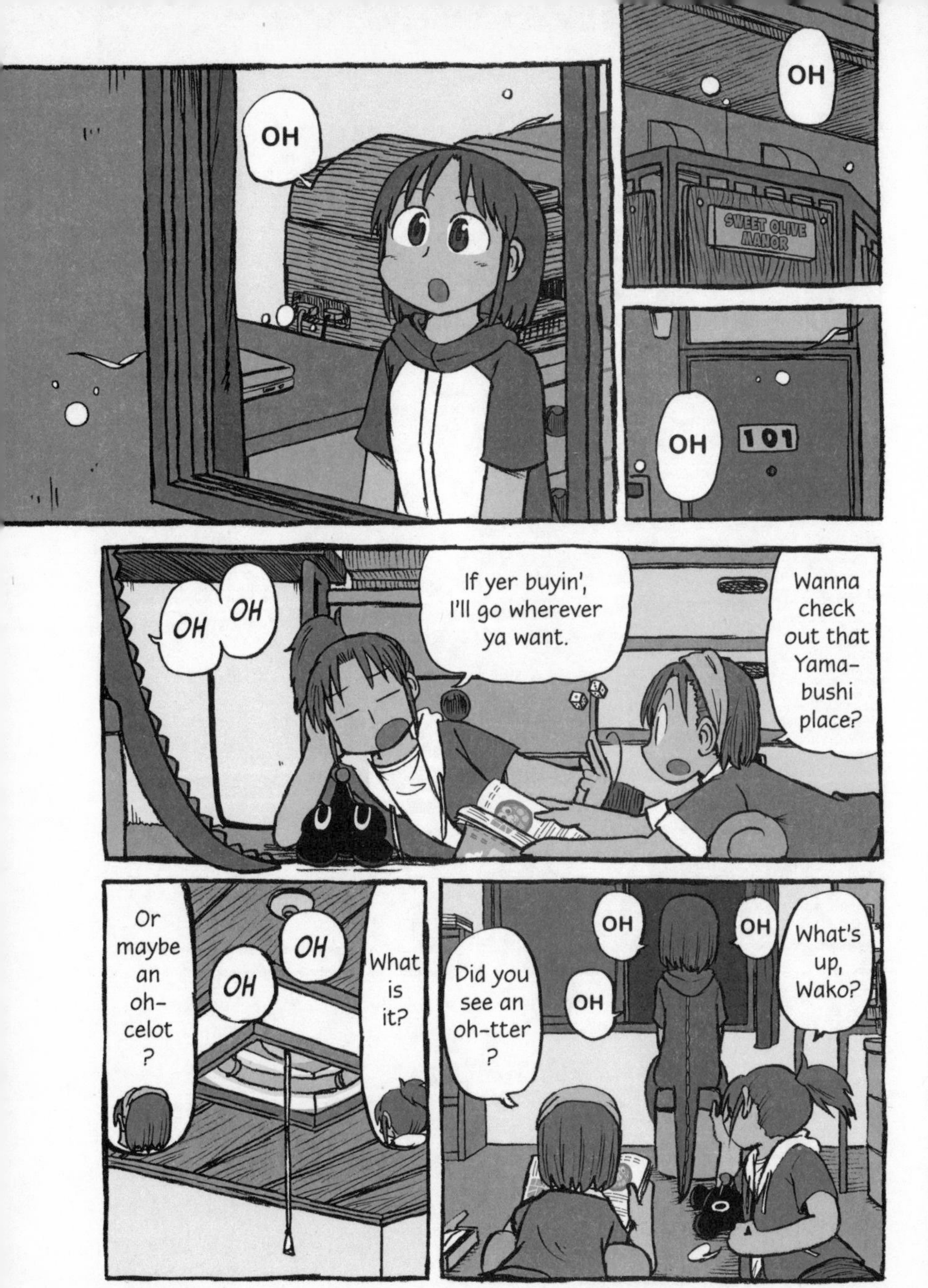
OH
SWEET OLIVE MANOR
OH
101
OH
Wanna check out that Yama-bushi place?
If yer buyin', I'll go wherever ya want.
OH
OH
What's up, Wako?
OH
OH
OH
Did you see an oh-tter?
What is it?
OH
OH
Or maybe an oh-celot?

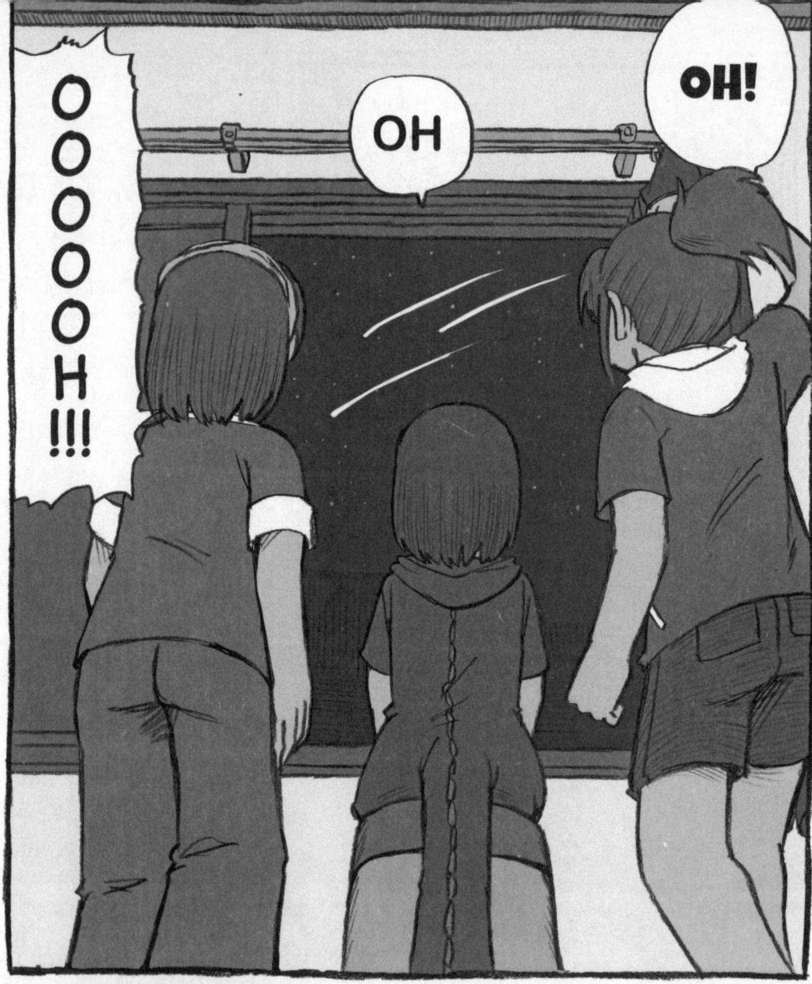
OH!
OH
OOOOOOH!!!

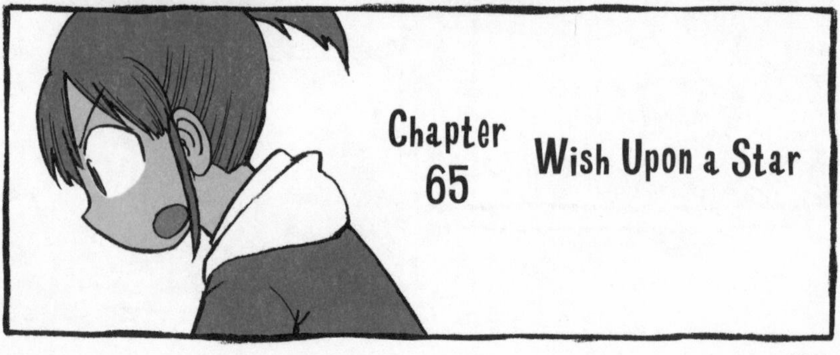

Chapter 65 Wish Upon a Star

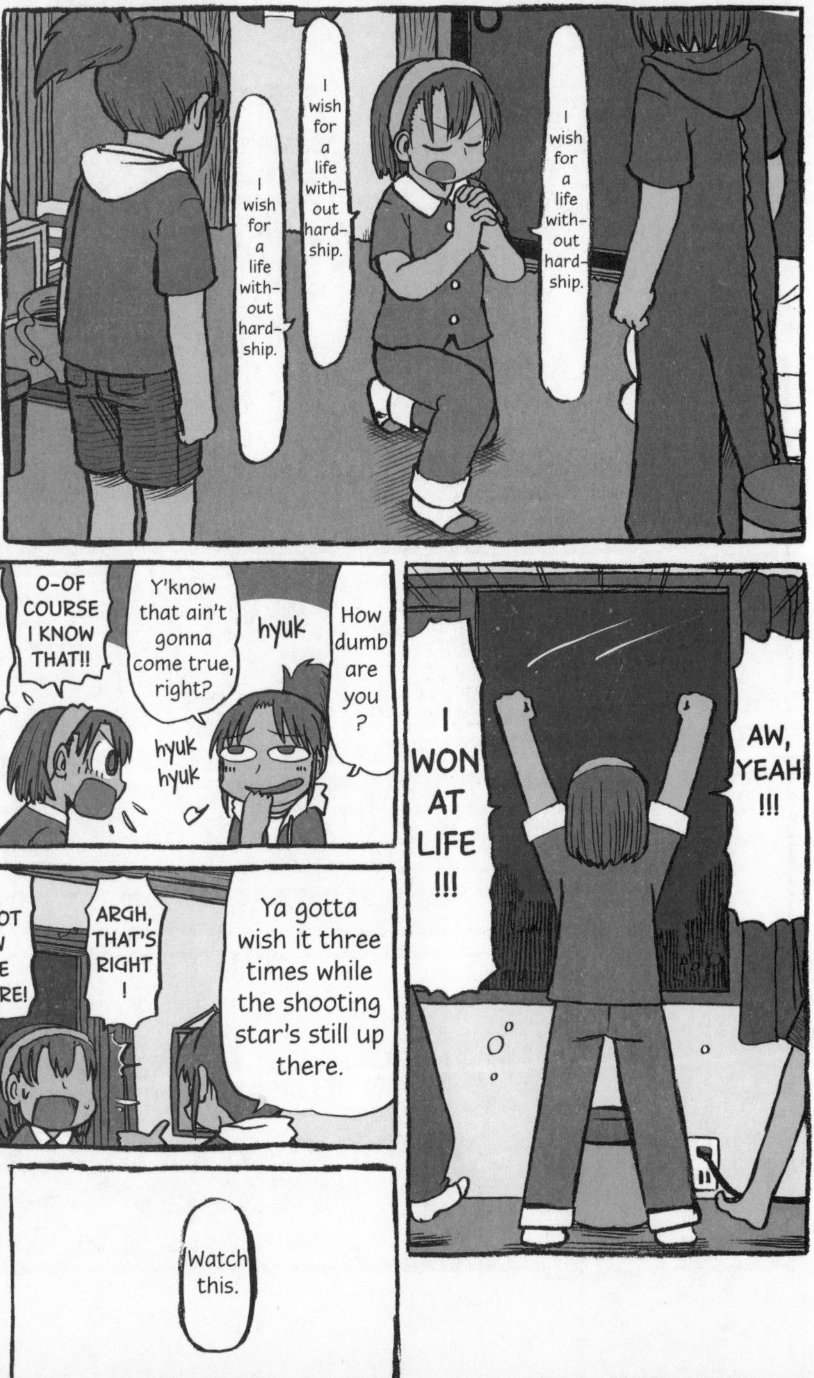
I wish for a life without hardship.
I wish for a life without hardship.
I wish for a life without hardship.
AW, YEAH!!!
I WON AT LIFE!!!
How dumb are you?
hyuk
Y'know that ain't gonna come true, right?
hyuk hyuk
O-OF COURSE I KNOW THAT!!
WHY'RE YOU BEING SO MATTER-OF-FACT?!!
Ya gotta wish it three times while the shooting star's still up there.
ARGH, THAT'S RIGHT!
I FORGOT HOW PURE YOU ARE!
Watch this.

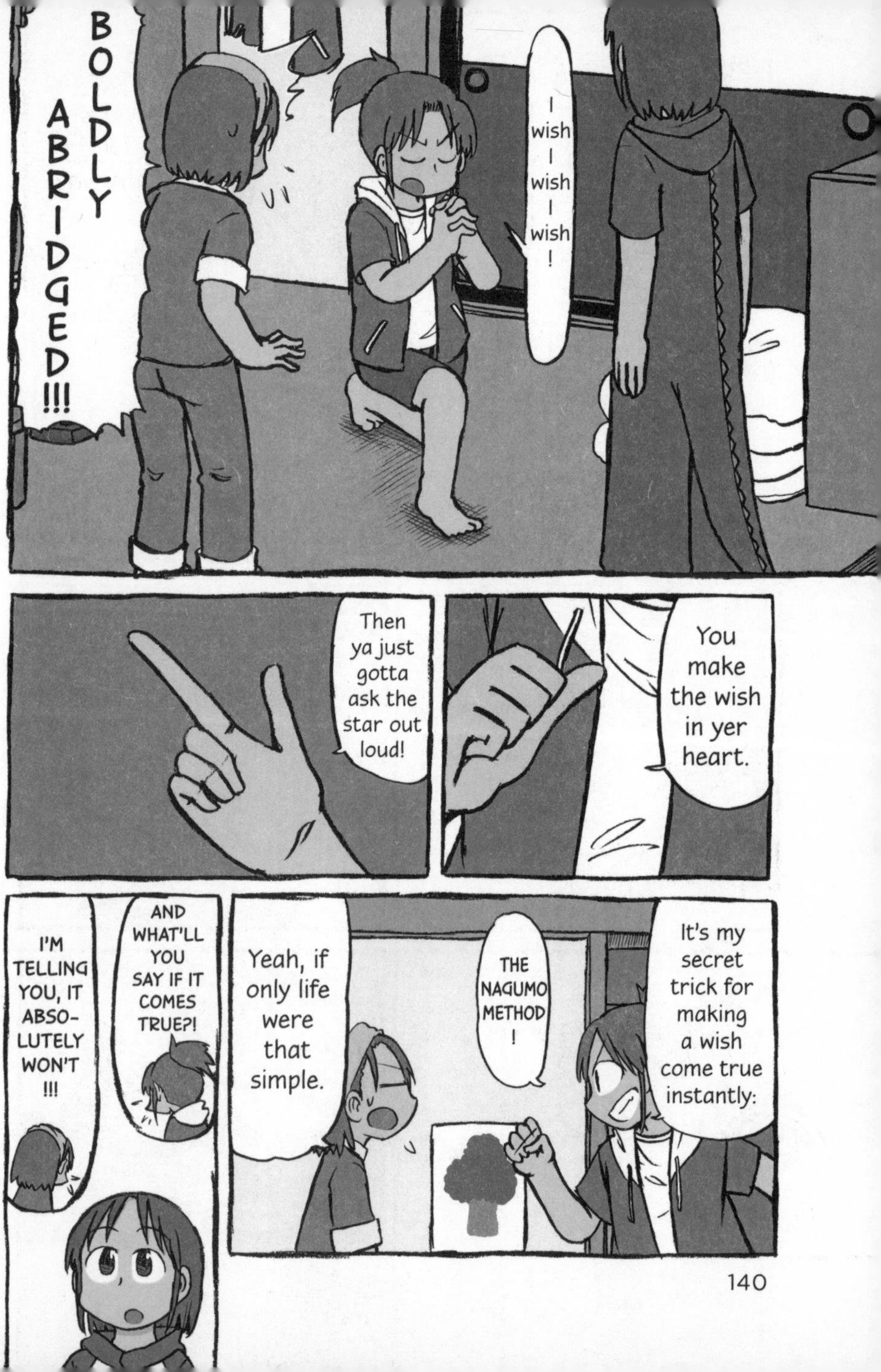
I wish I wish I wish!
BOLDLY ABRIDGED!!!
You make the wish in yer heart.
Then ya just gotta ask the star out loud!
It's my secret trick for making a wish come true instantly:
THE NAGUMO METHOD!
Yeah, if only life were that simple.
AND WHAT'LL YOU SAY IF IT COMES TRUE?!
I'M TELLING YOU, IT ABSO-LUTELY WON'T!!!

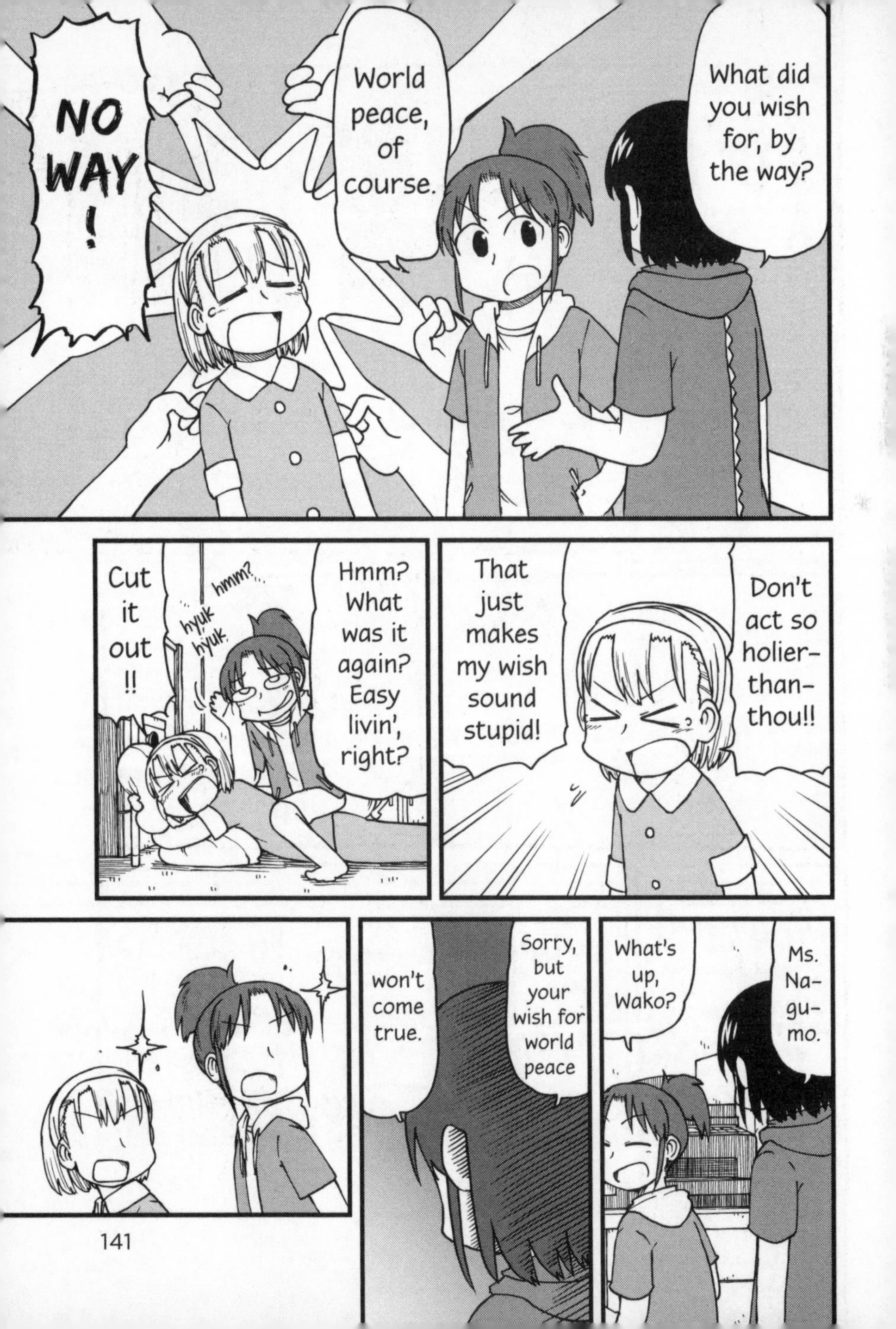

What did you wish for, by the way?
World peace, of course.
NO WAY!
Don't act so holier-than-thou!!
That just makes my wish sound stupid!
Hmm? What was it again? Easy livin', right?
hmm?
hyuk hyuk
Cut it out!!
Ms. Na-gu-mo.
What's up, Wako?
Sorry, but your wish for world peace
won't come true.

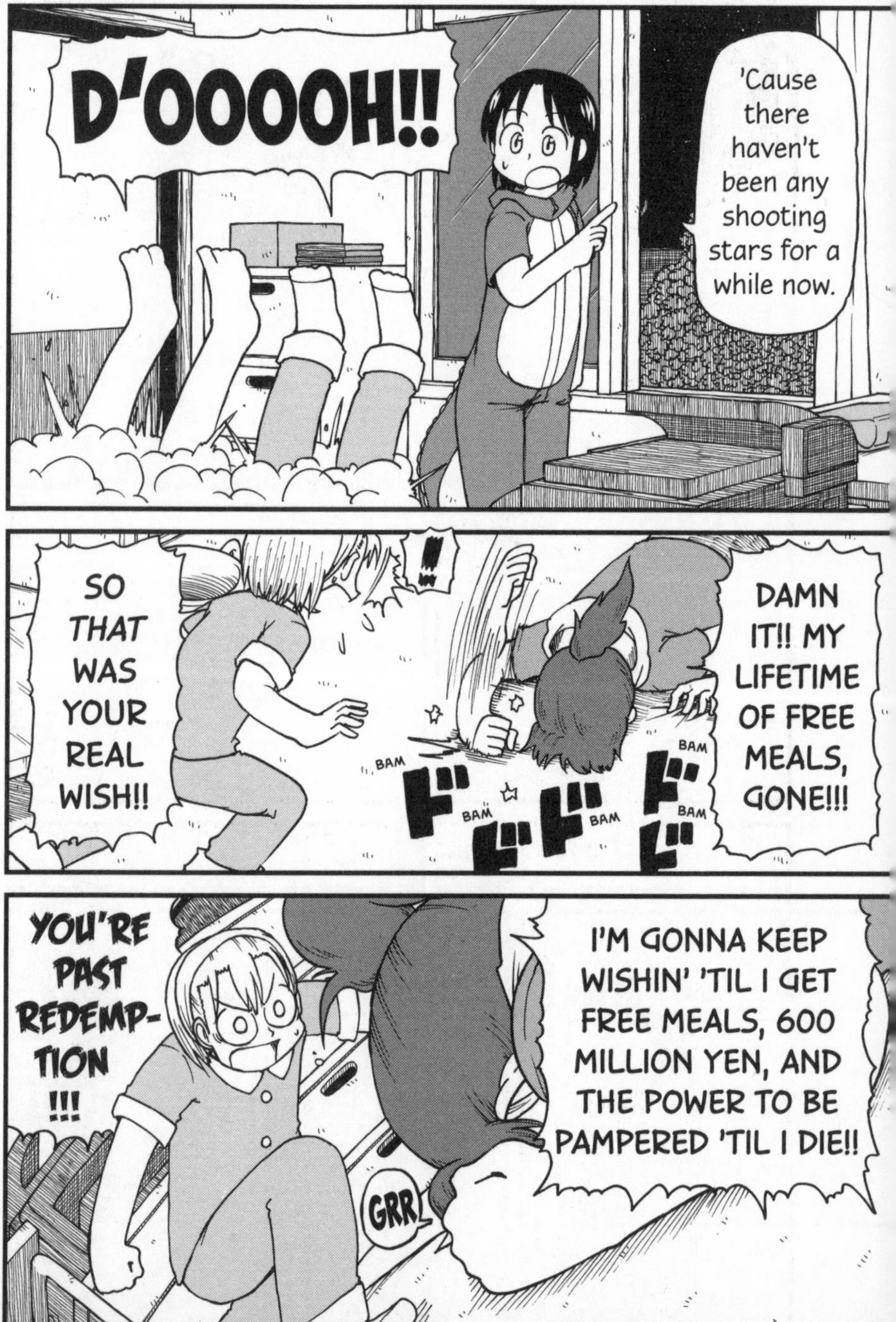
'Cause there haven't been any shooting stars for a while now.
D'OOOOH!!
DAMN IT!! MY LIFETIME OF FREE MEALS, GONE!!!
!!
BAM BAM BAM BAM BAM
ドドドドド
SO THAT WAS YOUR REAL WISH!!!
I'M GONNA KEEP WISHIN' 'TIL I GET FREE MEALS, 600 MILLION YEN, AND THE POWER TO BE PAMPERED 'TIL I DIE!!
GRR
YOU'RE PAST REDEMPTION!!!

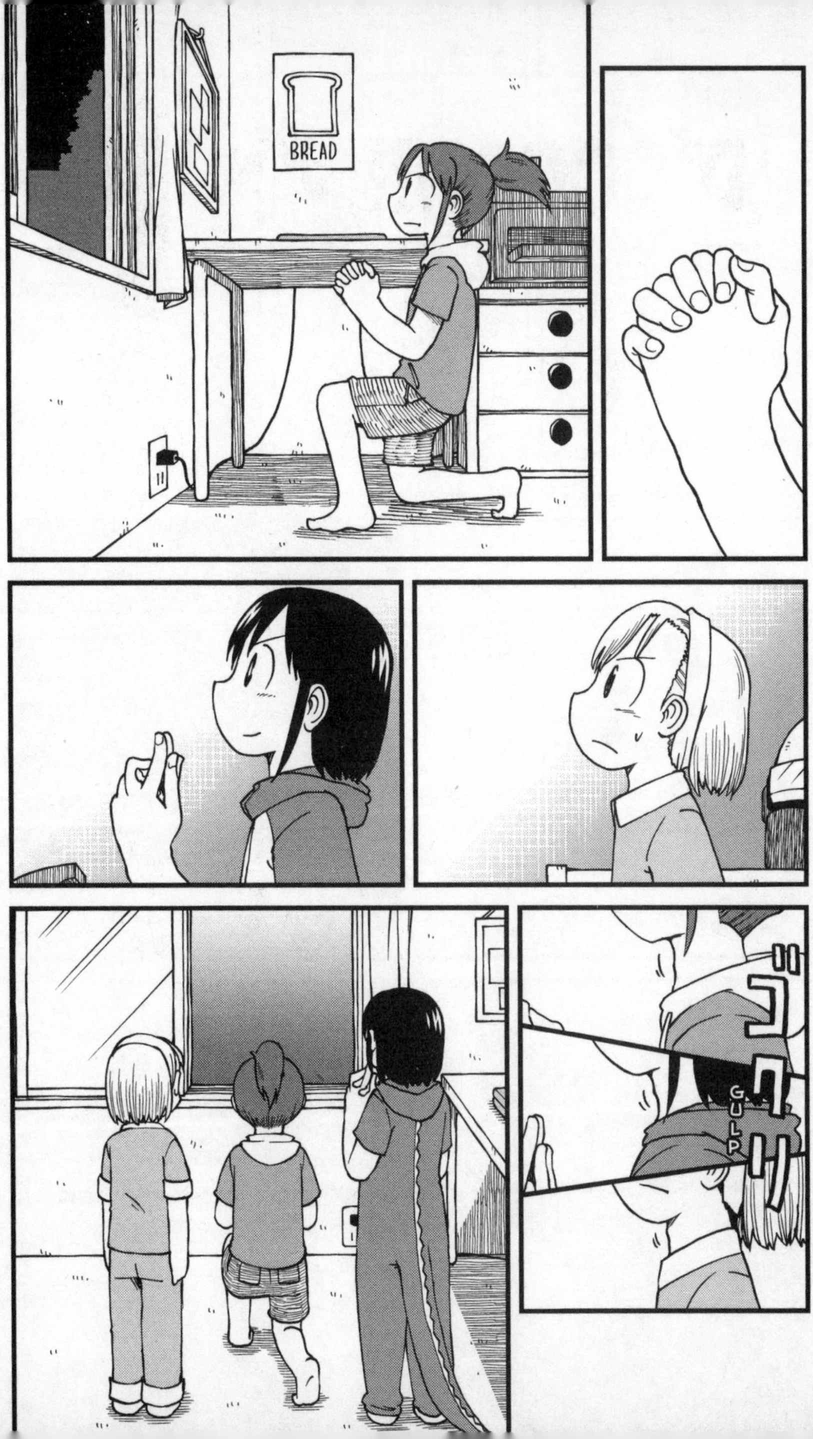
BREAD
ゴクリ
GULP

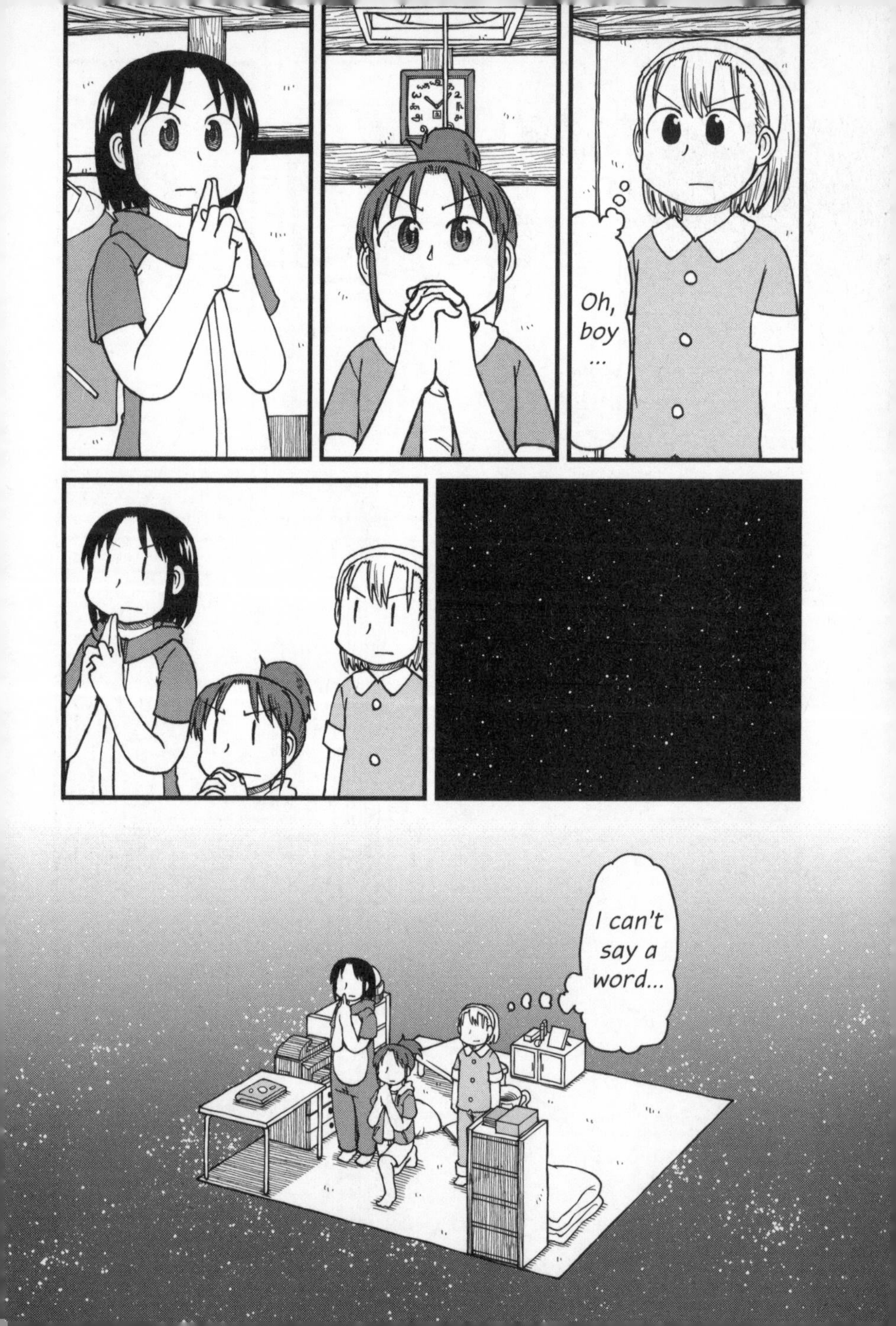
Oh, boy ...
I can't say a word...

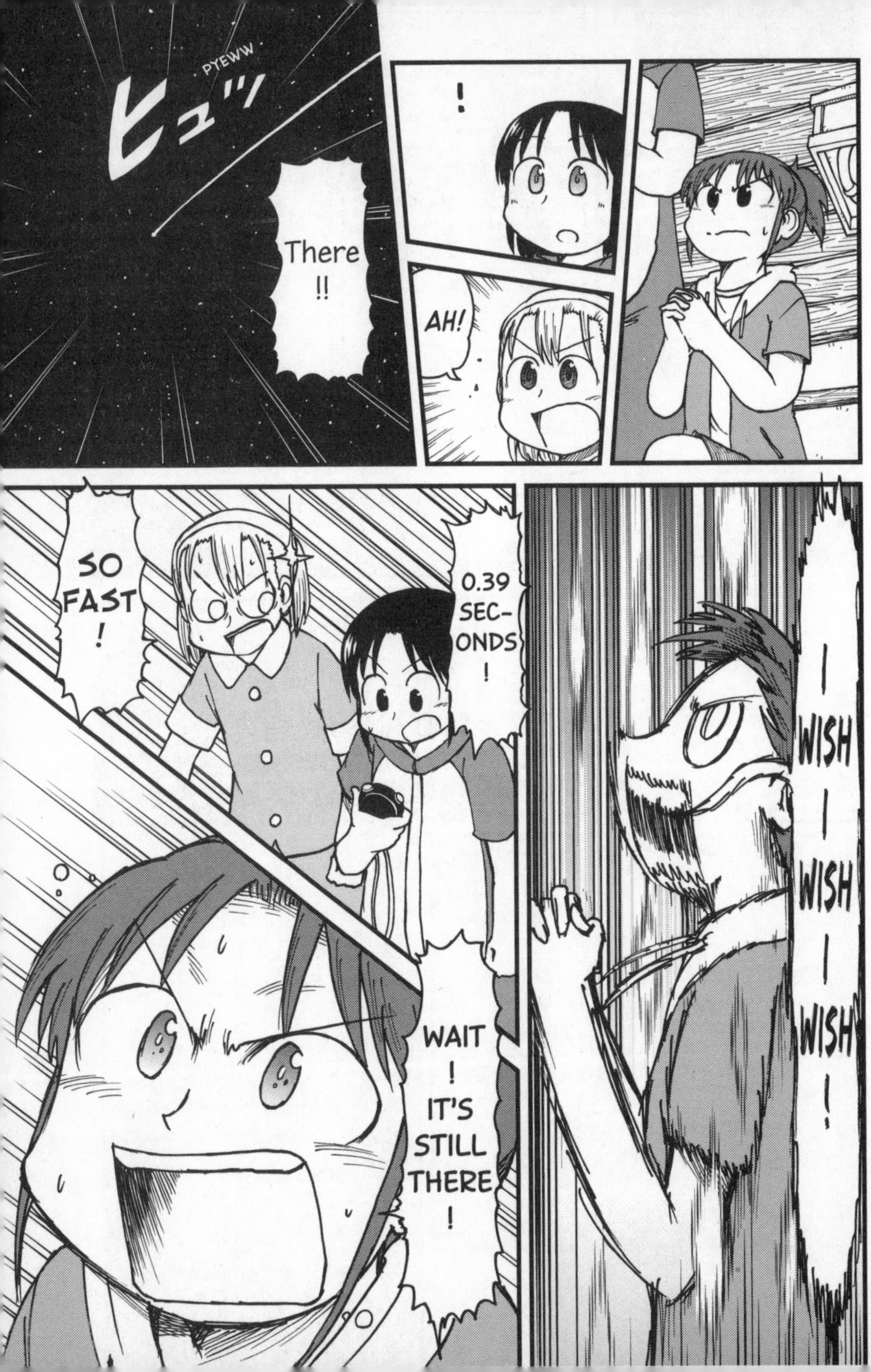
!
AH!
PYEWW
ヒュッ
There !!
I WISH I WISH I WISH!
0.39 SECONDS!
SO FAST!
WAIT! IT'S STILL THERE!

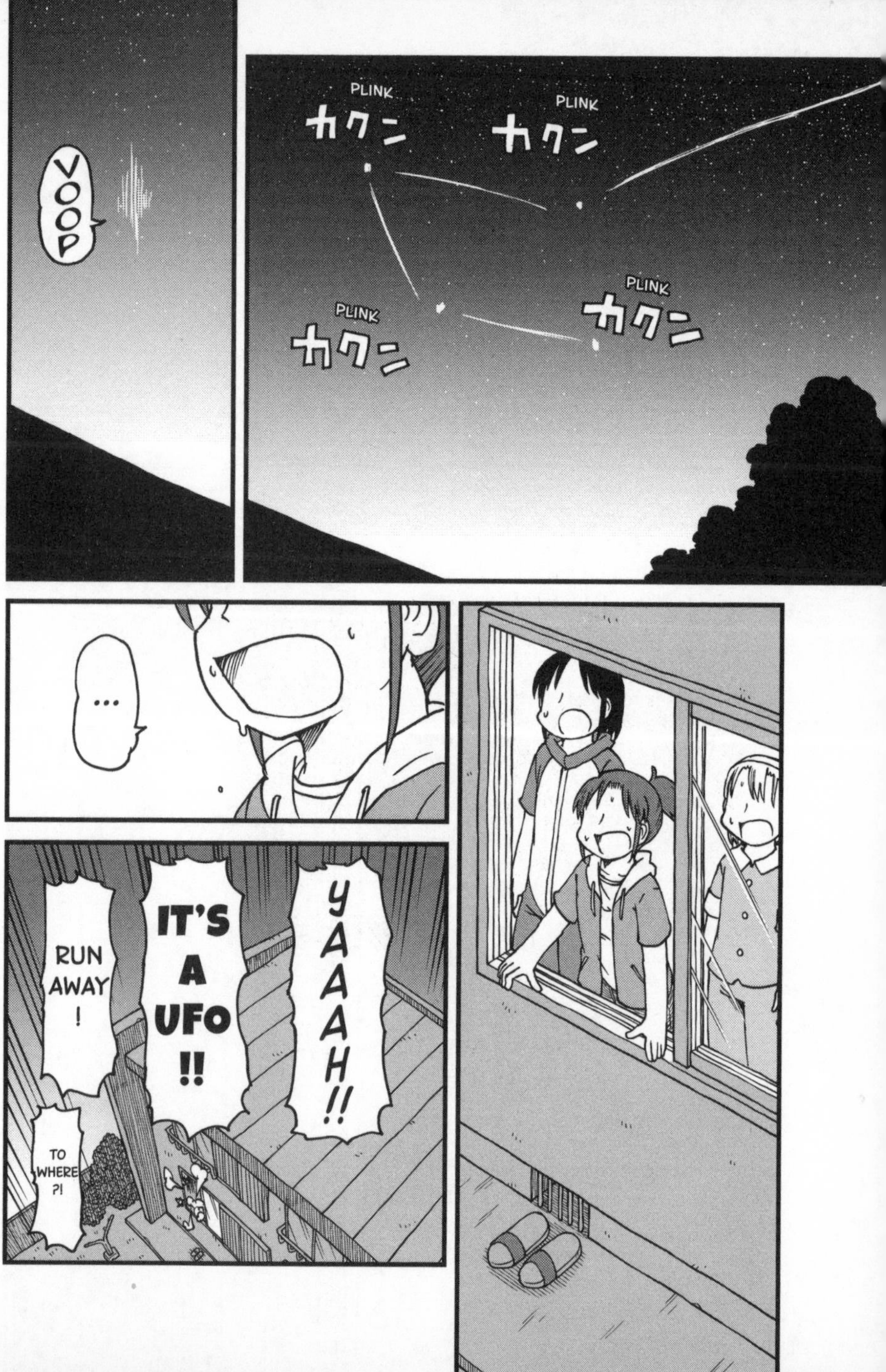
PLINK
カクン
PLINK
カクン
PLINK
カクン
PLINK
カクン
VOOP
...
YAAAAH!!
IT'S A UFO!!
RUN AWAY!
TO WHERE?!

CITY

CONTENTS

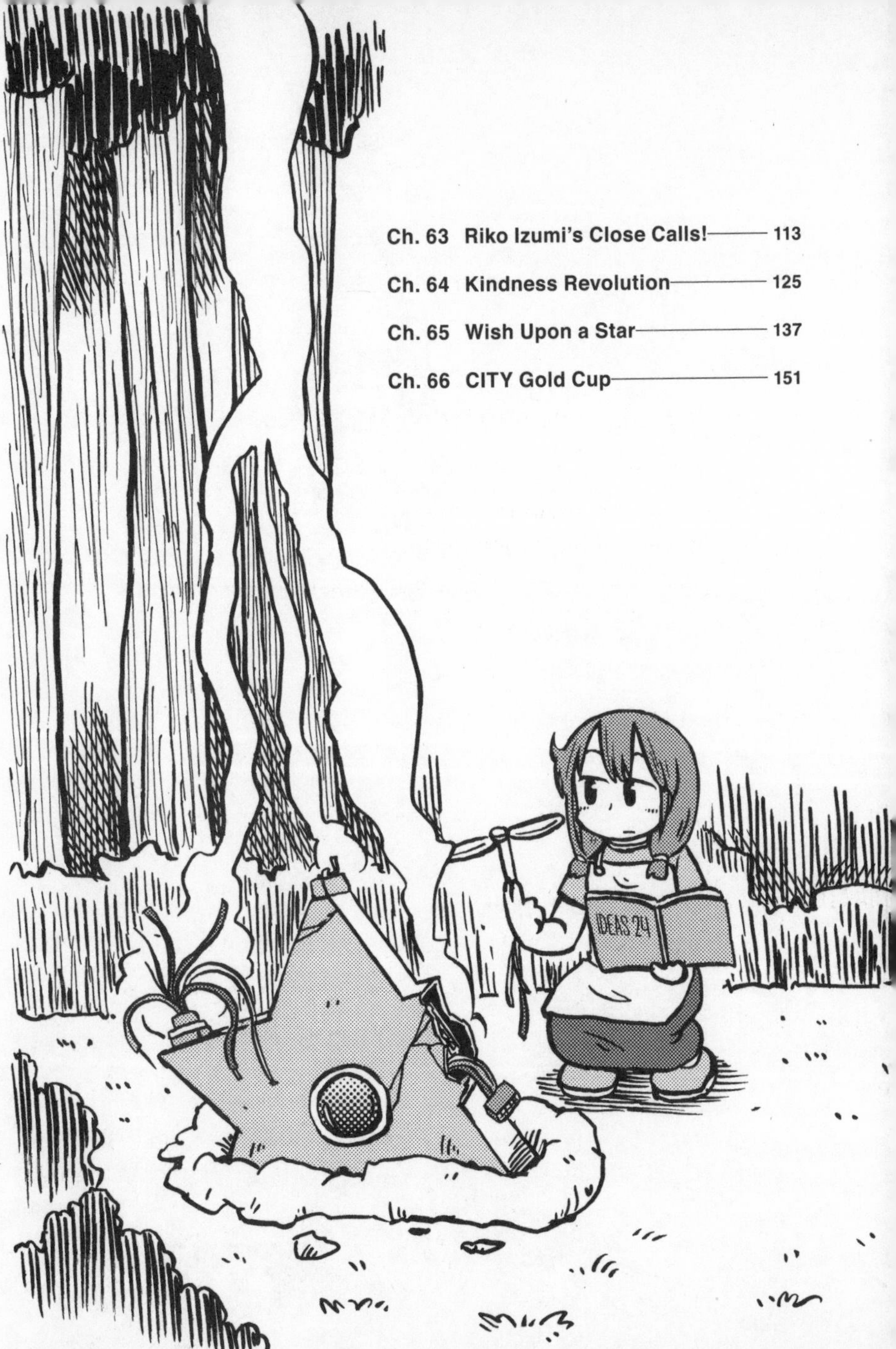
IDEAS 24

Here at the CITY racecourse, the smell of summer is drifting through the air.
Today, 8 contenders will race in the CITY Gold Cup.
CITY HORSE RACING
CITY
11 RACE
QUINELLA
2-3 ¥100
2-4 ¥100
2-7 ¥100
TOTAL ¥
#12 (G1)
CITY GOLD CUP
By far the favorite is Easy Death Machine, with 1-1 odds.
CITY HORSE RACING
2-34×7
LANE #
HORSE
EASY DEATH MACHINE
SANNANBOU
PICKLED LEEKS
MISS STRAWBERRY
SUPERCALI
FRAGILISTIC
EXPIALI
DON DYNAMITE
CITY 11
12TH CITY GOLD CUP
The rest might as well be pack-horses!
Did you choose the safe bet?
Or aim for a big win on a dark horse?
MAKABE
The race is about to begin.
MAKA

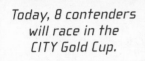

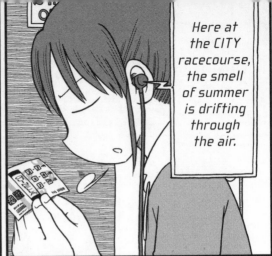

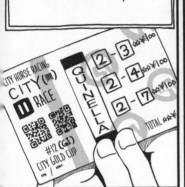

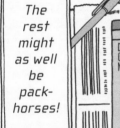

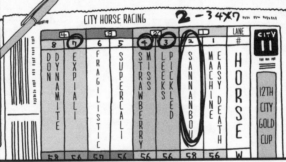

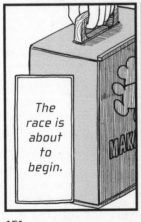

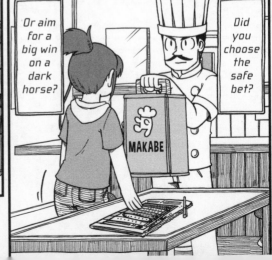

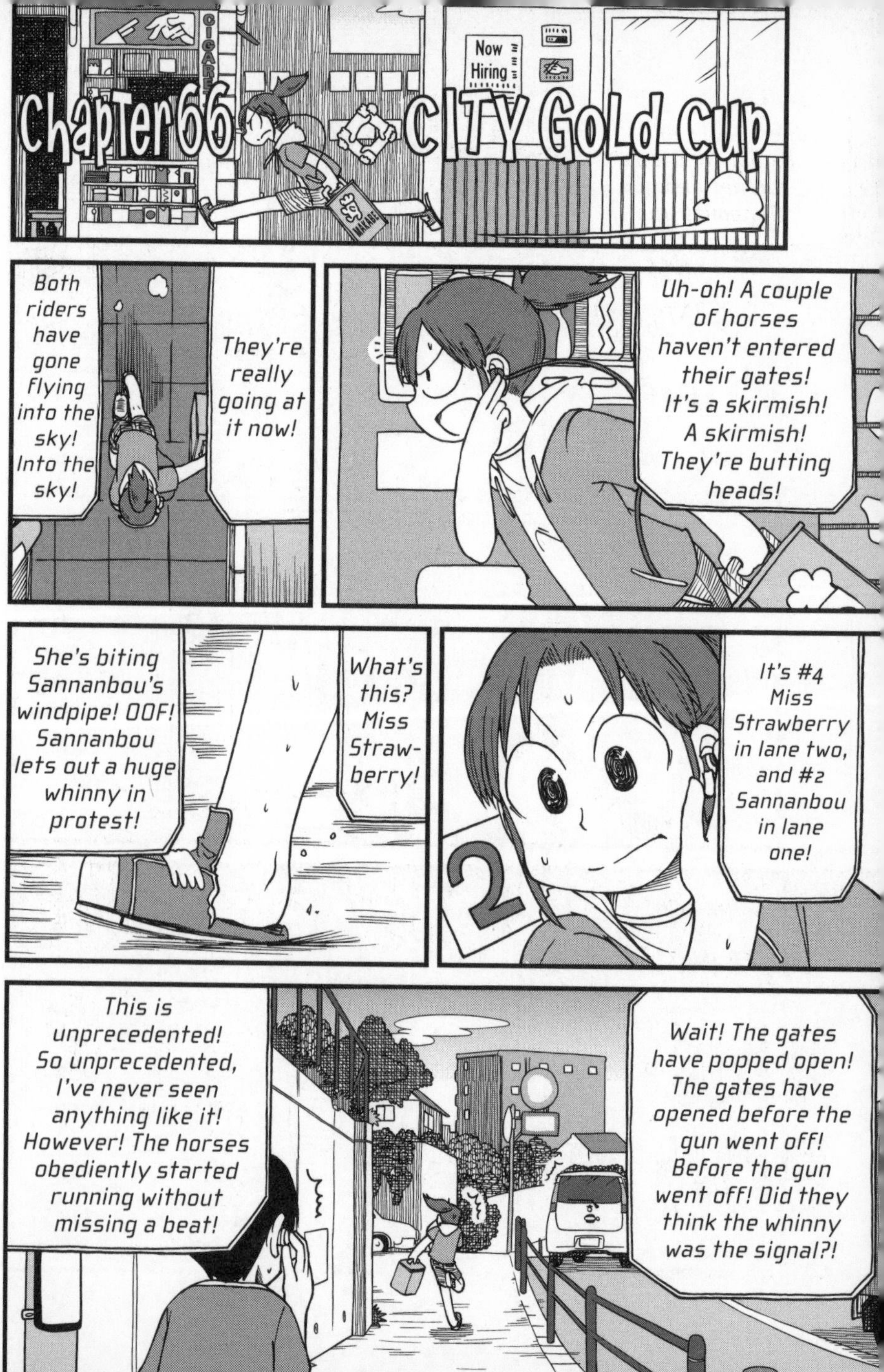
Chapter 66 CITY Gold Cup
Now Hiring
CIGARE
MAKADE
Uh-oh! A couple of horses haven't entered their gates! It's a skirmish! A skirmish! They're butting heads!
They're really going at it now!
Both riders have gone flying into the sky! Into the sky!
It's #4 Miss Strawberry in lane two, and #2 Sannanbou in lane one!
2
What's this? Miss Straw-berry!
She's biting Sannanbou's windpipe! OOF! Sannanbou lets out a huge whinny in protest!
Wait! The gates have popped open! The gates have opened before the gun went off! Before the gun went off! Did they think the whinny was the signal?!
This is unprecedented! So unprecedented, I've never seen anything like it! However! The horses obediently started running without missing a beat!

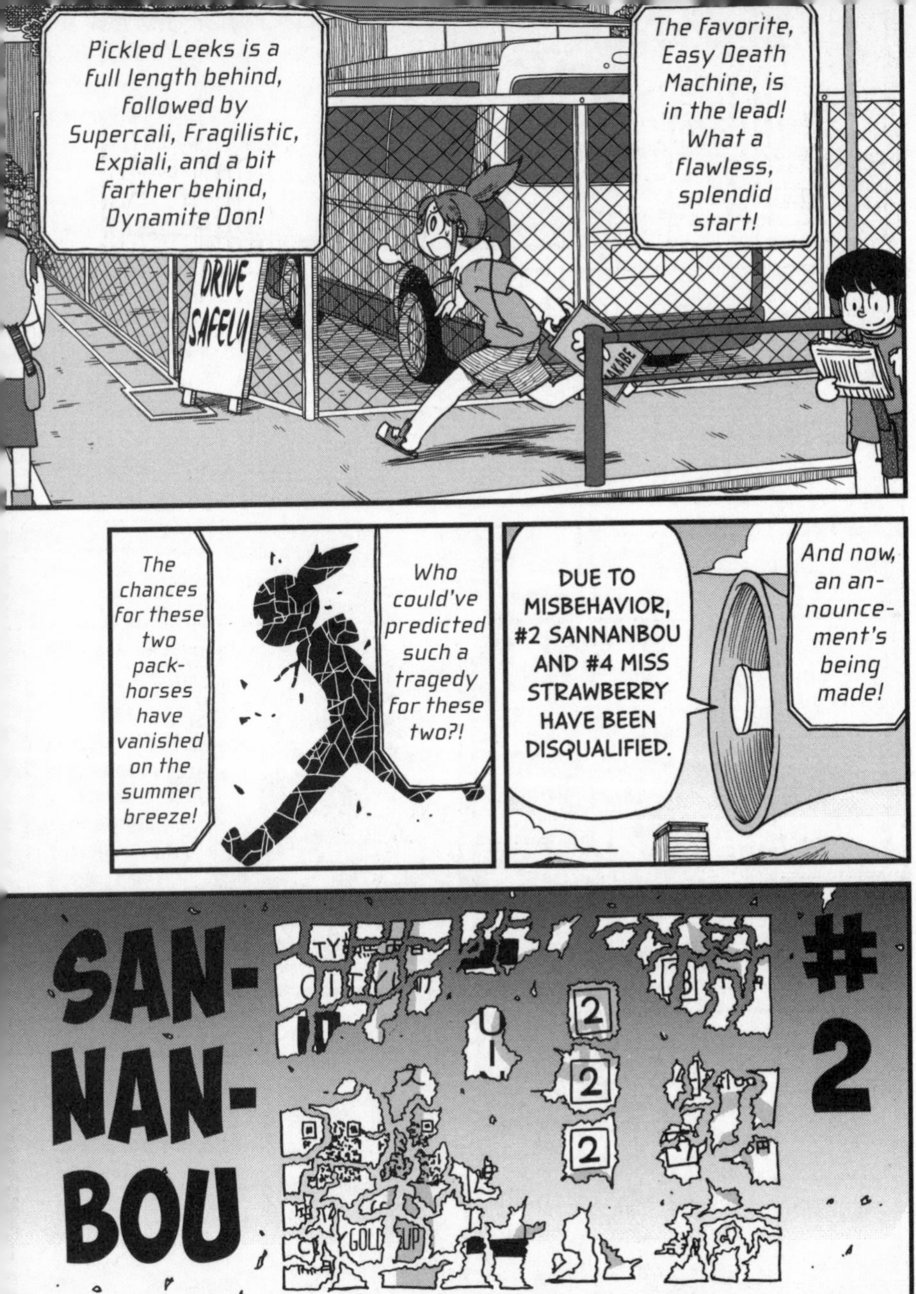
The favorite, Easy Death Machine, is in the lead! What a flawless, splendid start!
Pickled Leeks is a full length behind, followed by Supercali, Fragilistic, Expiali, and a bit farther behind, Dynamite Don!
DRIVE SAFELY
And now, an an-nounce-ment's being made!
DUE TO MISBEHAVIOR, #2 SANNANBOU AND #4 MISS STRAWBERRY HAVE BEEN DISQUALIFIED.
Who could've predicted such a tragedy for these two?!
The chances for these two pack-horses have vanished on the summer breeze!
#2
SAN-NAN-BOU

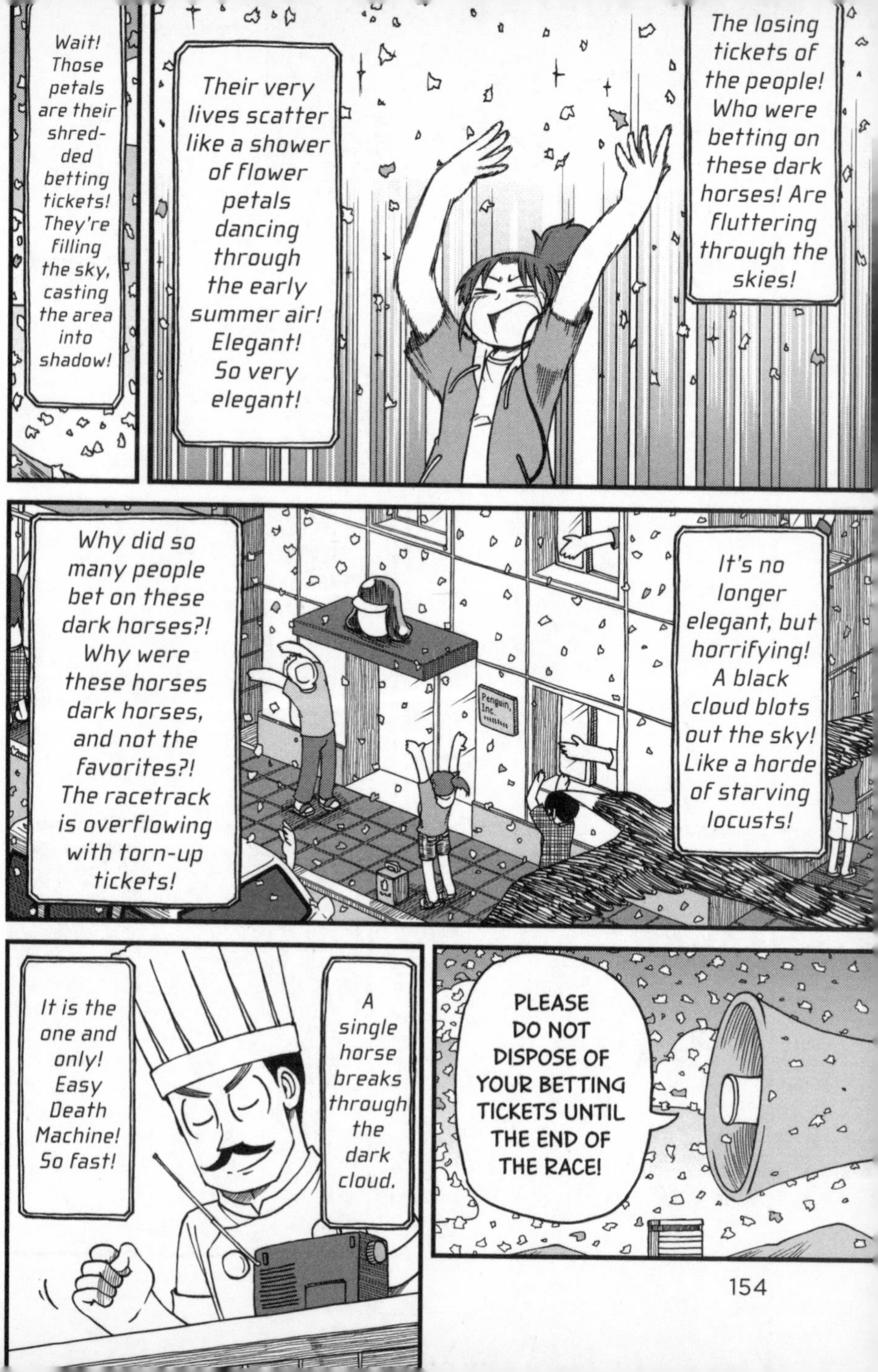

The losing tickets of the people! Who were betting on these dark horses! Are fluttering through the skies!
Their very lives scatter like a shower of flower petals dancing through the early summer air! Elegant! So very elegant!
Wait! Those petals are their shred-ded betting tickets! They're filling the sky, casting the area into shadow!
It's no longer elegant, but horrifying! A black cloud blots out the sky! Like a horde of starving locusts!
Why did so many people bet on these dark horses?! Why were these horses dark horses, and not the favorites?! The racetrack is overflowing with torn-up tickets!
Penguin, Inc.
PLEASE DO NOT DISPOSE OF YOUR BETTING TICKETS UNTIL THE END OF THE RACE!
A single horse breaks through the dark cloud.
It is the one and only! Easy Death Machine! So fast!

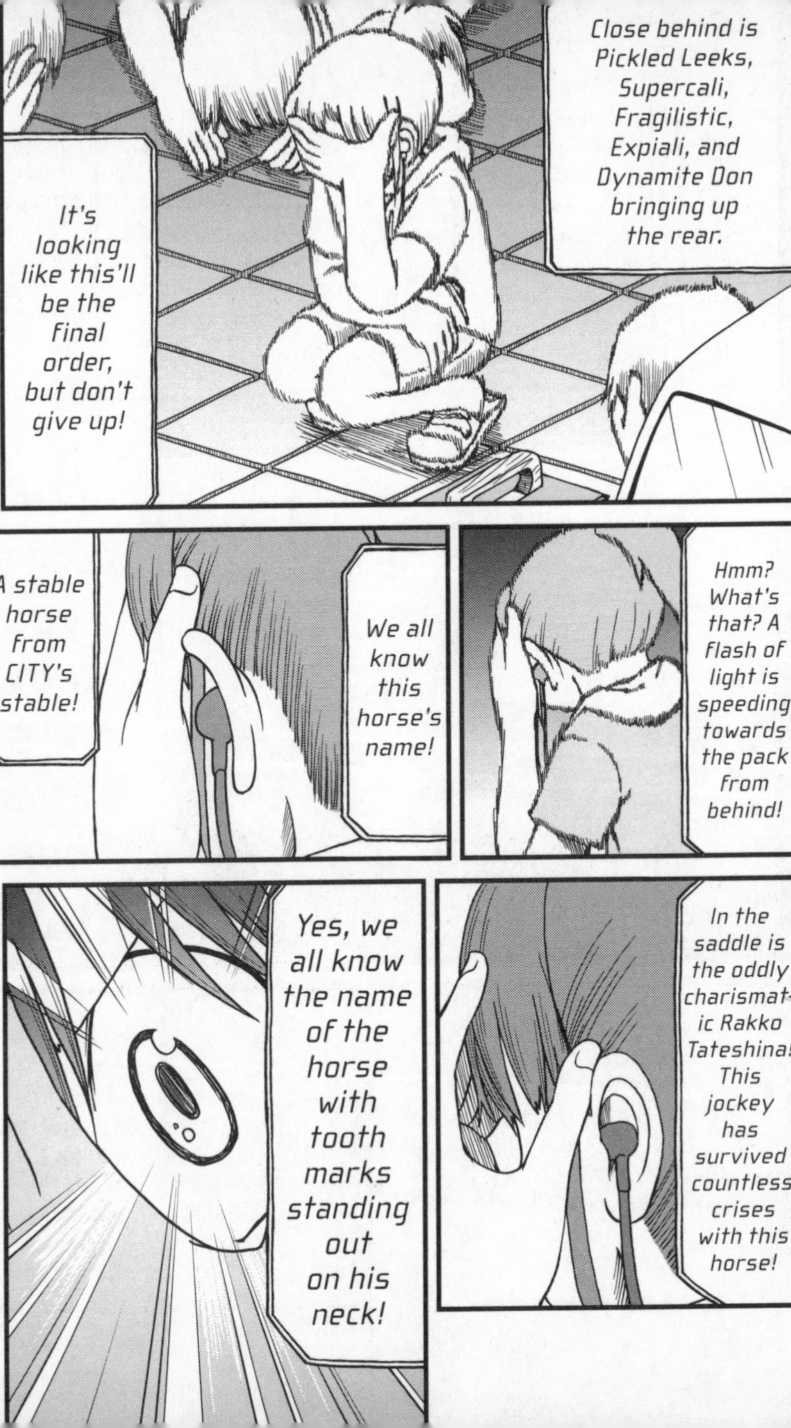
Close behind is Pickled Leeks, Supercali, Fragilistic, Expiali, and Dynamite Don bringing up the rear.
It's looking like this'll be the final order, but don't give up!
Hmm? What's that? A flash of light is speeding towards the pack from behind!
We all know this horse's name!
A stable horse from CITY's stable!
In the saddle is the oddly charismatic Rakko Tateshina! This jockey has survived countless crises with this horse!
Yes, we all know the name of the horse with tooth marks standing out on his neck!

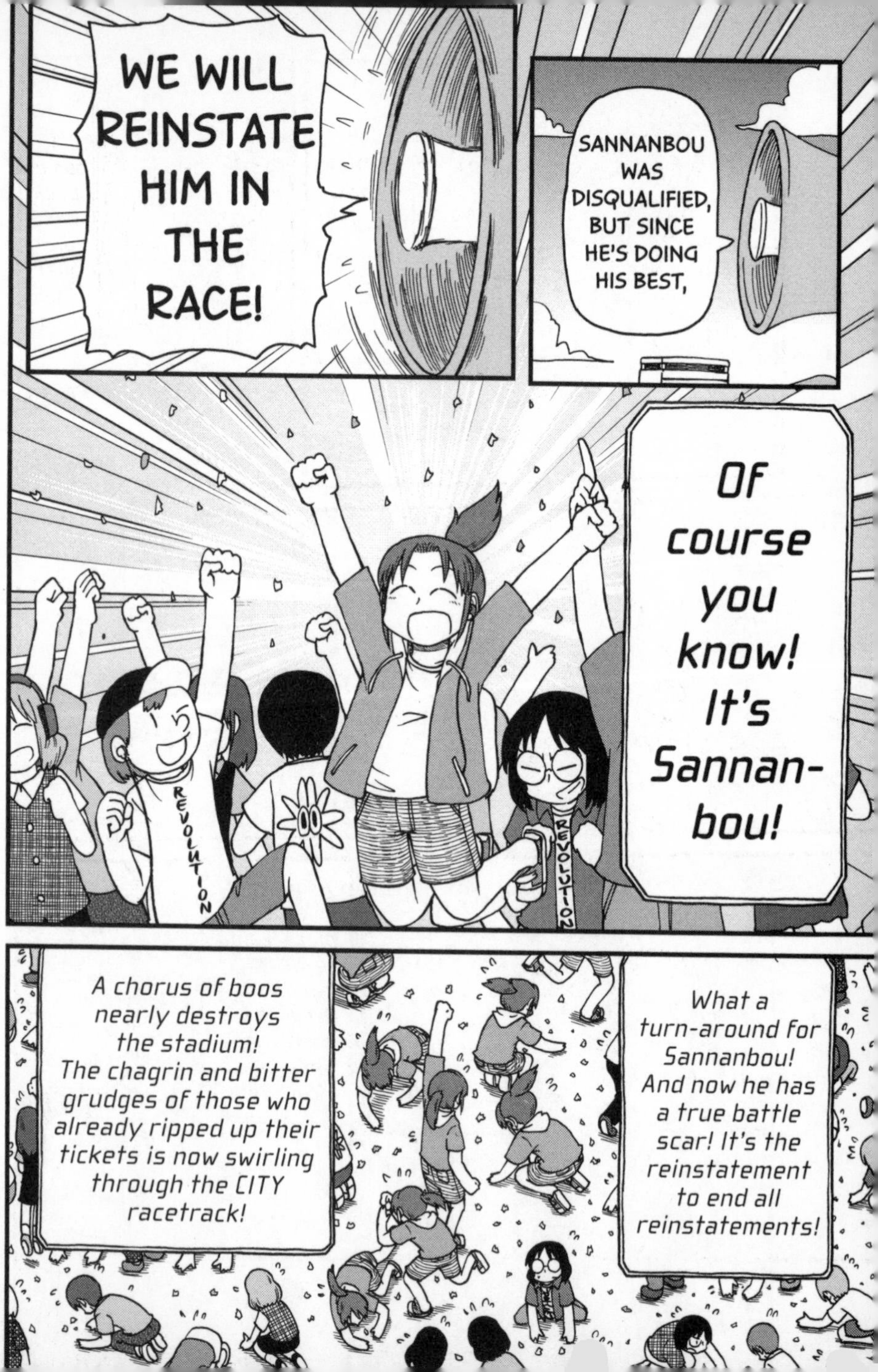
SANNANBOU WAS DISQUALIFIED, BUT SINCE HE'S DOING HIS BEST,
WE WILL REINSTATE HIM IN THE RACE!
Of course you know! It's Sannan-bou!
REVOLUTION
REVOLUTION
What a turn-around for Sannanbou! And now he has a true battle scar! It's the reinstatement to end all reinstatements!
A chorus of boos nearly destroys the stadium! The chagrin and bitter grudges of those who already ripped up their tickets is now swirling through the CITY racetrack!

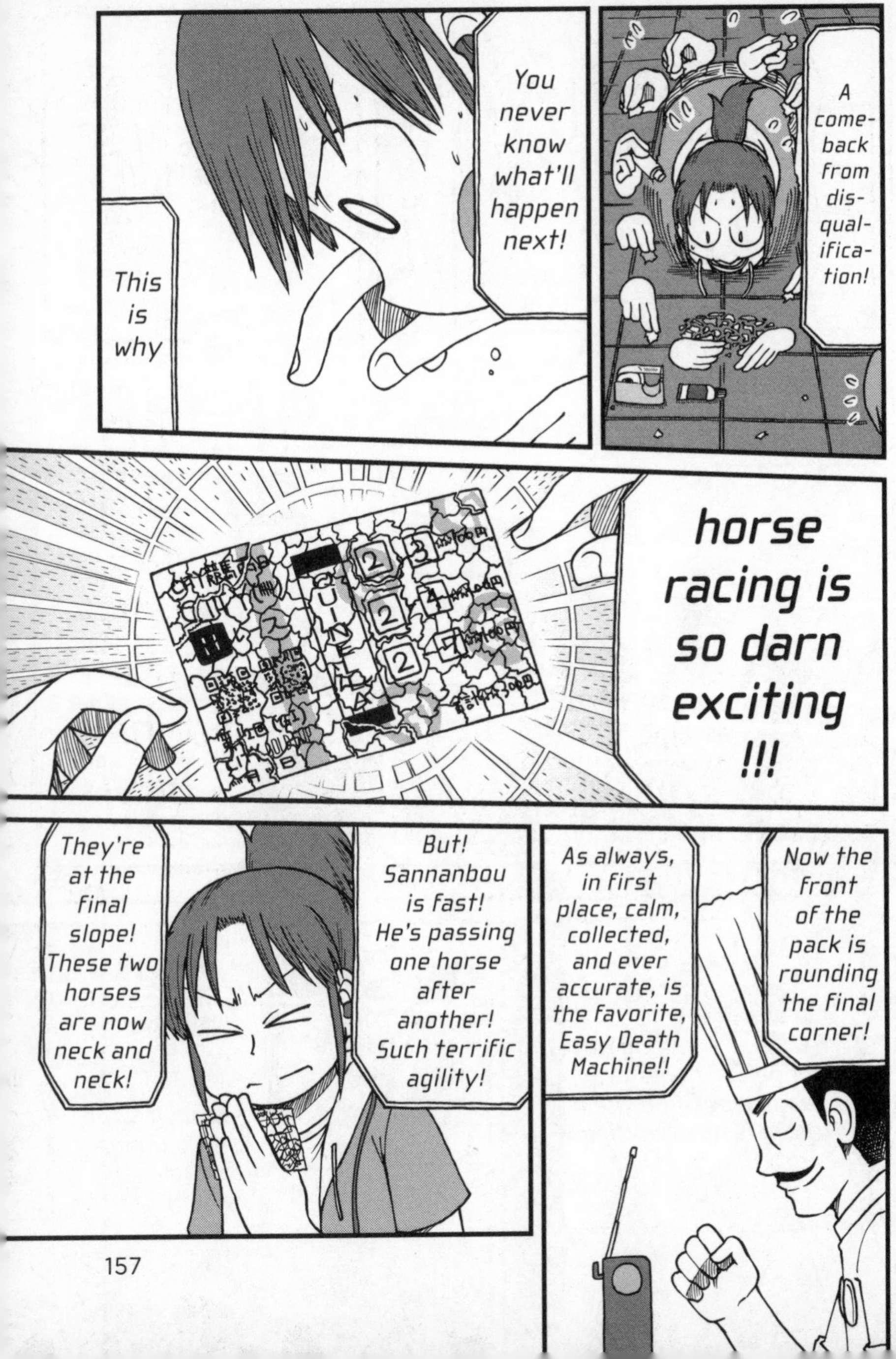
A comeback from disqualification!
You never know what'll happen next!
This is why
horse racing is so darn exciting!!!
Now the front of the pack is rounding the final corner!
As always, in first place, calm, collected, and ever accurate, is the favorite, Easy Death Machine!!
But! Sannanbou is fast! He's passing one horse after another! Such terrific agility!
They're at the final slope! These two horses are now neck and neck!

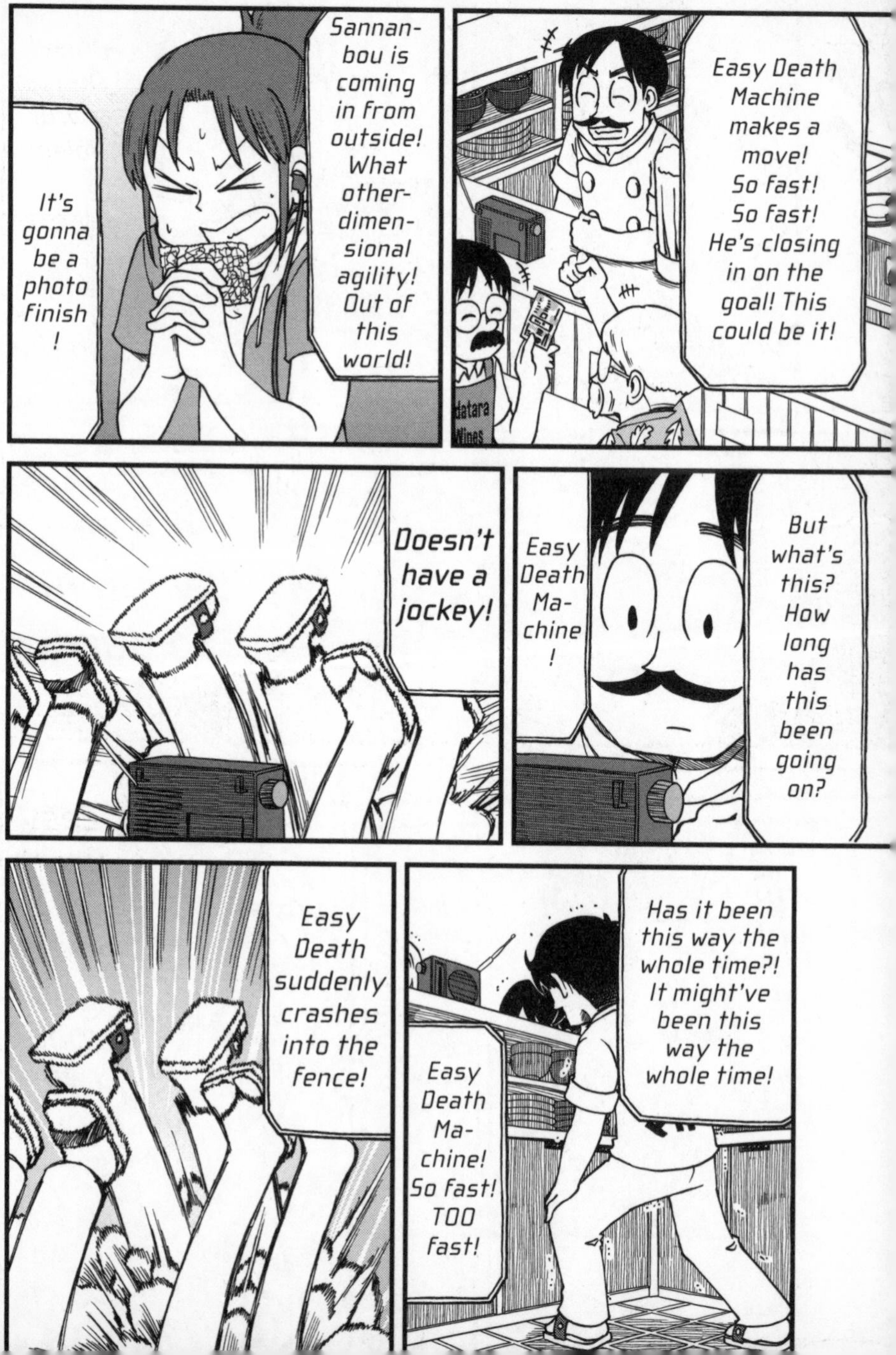
Easy Death Machine makes a move! So fast! So fast! He's closing in on the goal! This could be it!
Sannan-bou is coming in from outside! What other-dimen-sional agility! Out of this world!
It's gonna be a photo finish!
But what's this? How long has this been going on?
Easy Death Ma-chine!
Doesn't have a jockey!
Has it been this way the whole time?! It might've been this way the whole time!
Easy Death Ma-chine! So fast! TOO fast!
Easy Death suddenly crashes into the fence!

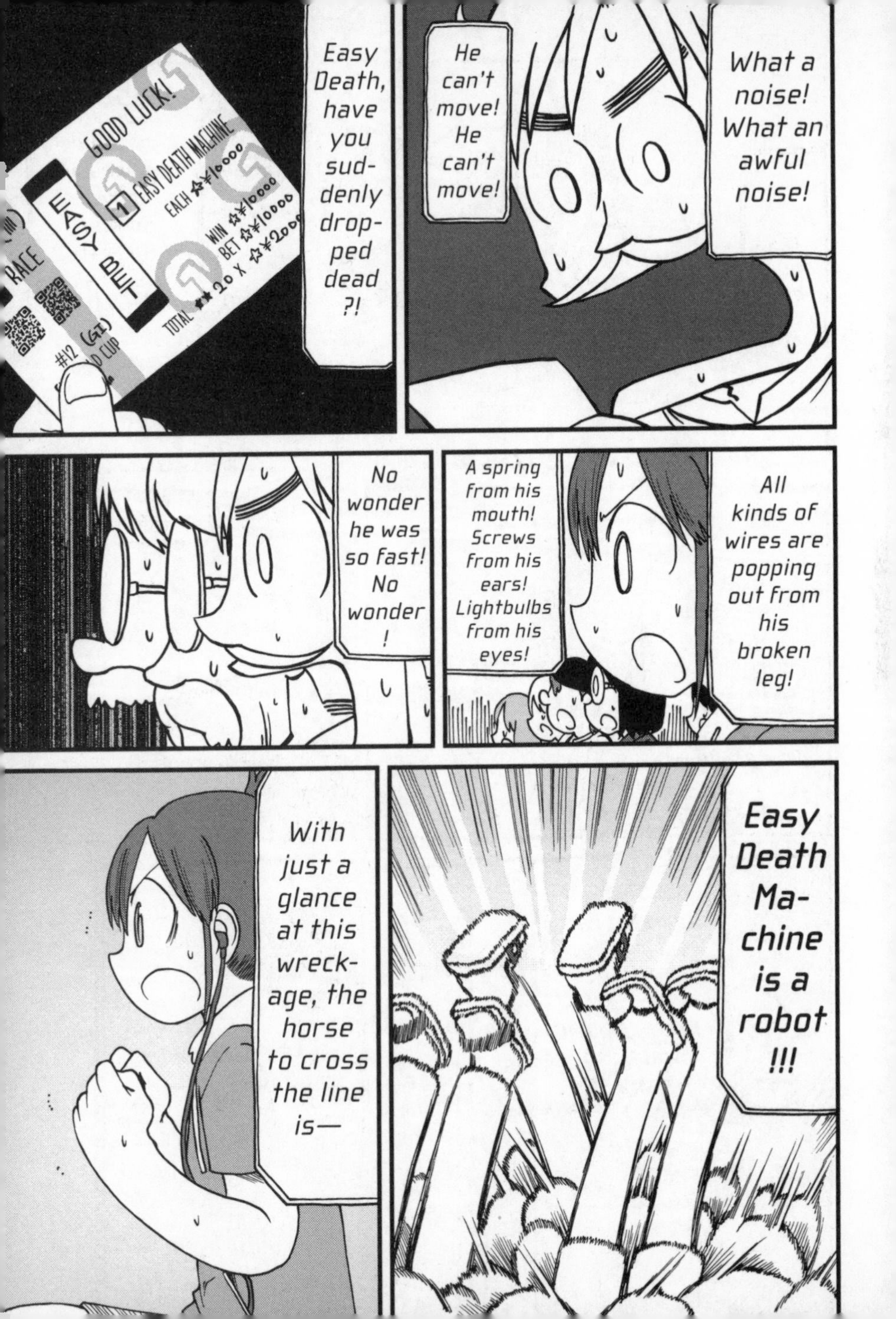
What a noise! What an awful noise!
He can't move! He can't move!
Easy Death, have you suddenly dropped dead?!
GOOD LUCK!
1 EASY DEATH MACHINE
EASY BET
RACE
#12 (G1)
All kinds of wires are popping out from his broken leg!
A spring from his mouth! Screws from his ears! Lightbulbs from his eyes!
No wonder he was so fast! No wonder!
Easy Death Machine is a robot!!!
With just a glance at this wreckage, the horse to cross the line is—

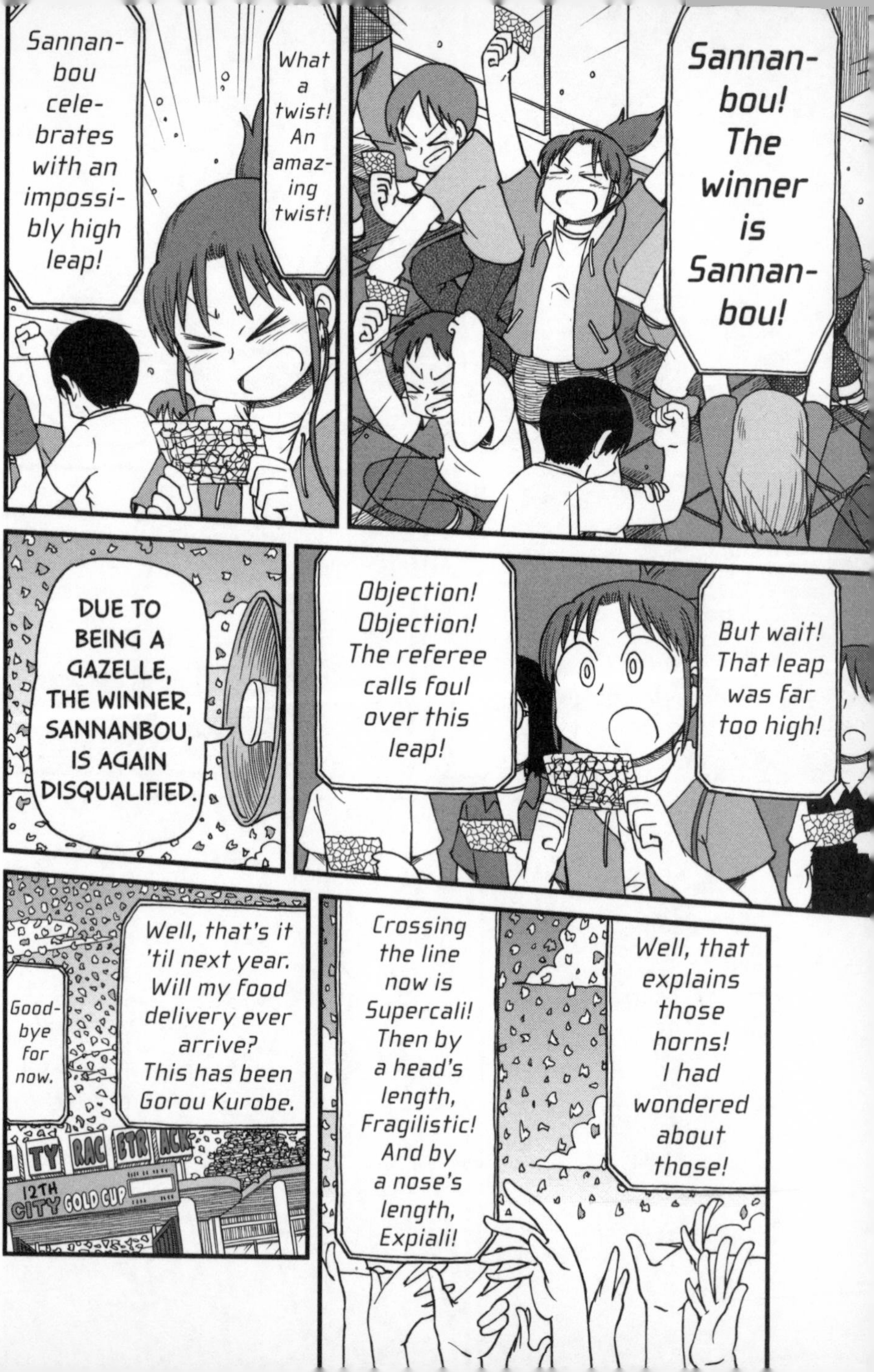
Sannanbou! The winner is Sannanbou!
What a twist! An amazing twist!
Sannanbou celebrates with an impossibly high leap!
But wait! That leap was far too high!
Objection! Objection! The referee calls foul over this leap!
DUE TO BEING A GAZELLE, THE WINNER, SANNANBOU, IS AGAIN DISQUALIFIED.
Well, that explains those horns! I had wondered about those!
Crossing the line now is Supercali! Then by a head's length, Fragilistic! And by a nose's length, Expiali!
Well, that's it 'til next year. Will my food delivery ever arrive? This has been Gorou Kurobe.
Goodbye for now.
12TH CITY GOLD CUP

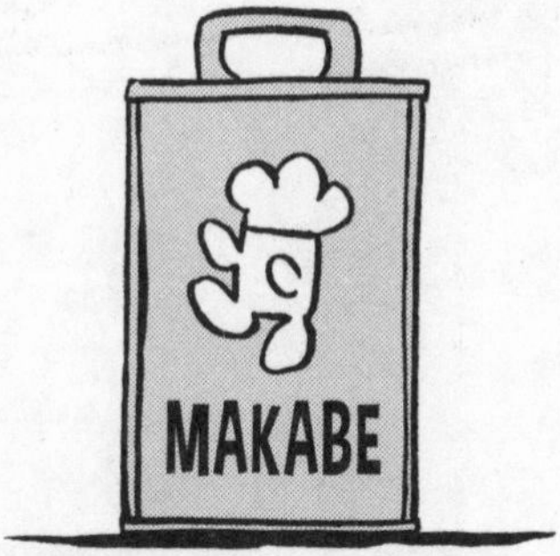
MAKABE

CITY

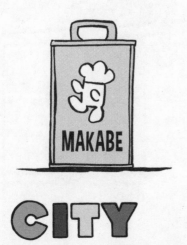

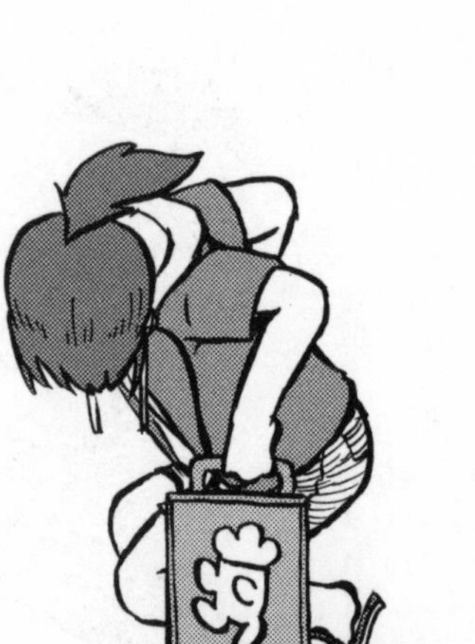
MAKABE

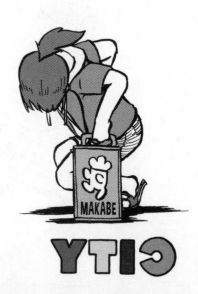

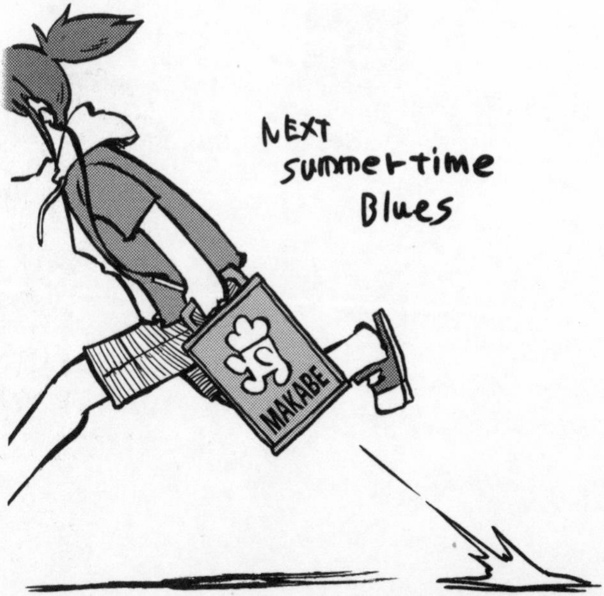
NEXT
summer time
Blues
MAKABE

Recent Author Photo

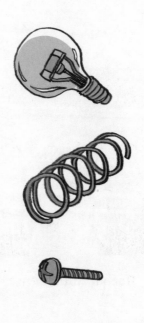

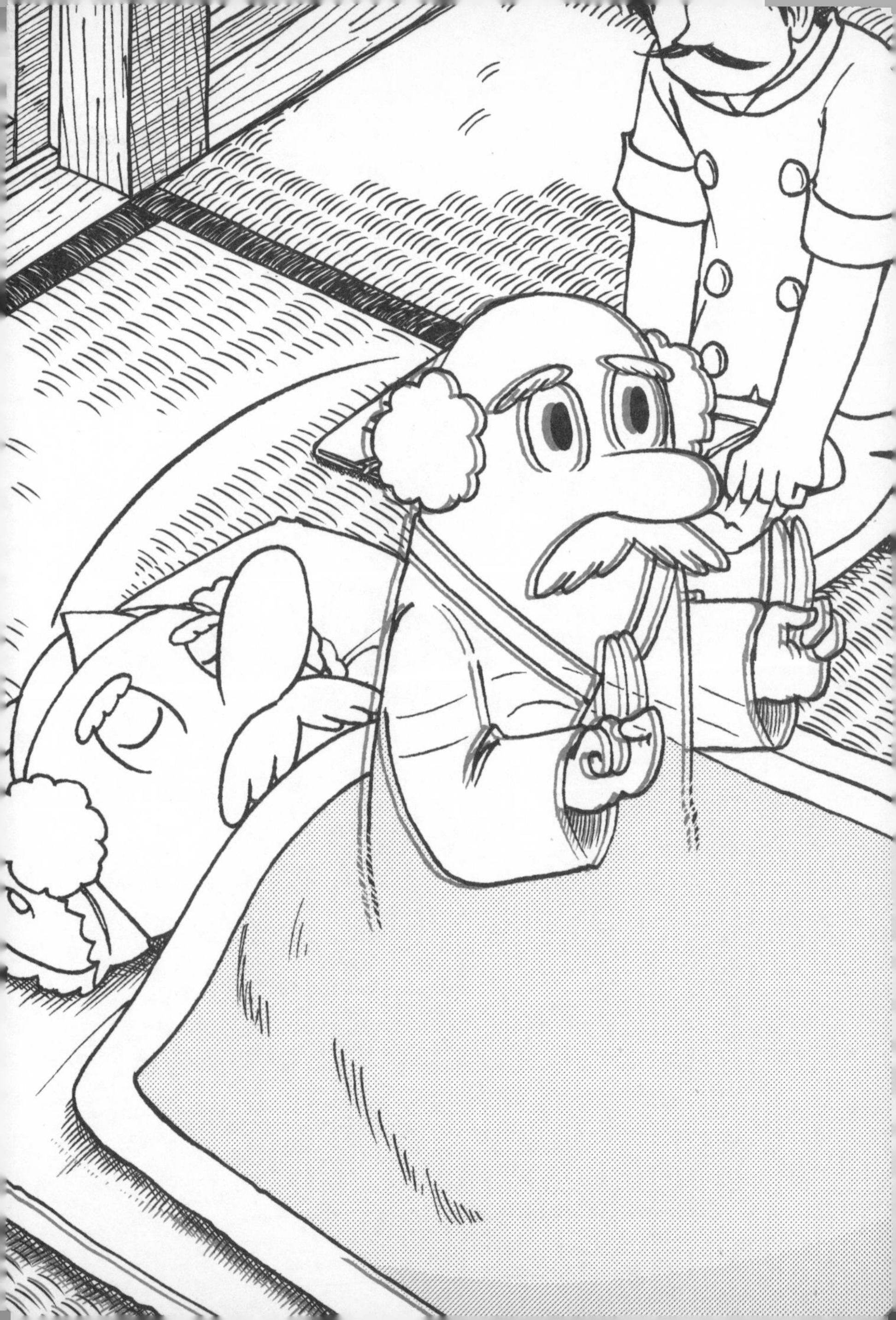

CITY

5

define "ordinary"

in this just-surreal-enough take on the "school genre" of manga, a group of friends (which includes a robot built by a child professor) grapples with all sorts of unexpected situations in their daily lives as high schoolers.

the gags, jokes, puns and random haiku keep this series off-kilter even as the characters grow and change. check out this new take on a storied genre and meet the new ordinary.

all volumes
available now!

nichijou

my ordinary life

keiichi
arawi

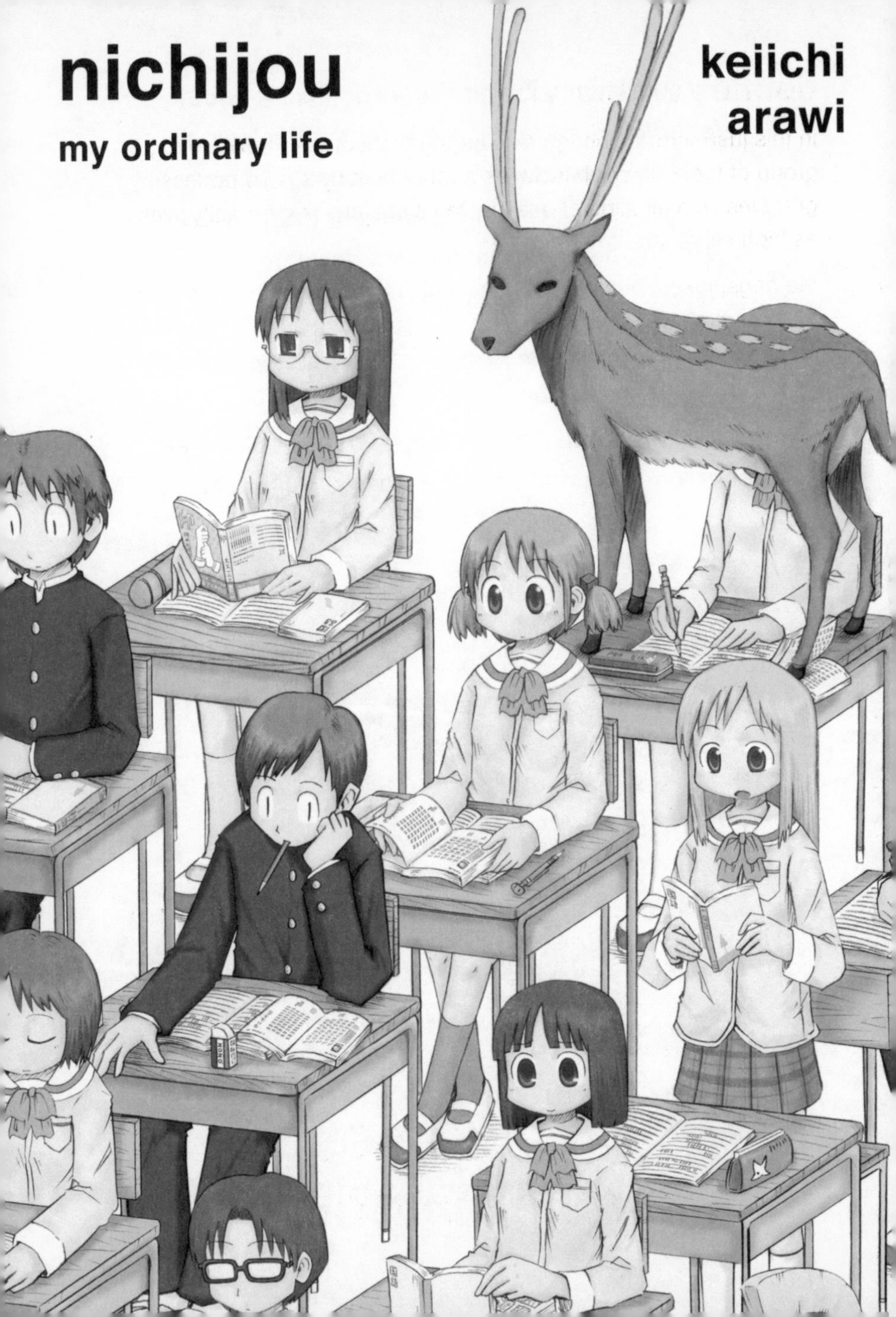

The follow up to the hit manga series *nichijou*, ***Helvetica Standard*** is a full-color anthology of Keiichi Arawi's comic art and design work. Funny and heartwarming, ***Helvetica Standard*** is a humorous look at modern day Japanese design in comic form.

Helvetica Standard is a deep dive into the artistic and creative world of Keiichi Arawi. Part comic, part diary, part art and design book, ***Helvetica Standard*** is a deconstruction of the world of *nichijou*.

Both Parts Available Now!

Keiichi Arawi

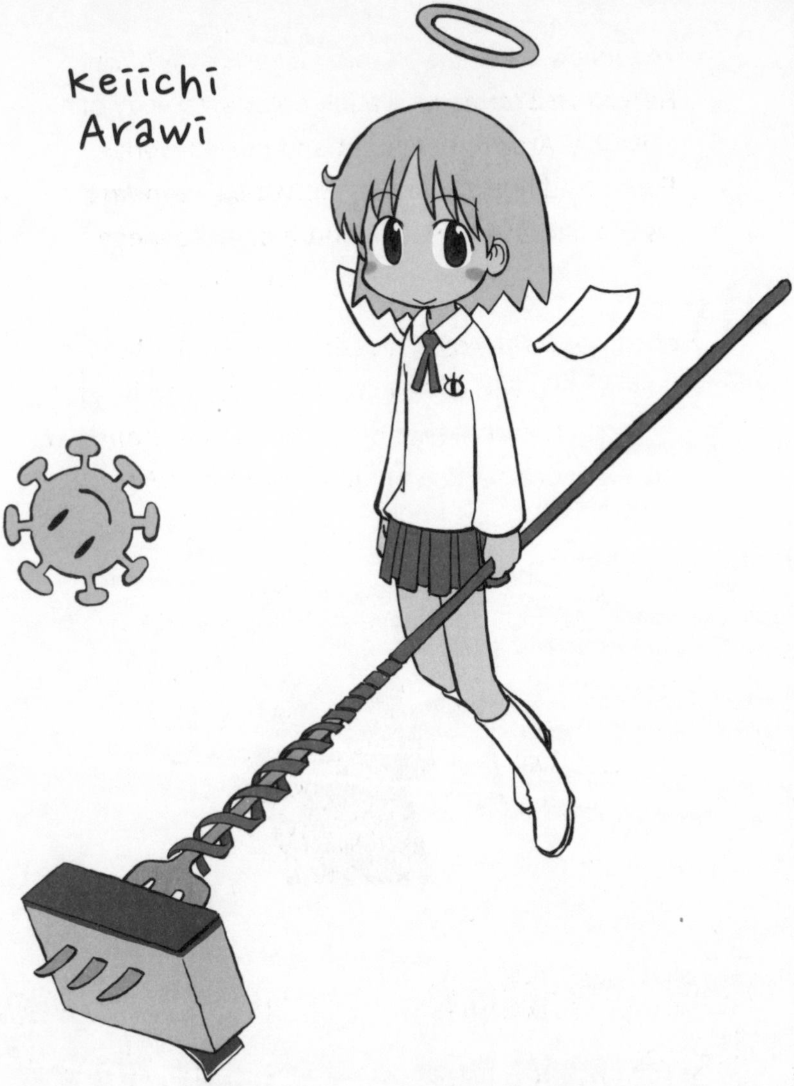

Helvetica Standard

CITY 5

A Vertical Comics Edition

Translation: Jenny McKeon
Production: Grace Lu
            Hiroko Mizuno

© Keiichi ARAWI 2018
First published in Japan in 2018 by Kodansha, Ltd., Tokyo
Publication rights for this English edition arranged through Kodansha, Ltd., Tokyo
English language version produced by Vertical, Inc.

Translation provided by Vertical Comics, 2019
Published by Vertical Comics, an imprint of Vertical, Inc., New York

Originally published in Japanese as CITY 5 by Kodansha, Ltd.
CITY first serialized in Morning, Kodansha, Ltd., 2016-

This is a work of fiction.

ISBN: 978-1-947194-73-1

Manufactured in Canada

First Edition

Vertical, Inc.
451 Park Avenue South
7th Floor
New York, NY 10016
www.vertical-comics.com

Vertical books are distributed through Penguin-Random House Publisher Services.